Facing Human Capital Challenges of the 21st Century

Education and Labor Market Initiatives
in Lebanon, Oman, Qatar,
and the United Arab Emirates

Gabriella Gonzalez | Lynn A. Karoly | Louay Constant
Hanine Salem | Charles A. Goldman

This study was conducted by researchers in RAND Education and RAND Labor and Population in the United States and at the RAND-Qatar Policy Institute (RQPI) in Doha, Qatar. This study results from the RAND Corporation's continuing program of self-initiated research. Support for such research is provided, in part, by the generosity of RAND's donors and by the fees earned on client-funded research.

Library of Congress Cataloging-in-Publication Data

Facing human capital challenges of the 21st century : education and labor market initiatives in Lebanon, Oman, Qatar, and the United Arab Emirates / Gabriella Gonzalez ... [et al.].
  p. cm.
  Includes bibliographical references.
  ISBN 978-0-8330-4516-4 (pbk. : alk. paper)
  1. Labor market—Arab countries. 2. Human capital—Arab countries.
  3. Education and state—Arab countries. 4. Manpower policy—Arab countries.
  5. Manpower planning—Arab countries. I. Gonzalez, Gabriella C., 1972– II. Title: Education and labor market initiatives in Lebanon, Oman, Qatar, and the United Arab Emirates.

HD5812.3.A6F33 2008
331.10953—dc22

2008032855

The RAND Corporation is a nonprofit research organization providing objective analysis and effective solutions that address the challenges facing the public and private sectors around the world. RAND's publications do not necessarily reflect the opinions of its research clients and sponsors.

RAND® is a registered trademark.

Cover design by Peter Soriano

© Copyright 2008 RAND Corporation

All rights reserved. No part of this book may be reproduced in any form by any electronic or mechanical means (including photocopying, recording, or information storage and retrieval) without permission in writing from RAND.

Published 2008 by the RAND Corporation
1776 Main Street, P.O. Box 2138, Santa Monica, CA 90407-2138
1200 South Hayes Street, Arlington, VA 22202-5050
4570 Fifth Avenue, Suite 600, Pittsburgh, PA 15213-2665
RAND URL: http://www.rand.org/
To order RAND documents or to obtain additional information, contact
Distribution Services: Telephone: (310) 451-7002;
Fax: (310) 451-6915; Email: order@rand.org

Preface

Many nations are making efforts to address human resource development challenges and any existing mismatch between the skills and technical knowledge of their secondary and post-secondary education graduates and the needs of the labor market. RAND recently examined such efforts in four Middle Eastern countries: Lebanon, Oman, Qatar, and the United Arab Emirates (UAE). The study focused on reforms enacted or under way that were designed to improve the nation's human capital, or skills and technical knowledge, of its population, or to facilitate the employment of human capital in diverse sectors of the economy. The case study approach juxtaposed three Arab Gulf countries (Oman, Qatar, and the UAE) and one non-Gulf country (Lebanon) to showcase similarities and differences in the reform strategies these countries were employing as of 2006. The nations were compared in terms of challenges they faced, reforms enacted, and efforts to assess reform impacts.

The study is documented in this monograph in English. Research briefs describing the study in English and in Arabic are also available, as is a bilingual executive summary. All of these documents can be accessed in full text on the RAND website: www.rand.org.

This monograph should be of interest to policymakers in the Arab world who want to understand the evolution and progress of education and labor market reforms designed to advance human capital development and to enhance workforce competitiveness in the 21st century global economy. It will also be useful for readers with a general interest in human capital and economic initiatives.

The study was conducted by researchers in two units of the RAND Corporation—RAND Education and RAND Labor and Population—both in the United States and at the RAND-Qatar Policy Institute (RQPI) in Doha, Qatar. This study resulted from RAND's continuing program of self-initiated research, support for which is provided in part by the generosity of RAND's donors and by fees earned on client-funded research.

Contents

Preface iii
Figures xi
Tables xiii
Summary xvii
Acknowledgments xxvii
Abbreviations xxix

CHAPTER ONE
Introduction 1
Human Resource Challenges Faced by the Arab Region 1
Research Questions 5
Analytic Approach 6
    Diagnosis and Articulation of the Problem: What Are the Human
        Resource Challenges That Each Country Faces? 6
    Approaches to Addressing the Problem: What Reforms Have Been
        Developed or Are Under Way? 7
    Availability of Resources for Policy Evaluation: What Mechanisms
        Are in Place for Evaluating Policy? 9
Approach to Data Collection and Interviews 9
Rationale for Country Selection 12
Limitations of the Study 13
Organization of This Document 14

CHAPTER TWO
Economic and Sociopolitical Context for Reform in the Four Study Countries 17
Reliance on Natural Resources for National Wealth 17
Sociopolitical System: The Role of Participatory Democracy................ 21
Diversity of the Economy 24
Composition of the Labor Pool.. 26
The Case-Study Approach 30

CHAPTER THREE
Qatar 31
Overview of Qatar 33
    Political History... 35
    Economic Development... 36
    Population Composition and Change..................................... 38
    Advances in Education.. 41
    Labor Force Trends 44
Human Resource Challenges Faced by Qatar................................. 45
    Non-Qataris Compose the Bulk of the Labor Force 46
    Qatari Employees Are Concentrated in Government Sector 49
    Unemployment Rates Are High Among Young, First-Time Workers.... 52
    Qataris Are Not Obtaining the Types of Education Needed to
        Compete in Qatar's Economy 55
Approaches to Reform in Qatar 61
    Qatar Introduces a Comprehensive Primary and Secondary
        Education Reform 65
    Post-Secondary Education Reforms Are Also Considered a Priority 69
    Efforts to Train Qatari Secondary School Graduates 72
    Privatization and Economy Diversification Efforts 75
Efforts to Collect Demographic, Economic, Labor Market, and
    Education Data Are Expanding.. 79
    Principal Data Provider: The Qatar Planning Council.................... 80
    New Source of Education Statistics.. 81
    Other Activities to Extend Statistical Resources 82
Summary... 83

CHAPTER FOUR
The United Arab Emirates 87
Overview of the UAE..89
   Political History..91
   Economic Growth 93
   Population Composition and Change..95
   Education Advances and Gender Differences 99
   Labor Force Trends... 105
Human Resource Challenges Faced by the UAE 106
   Expatriates Dominate the Workforce and Emiratis Participate
      at Low Rates.. 108
   The Education and Training System Is Not Preparing Emiratis
      to Meet the Needs of Employers....................................... 112
   Efforts to Train Emiratis Have Been Piecemeal......................... 115
   Emiratis Prefer Working in the Government Sector..................... 116
   Implications of Overdependence on a Non-National Workforce 117
Approaches to Reform in the UAE 120
   Post-Secondary Education and Training Reforms 124
   Emiratisation: Nationalizing the Workforce............................. 131
   Private-Sector Promotion and Economic Diversification 137
   Broad-Level Policy Goals Remain Focused on Improving the
      Performance of the Federal Government 139
Efforts at Data Collection and Dissemination to Improve
      Policymaking Are in the Early Stages 141
   Data Collection Efforts at the National Level........................... 141
Summary.. 143

CHAPTER FIVE
Sultanate of Oman... 147
Overview of Oman 148
   Political History... 150
   Economic Development... 153
   Population Composition and Change................................... 155
   Advances in Education 156
   Labor Force Trends: The Labor Force Is Growing and the Share
      of Females Is Rising 158

Human Resource Challenges Faced by Oman 162
  Omani Employees Are Concentrated in the Public Sector 162
  Oman Has Relatively High Unemployment Rates, Particularly
    for Its Youth 164
  Omanis Are Not Obtaining the Types of Education Needed to
    Compete in Oman's Economy 165
  Income Inequality Is Another Area of Concern for Human
    Capital Development 169
Approaches to Reform in Oman 170
  Efforts to Reform the Education System and Develop Human
    Resources Are Under Way 172
  Changes in Primary and Secondary Government-Funded
    Education 174
  Post-Secondary Education Reform Efforts 178
  Vocational Training Programs 181
  Labor Market Initiatives: Economy Diversification and
    Privatization Efforts 186
Foundation for Data Collection in Support of Decisionmaking Is
  in Place 192
Summary 195

CHAPTER SIX
Lebanon 199
Overview of Lebanon 201
  Political History 203
  Economic Development 205
  Population Composition and Change 208
  Advances in Education 212
  Labor Force Trends 217
Human Resource Challenges Faced by Lebanon 220
  Outcomes of Primary and Secondary Education System Are Not
    Up to International Standards 221
  The Higher Education System Is Strong and Depends on the
    Private Sector 223
  Brain Drain Has Diminished the Benefit of a Strong Higher
    Education Sector 226

Unemployment Is High Among Youth in Particular and Foreign
    Workers Compete with Lower-Skilled Lebanese..................... 227
Material Deprivation Is High and Disparities in the Standard of
    Living Are Large 230
Approaches to Reform in Lebanon 232
    Economic Reforms Are Under Way 234
    Efforts to Reform Public Institutions Are Concurrent with
        Economic Reform... 236
Only Limited Demographic, Economic, and Labor Market Data
    Are Available to Monitor and Evaluate Progress 240
Summary.. 241

CHAPTER SEVEN
Conclusions.. 245
Significant Human Resource Challenges 246
Active Engagement with Reforms to Education and Training
    Systems, Labor Markets, and the Economy............................ 249
    Education and Training Reforms... 249
    Reforms to the Labor Market and Economy 254
Lack of High-Quality Data and Evaluation Systems....................... 257
The Value of Policy Evaluation 261

APPENDIXES
A. **Interviews Conducted**.. 263
B. **Interview Protocol**... 265
C. **Qatar Higher Education Institute Scholarship Programs** 269
D. **Private Institutions of Higher Education in Oman** 273
E. **Recent Economic Reform Efforts in Oman**......................... 277

References... 283

Figures

2.1.	Classification of Study Countries	18
3.1.	Map of Qatar	34
3.2.	Trends in Population Total and Growth Rate in Qatar, 1960 to 2006	39
3.3.	Trends in Working-Age Population, Labor Force, and Labor Force Participation Rate in Qatar, 1960 to 2006	45
3.4.	Student Results on Multiple Choice Component of QCEA, 2004	59
3.5.	Qatari Graduates from Qatar University in Humanities, Business, and Sciences, 1998–1999 to 2004–2005	60
3.6.	Schematic of Challenges Faced by Qatar: Need to Address an Underqualified and Unprepared National Workforce	63
4.1.	Map of the United Arab Emirates	90
4.2.	Trends in GDP and GDP Growth in the UAE, 1973 to 2005	94
4.3.	Trends in GDP per Capita and GDP per Capita Growth in the UAE, 1973 to 2005	96
4.4.	Trends in Population Total and Growth Rate in the UAE, 1960 to 2006	97
4.5.	Trends in Working-Age Population, Labor Force, and Labor Force Participation Rate in the UAE, 1980 to 2006	105
4.6.	Graduates of UAE University, by College, 1998–1999 to 2004–2005	114
4.7.	Schematic of Challenges Faced by the UAE: Need to Balance Nationalization Efforts with Policies Promoting Economic Growth	120
5.1.	Map of Sultanate of Oman	149

5.2.	Trends in GDP per Capita and GDP per Capita Growth in Oman, 1970 to 2004	154
5.3.	Trends in Population Total and Growth Rate in Oman, 1960 to 2006	156
5.4.	Trends in Working-Age Population, Labor Force, and Labor Force Participation Rate in Oman, 1980 to 2006	159
5.5.	Schematic of Challenges Faced by Oman: Need to Meet the Challenges of a Changing Economy	171
5.6.	Omanization Rates, by Area of Private Sector, 2005	192
6.1.	Map of Lebanon	202
6.2.	Trends in GDP per Capita and GDP per Capita Growth in Lebanon, 1989 to 2006	206
6.3.	Trends in Population Total and Growth Rate in Lebanon, 1960 to 2006	209
6.4.	Trends in Working-Age Population, Labor Force, and Labor Force Participation Rate in Lebanon, 1980 to 2006	218
6.5.	Schematic of Challenges Faced by Lebanon: Need to Achieve Political Stability While Addressing Human Resource Issues	232

Tables

1.1.	Categories of Human Capital Reforms Covered in Study	7
1.2.	Interviews Conducted, by Sector and Country	11
2.1.	Key Economic Indicators of Study Countries, 2004	21
2.2.	Governance Models in Study Countries	22
2.3.	Key Demographic Indicators of Study Countries, 2004	27
2.4.	Key Labor Market Indicators of Study Countries, 2004	28
2.5.	Key Education Indicators of Study Countries	30
3.1.	Human Capital Reforms Covered in Qatar Case Study	32
3.2.	Population in Qatar, by Age Group and Gender, 1986, 1997, and 2004	40
3.3.	Enrollment in Grades 1–12 in Qatar Public Schools, by Academic Year and Gender	43
3.4.	Gross and Net Enrollment Ratios in Qatar, by Education Level and Gender, 2005	44
3.5.	Working-Age Population in Qatar, by Nationality and Gender, 2004	47
3.6.	Labor Force in Qatar, by Nationality and Gender, 2004	47
3.7.	Labor Force Participation Rates in Qatar, by Nationality and Gender, 2004	48
3.8.	Distribution of Labor Force in Qatar, by Nationality and Sector, 2004	50
3.9.	Percent Distribution of Persons Employed in Qatar, by Economic Activity and Nationality, 2004	51
3.10.	Number of Unemployed and Unemployment Rate in Qatar, by Age Group and Gender, 2001	54
3.11.	Unwillingness of Unemployed Qataris to Work in the Private and Mixed Sectors and Reasons for Unwillingness, by Gender, 2001	55

3.12.	Fields of Study of Qatari Secondary School Graduates, by Gender, 1980–1981 to 2004–2005	57
3.13.	Breakdown of First University Degrees Granted in Qatar, 2002	61
3.14.	Educational Attainment of Employed Qataris, by Education Level and Gender, 2004	62
3.15.	Institutes of Higher Education on Qatar's Education City Campus	71
3.16.	Labor Force Participation Rates in Qatar, by Gender, 1986 to 2004	77
3.17.	Summary of Education and Labor Market Reforms Under Way in Qatar	84
4.1.	Human Capital Reforms Covered in UAE Case Study	89
4.2.	Population in the UAE, by Nationality and Age Group, 1995 and 2005	98
4.3.	Gross and Net Enrollment Ratios in the UAE, by Education Level and Gender, 2005	101
4.4.	Enrollment of Emiratis in Government and Private Education Systems, by Gender and Education Level, 2005–2006	102
4.5.	Enrollment in Higher Education Institutions in the UAE, by Nationality and Gender, 2001–2002	104
4.6.	Emirati Graduates from Higher Education Institutions in the UAE, by Gender, 2001–2002	104
4.7.	Labor Force Participation Rates in the UAE, by Gender, 1980 to 2006	106
4.8.	Distribution of Labor Force in the UAE, by Nationality, 1995 and 2005	108
4.9.	Labor Force Participation Rates in the UAE, by Gender and Nationality, 2005	109
4.10.	Gender Distribution in the UAE Labor Force, 1995 and 2006	110
4.11.	Gender Distribution in the UAE Labor Force, by Nationality, 1995 and 2005	110
4.12.	Secondary School Graduates of Government Schools in the UAE, by Major, 1998–1999 to 2005–2006	113
4.13.	Underlying Factors Driving Growth in Non-National Labor Force in the UAE	118

4.14.	Summary of Education and Labor Market Reforms Under Way in the UAE	145
5.1.	Human Capital Reforms Covered in Oman Case Study	148
5.2.	Population in Oman, by Nationality and Age Group, 1993 and 2003	157
5.3.	Gross and Net Enrollment Ratios in Oman, by Education Level and Gender, 2006	159
5.4.	Distribution of Labor Force in Oman, by Nationality, 1993 and 2003	160
5.5.	Labor Force Participation Rates in Oman, by Nationality and Gender, 1993 and 2003	161
5.6.	Gender Distribution in Oman Labor Force, by Nationality, 1993 and 2003	161
5.7.	Distribution of Persons Employed in Public and Private Sectors in Oman, by Nationality, 2003	162
5.8.	Percent Distribution of Persons Employed in Oman, by Economic Activity and Nationality, 2003	163
5.9.	Gross Rates of Student Dropout, Grade Failure, and Grade Repetition in Oman, by Education Level and Gender, 1999–2000	166
5.10.	Breakdown of First University Degrees Granted in Oman, 2000	167
5.11.	Number of Students Registered for Bachelor's Degree in Oman, by College, Field of Study, and Gender, 2004–2005	168
5.12.	Gross Rates of Student Dropout and Grade Repetition in Oman, by Education Level and Gender, 2005	178
5.13.	Summary of Education and Labor Market Reforms Under Way in Oman	196
6.1.	Human Capital Reforms Covered in Lebanon Case Study	200
6.2.	Population in Lebanon, by Age Group and Gender, 2004	211
6.3.	Population in Lebanon, by Nationality and Age Group, 2004	211
6.4.	Gross and Net Enrollment Ratios in Lebanon, by Education Level and Gender, 2004	213
6.5.	Student Enrollment in Lebanon, by Education Level and Type of School, 2004–2005	215

6.6.	Labor Force Participation Rates in Lebanon, by Gender, 1970 to 2004	219
6.7.	Distribution of Workforce in Lebanon, by Sector and Gender, 1970 and 2001	220
6.8.	Average Scale Scores on the 2003 TIMSS Assessment for Lebanon and Comparison Countries	222
6.9.	Breakdown of First University Degrees Granted in Lebanon, 2001	224
6.10.	Educational Attainment of Labor Force in Lebanon, 2004	228
6.11.	Unemployed and Unemployment Rates in Lebanon for Economically Active Population, by Gender, Age Group, and Educational Attainment, 2004	229
6.12.	Summary of Education and Economic Reforms Under Way in Lebanon	242
7.1.	Human Resource Challenges Affecting Study Countries	246
7.2.	Education and Training Reforms in Study Countries	250
7.3.	Labor Market and Other Economic Reforms in Study Countries	255
7.4.	Censuses and Specialized Surveys in Study Countries	259
C.1.	Number of Students in Qatar HEI Scholarship Programs, 2005–2006	270
C.2.	Highest Concentrations in HEI Scholarships, by Field of Study, 2005–2006	271
D.1.	Information on Private Institutions of Higher Education Operating in Oman, 2006–2007	274

Summary

A key challenge faced by countries in the Arab world today is promoting human capital development of the region's population. The 2003 *Arab Human Development Report* (United Nations Development Programme, 2003), with its call to build a "knowledge society" in response to economic globalization and technological change, spotlighted the deficits in education systems and workforce skills throughout much of the Arab region. There is a need for the economies in the region to be diversified—especially away from sectors built on natural resources such as oil and gas—the private sector to be expanded, and entrepreneurship to be fostered.

Progress in raising literacy and enrollment rates—especially at the primary level—has been considerable in recent decades in the Arab world, but education outcomes continue to lag those of other regions of the world. Even in cases in which education outcomes have been on a par with those of other developed countries, the education systems themselves do not consistently produce graduates who possess the skills needed for a 21st century global economy.

One consequence is that the demand for a qualified workforce is outpacing the supply of skilled workers—both in sectors that are already important in the economies of Arab countries and in areas of new opportunity. For some countries in the region, the citizen population is too small to support the economy, so skilled labor must be imported; in other countries, high population growth leads to a large youth population that must be educated and transitioned to productive work.

This monograph outlines the measures taken by Lebanon, Oman, Qatar, and the United Arab Emirates (UAE) to address the human resource and labor market issues that these countries face as they enter the 21st century global economy. These focal countries provide examples of the diversity and similarity of challenges faced by the Arab region and responses to those challenges. Three countries—Oman, Qatar, and the UAE—are in the Gulf; the fourth, Lebanon, provides a contrasting, non-Gulf country. Specifically, for these four countries, we attempted to answer the following questions:

- What are the human resource challenges they face?
- What education, human capital, and labor market reforms have recently been implemented or are under way to address these challenges?
- What mechanisms and information are used to assess whether reforms are meeting their objectives, and is there evidence of success?

Our approach involved reviewing relevant literature, collecting the most recent population and labor force data from international and in-country sources, and conducting a series of elite interviews with government officials and individuals in private organizations in the study countries (from January to August 2006 in Lebanon, Oman, and the UAE; from 2001 through 2006 in Qatar).

In discussing the human resource challenges faced by these four countries and their approaches to reform, it is important to keep in mind some basic distinctions. The World Bank classifies Lebanon and Oman as "middle income" in stage of economic development, whereas Qatar and the UAE are classified as "high income." Because Qatar, the UAE, and Oman derive much of their wealth from natural resources, their industrial sectors are a larger part of their economies than is Lebanon's. Notably, two of these countries, Qatar and the UAE, rely heavily on an expatriate workforce—88 and 91 percent, respectively.

In the remainder of this summary, we highlight what we learned about our four focal countries in terms of human resource challenges they face, range of reforms and other initiatives implemented or under way, and extent to which the changes are being or can be evaluated with existing data. We also highlight the benefits of making policy evaluation an integral part of the reform process, in the hope that all countries in the region can benefit from the lessons learned and knowledge gained from the extensive changes under way.

Human Resource Challenges

The first challenge, which is relevant for the three Gulf countries and most prominently affects the labor-importing resource-rich countries of Qatar and the UAE, is heavy reliance on non-nationals (i.e., non-citizens, in contrast to nationals, or citizens) to meet workforce needs for both skilled and unskilled labor. Foreign workers dominate in the workforce because of the relatively small population base from which rapid economic growth took place following the discovery of oil and gas, and because of nationals' relatively low rate of participation in the labor force. In Oman, Qatar, and the UAE, labor force participation rates for male and female nationals are 15 to 40 percentage points lower than the rate for non-nationals. And cultural and religious reasons keep the rate of labor force participation for female nationals considerably lower than that for male nationals, despite the fact that female nationals attain higher educational levels. Thus, the labor capacity of the citizen population—both male and female—is underutilized.

A second challenge—again, for the same three countries, particularly Qatar and the UAE—is the proportion of nationals working in the public sector. This issue reflects the preferential treatment nationals have historically received in the public sector, where the compensation, working conditions, job security, and prestige are better than the private sector offers. In effect, employment in government jobs is another form of the social welfare system put in place by the ruling elite in the resource-rich Gulf countries.

The third challenge is high rates of unemployment among young, first-time workers. Although data on unemployment rates by age were not available for each country (notably Oman and the UAE), this issue was consistently raised in our meetings with officials. These high rates signal a problem with matching workers to jobs at young ages, in part because of a mismatch between the skills of labor market entrants and the needs of employers, especially in the private sector. Compared with female nationals, male nationals in our Gulf countries tended to be particularly vulnerable to unemployment because of their lower rates of post-secondary degree attainment.

The skill mismatch is a symptom of the fourth challenge, which is universal for our study countries: the perception that the existing education and training systems do not effectively prepare students for the needs of the 21st century global economy. Our study countries have successfully expanded the primary-level education opportunities to all citizens, and literacy rates have risen rapidly, but there is general acknowledgment that the quality of the primary and secondary education systems in these countries is not up to international standards. Secondary school graduates are considered unprepared to directly enter the labor market with relevant skills or to enter competitive university programs. These concerns are validated by different forms of evidence: low levels of performance on internationally benchmarked student assessments; low shares of students whose studies at the secondary and post-secondary level concentrate in the critical fields of science, mathematics, engineering, and technology; and low rates of obtaining post-secondary degrees.

Two other challenges also pertain. One of these is the outmigration in Lebanon of university-level graduates in recent decades because of civil war and ongoing political and economic instability. As a result, the benefits of producing graduates from what is considered one of the region's finer higher education systems have diminished. The other challenge, which applies to both Lebanon and Oman because of their lower per capita income and higher disparities in living standards, is the disparities in access to and quality of educational opportunities for their populations.

Reforms to Education and Training Systems, Labor Markets, and the Economy

The human resource challenges motivated a series of reforms that have been implemented or are under way in the four study countries. Our analysis of government documentation of policies and reform efforts and our interviews with government officials and members of the private sector led us to group reforms into two broad categories: changes in the education and training system that are designed to raise the skills of the population, and changes to the labor market and economy that aim to facilitate the use of human capital in diverse sectors of the economy.

Education and Training Reforms

Education and training reforms are generally aimed at increasing access to or quality of the education and training being provided. It is evident that Lebanon has not been actively engaged in reforms to its education and training system with the exception of its participation in international student assessments. This does not indicate that the country's leadership has failed to recognize the importance of an effective education system for future economic success, but, rather, that the country's basic infrastructure and pubic sector institutions must be rebuilt before fundamental changes can be made to the education and training system. The three Gulf countries also recognize the importance of advancing their education and training systems. The greater resources these three have available to devote to reform at all levels—primary and secondary education, higher education, and training—have enabled them to engage in more-extensive reforms.

Primary and Secondary Education Reforms. Oman and Qatar are engaged in broad-based reforms to their primary and secondary education systems. Qatar's education reforms are arguably the most comprehensive in the region; changes initiated in 2002 address the management and delivery of educational services, the curriculum, and the quality of teachers and other critical resources. Qatar's education reform provides for a decentralized, "independent" primary and secondary school system that operates alongside the country's traditional Ministry of Education schools. Independent schools use newly developed curriculum standards in mathematics, science, and English (benchmarked to international standards) and in Arabic (the first of their kind). The standards encourage critical thinking and problem solving as part of their learning tools. Another part of the education reform is a system for evaluating the progress of students in all publicly funded schools that includes annual standards-based assessments and surveys administered to all students, their parents, teachers, and school administrators. Results from the assessments and surveys are distributed to all schools in the form of a school report card.

Faced with the prospect of dwindling natural resources and spurred by Vision 2020, a map for Oman's economic development that originated in a 1995 conference (Oman Ministry of Education, 2004), Oman initiated reforms to its publicly funded education system earlier than the other Gulf countries in our study. In 1998, Oman's Ministry of Education initiated its Basic education school system, which runs parallel to the Ministry's General education school system, beginning with students in grades 1 and 2 in 17 primary schools. The number of students and schools participating in the Basic education school system grows each year. The new system restructured schooling as two cycles: Cycle 1 covers students in grades 1 through 5; cycle 2 covers students in grades 6 through 10. After grade 10, students have the option of entering the labor market or continuing with grades 11 and 12, which prepare them for higher education. Other changes in the Basic education reform include lengthening the school year, school day, and class period; changing the curriculum to emphasize critical thinking, English language, information and communication technology, mathematics, and science; encouraging the use of formative and continuous assessments in the classroom so that teachers can receive feedback on student performance and skills; and raising teacher qualifications and the classroom supports teachers receive.

UAE policymakers recently brought primary and secondary education reform to the forefront in their nation. The formation of the Abu Dhabi and Dubai Education Councils to set new priorities for the government education system signals a commitment to fundamental change in the UAE's education system. Early activities include a pilot program in Abu Dhabi for an alternative governance model, one involving the establishment of government school clusters administered by a number of carefully selected Education Management Organizations, and reforms in how the Ministry of Education runs the traditional government schools. The Ministry of Education itself, under the leadership of a new minister, is considering granting more autonomy to the individual emirate states to allow them to manage their own education affairs with the support and guidance of the Ministry. In the 2007–2008 academic year, the Ministry launched new programs in select kindergarten through grade 12 (K–12) schools, known as "Al Ghad" schools (or Schools of Tomorrow). These schools are gradually implementing new curricula emphasizing bilingual education (Arabic and English) and are providing more-comprehensive leadership and teacher training. Although the development of new schools is a significant step, the reform effort is still in its early stages.

Higher Education and Training Reforms. The higher education and training reforms are a mix of strategies designed to focus on quality through curricular changes, international accreditation, and other reforms; to expand access by introducing new higher education institutions and providing scholarships; and to strengthen links to the labor market through job placement programs. The three Gulf countries in our study reexamined the quality of post-secondary options available in-country and adopted several approaches to enhance quality within existing institutions and to increase the number of quality post-secondary programs available to students. For example, all three Gulf countries are increasingly relying on foreign universities and the private sector to meet their growing post-secondary education needs. Qatar and the UAE have instituted education and "knowledge" centers that have enticed international colleges and universities to establish satellite campuses in their countries. In addition, scholarships are being used—in Oman as a tool to allow students from low-income families to attend higher education and in Qatar to provide incentives for university students to major in high-priority fields. In the UAE, another focus at the post-secondary level is matching students to jobs.

Raising the skills of the current and future workforce requires a focus not just on primary, secondary, and post-secondary education, but on the training system as well. While changes in the training domain are under way in the three Gulf countries, efforts to address training needs are not as systematic or sustained as those in the education domain. In the UAE, training issues are one focus of the coordinating education councils, which also focus on primary, secondary, and higher education reforms. All three Gulf countries are making an effort to expand the number of technical and vocational colleges and to forge public-private partnerships to increase nationals' opportunities for training, especially in skills required for the private sector. In Qatar, officials have established an independent certification of training programs to ensure their quality.

Reforms to the Labor Market and Economy

The countries in our study have initiatives targeting the labor market and the economy more generally. The labor market reforms are specific to the three Gulf countries; they aim to address some of the labor market barriers that have precluded employment of nationals in the private sector. The broader economic reforms seek to diversify and privatize the economy and, in the case of Lebanon, provide for a more efficient public sector. These reforms potentially allow the country's human capital to be used throughout the economy.

The labor market reforms in the Gulf countries take different forms. One approach gives employers incentives to hire nationals through quotas or sanctions; another approach aims to make private-sector employment more attractive to nationals by equalizing public- and private-sector employment conditions. A third approach entails inducing institutions to facilitate the transition of nationals to private-sector work through training and financial support or through job matching. In contrast, Lebanon is not instituting labor market reforms designed to encourage their citizens to work in the private sector, largely because the country does not face the challenge of nationals being concentrated in public-sector employment.

Our study countries are pursuing a variety of measures to diversify their economies, promote their private sectors, and raise public-sector efficiency as a way to employ the citizenry and enhance the sustainability of their economies. These measures include offering tax incentives to foreign companies to open branch offices and plants in the country, privatizing public utilities and other government-owned firms, relaxing restrictions on foreign ownership of companies in targeted sectors, opening free zones to expand and create new areas of economic activity, and creating a more efficient public sector.

Need for and Value of Policy Evaluation

Common across the study countries is a disconnect between implementation of reforms and evaluation to ascertain whether reforms are having the intended effects. In many cases, reforms have only recently gotten under way, so it may be too early to measure their impact. In other cases, however, the lack of systematic assessment stems from gaps in the data needed to track the effects of policy changes. In sum, for both recent reforms and those implemented up to a decade ago, analysis and evaluation have generally not been an integral part of planning for or implementing policy changes.

In responding to the human resource challenges they face, the Arab countries are devoting tremendous energy and resources to initiatives aimed at raising the skills of their populations and ensuring that the resulting human capital is fully used throughout the economy. To ensure that this energy and these resources are wisely invested, it is critical that evaluations be carried out to determine whether the policy changes and other initiatives are having their intended effects and whether the reforms are having unintended consequences. The extensive range of reforms under way throughout the Arab world provides a tremendous opportunity to learn from cross-county experimentation and to build a knowledge base of lessons learned and strategies that can be transferred from one county to another. To make policy evaluation an integral part of reform, there must be an investment in collecting data, a commitment to using evaluation results in decisionmaking, and opportunities to share lessons learned across countries so that Arab world governments can benefit from investments in research. If these requirements are met, and policy evaluation is made integral to reform, the countries in the Arab world will have the information they need to make the best investments in their human capital in the decades to come.

Acknowledgments

We gratefully acknowledge the participation of a number of officials and other individuals from the countries analyzed in our study. These people generously provided their time and made resources and materials available to us to facilitate our analysis; they also reviewed early drafts of the country chapters to check for factual errors. They include officials representing the Ministry of Manpower (Oman), the Dubai Education Council (UAE), Ministry of Higher Education (Oman), Ministry of Education (Lebanon, Oman, Qatar), Knowledge Village (UAE), Academic City (UAE), Supreme Education Council (Qatar), Education City (Qatar), Ministry of Civil Service (Oman, Qatar), Ministry of Economy (Lebanon), Ministry of Finance (Lebanon), Ministry of National Economy (Oman), Ministry of Economy and Planning (Lebanon, UAE, Qatar), Ministry of Reform (Lebanon), Ministry of Social Affairs (Lebanon), College of Business and Economics of UAE University, Office of the Prime Minister (Lebanon), Gulf Research Center (UAE), and Qatar University, and representatives of the petroleum industry (UAE, Qatar).

We wish to thank several RAND colleagues who provided early direction and support and pointed us to sources of information and data. They are Claude Berrebi, Keith Crane, Cassandra Guarino, Francisco Martorell, C. Richard Neu, Cathleen Stasz, and Gail Zellman. We also gratefully acknowledge the comments and suggestions of Sue Bodilly, Brent Bradley, Michael Rich, and James Thomson that stemmed from an interim project briefing given in April 2006, as well as the comments and suggestions we received from members of the

Board of Overseers of the RAND-Qatar Policy Institute at a briefing given in May 2007. Catherine Augustine, Dominic Brewer, and Elaine Reardon reviewed the report and provided helpful comments on its direction and analytic framework. We are grateful for their comments.

We also thank Lawrence Tingson and Reham Al Sayed, both of whom provided us with administrative, logistical, and research support. We alone, however, claim full responsibility for any errors within.

Abbreviations

ABP	Academic Bridge Program (Qatar)
bbl/day	barrels per day (of oil production)
CERT	Centre of Excellence for Applied Research and Training (UAE)
CLMRI	Centre for Labour Market Research and Information (UAE)
CNA-Q	College of North Atlantic–Qatar
EU	European Union
GCC	Gulf Cooperation Council
GDDS	General Data Dissemination System (IMF)
GDP	gross domestic product
GNI	gross national income
HCP	Higher Council for Privatization (Lebanon)
HCT	Higher Colleges of Technology (UAE)
HDI	human development index
HEI	Higher Education Institute (Qatar)
IAD	Institute of Administration Development (Qatar)
IDAL	Investment Development Authority of Lebanon

IMF	International Monetary Fund
K–12	kindergarten through grade 12
KOM	Knowledge Oasis Muscat (Oman)
LMIS	Labor Market Information System (UAE)
MENA	Middle East and North Africa (region)
MoCSAH	Ministry of Civil Service Affairs and Housing (Qatar)
n.a.	not available
N/A	not applicable
NGO	non-governmental organization
NSF	National Science Foundation
O.R.	Omani rials
OECD	Organisation for Economic Co-operation and Development
OMSAR	Office of the Minister of State for Administrative Reform (Lebanon)
OPEC	Organization of the Petroleum Exporting Countries
OVQ	Oman Vocational Qualification
PANDE	Public Authority for National Development and Employment (UAE)
PEIE	Public Establishment for Industrial Estates (Oman)
PIRLS	Progress in International Reading Literacy Study
PISA	Programme for International Student Assessment
QCEA	Qatar Comprehensive Educational Assessment
QNEDS	Qatar National Education Data System
QSTP	Qatar Science and Technology Park

RQPI	RAND-Qatar Policy Institute
SDDS	Special Data Dissemination Standard (IMF)
TIMSS	Trends in International Mathematics and Science Study
UAE	United Arab Emirates
UN	United Nations
UNDP	United Nations Development Programme
UNESCO	United Nations Education, Scientific, and Cultural Organization
UNFPA	United Nations Population Fund
UNICEF	United Nations Children's Fund
VAT	value-added tax
WTO	World Trade Organization

CHAPTER ONE

Introduction

Human Resource Challenges Faced by the Arab Region

According to the Framework for Action adopted for Arab states by the 2000 Regional Conference on Education for All (United Nations Education, Scientific, and Cultural Organization [UNESCO], 2000b), millions of individuals in the Arab region[1] are being deprived of education, and millions are receiving education of poor quality. In addition, most of those receiving an education are not being appropriately prepared for the technological era or the potential for international competition in the new millennium. While primary education enrollments are relatively high (90 percent or higher), secondary and postsecondary education remains elusive for most. And illiteracy rates in the region are high—68 million illiterate people, 63 percent of them females—largely due to the lack of education for older groups. For many countries in the region (Egypt, Sudan, Morocco, Mauritania, Yemen, Tunisia, Algeria, Djibouti, Iraq, and Oman), illiteracy is the number one challenge.

Many other of the region's countries have addressed the basic education needs of their populations, overcoming the problem of illiteracy and the gender gap related to it (e.g., the UAE, Bahrain, Jordan, Kuwait, Lebanon, Libya, Palestine, Qatar, Saudi Arabia, and Syria) (UNESCO, 2000b). However, the workforce in the vast majority of

---

[1] According to UNESCO, the Arab region countries are Algeria, Bahrain, Djibouti, Egypt, Iraq, Jordan, Kuwait, Lebanon, Libya, Malta, Mauritania, Morocco, Oman, Qatar, Saudi Arabia, Somalia, Sudan, Syria, Tunisia, the United Arab Emirates (UAE), and Yemen.

Arab nations either lacks the skills needed for important sectors of industry and the economy or does not have the skills essential for fueling entrepreneurship and growth in new areas of opportunity. Labor market and economic reforms are needed to increase the role of the private sector, to diversify economies (especially away from oil domination), and to reduce unemployment, particularly among young nationals (World Bank, 2004).

The 2003 *Arab Human Development Report*, which carries the subtitle *Building a Knowledge Society,* cites lack of knowledge capital as the main long-term problem faced by the Arab world and calls declining quality the most important challenge faced by Arab education (United Nations Development Programme [UNDP], 2003). A key component of a knowledge society, or knowledge economy, is reliance on the intellectual capabilities of the workforce, rather than on material products or national resources (Powell and Snellman, 2004). The 2003 report notes that the knowledge gap, not the income gap, "determines the prospects of countries in today's world economy" (UNDP, 2003, p. 35).

Human capital—the learning, abilities, skills, and knowledge of an individual—can be used in the labor market as a form of currency (or capital) in exchange for wages or earnings. Human capital is often considered a key predictor of a person's employment and wages. Human capital theory (Becker, 1964) suggests that investments in human capital can be through formal schooling or on-the-job training, both of which raise workers' productivity and therefore increase their wages or earnings. Most studies show that formal schooling is an important factor in explaining variations of salary and wages in well-developed countries (Cohn and Addison, 1998) and in some less-developed countries (Psacharopoulos, 1985, 1994). One expectation is that widespread investment in human capital will create the skill base in the labor force that is indispensable for a country's economic growth.

Globalization and technological changes have made human capital development increasingly important for a nation's economic progress (Korpi and Tahlin, 2006). Labor markets around the world are going beyond countries' borders, calling for individuals to have specific technology-based skills. However, recent studies found that those educated in the Arab region are ill prepared to enter the world of work in a global economy. According to the results of the Monitoring Learning Achievement project conducted by UNESCO and the United Nations Children's Fund (UNICEF) between 1993 and 1998, primary education in the Arab states appears to be of poor quality and fails to provide for students' basic learning needs (UNESCO, 2000a). For example, the project's study of English language found that despite English being the language of technology, students in the Arab region were not receiving the amounts and kinds of English instruction needed to communicate effectively and to keep up with advances in information technology. Given that human capital needs of countries change over time with the advent of new technology, improving the quality of education now constitutes a main challenge to the Arab states.[2]

Labor demand in both growing and emerging economic sectors is outpacing the supply of local populations' workforce skills.[3] This skill mismatch can lead to either low wages or unemployment. Research shows that labor demand and supply imbalances (skill mismatch) that affect workers with the poorest labor market prospects (i.e., those with the lowest education levels) worsen the overall performance of a country's economy by increasing the unemployment rate (Manacorda and Petrongolo, 1999). Because of the limits in the quality of education that students in the Arab world receive, a large gap exists between the

---

[2] The World Education Forum (held in Dakar, Senegal, in 2000) set the following six goals for achieving "Education for All" by 2015 and called on states in the Arab region to establish national plans to reach those goals: (1) expand and improve comprehensive early childhood care and education, especially for the most vulnerable and disadvantaged children; (2) ensure that by 2015 all children, particularly girls, in difficult circumstances and those belonging to ethnic minorities have access to and complete free and compulsory primary education of good quality; (3) ensure that the learning needs of all young people and adults are met through equitable access to appropriate learning and life skills programs; (4) achieve a 50 percent improvement in levels of adult literacy by 2015, especially for females, and equitable access to basic and continuing education for all adults; (5) eliminate gender disparities in primary and secondary education by 2005, and achieve gender equality in education by 2015, with a focus on ensuring females' full and equal access to and achievement in basic education of good quality; (6) improve all aspects of the quality of education and ensure excellence for all so that recognized and measurable learning outcomes are achieved by all, especially in literacy, numeracy, and essential life skills (UNESCO, 2000a).

[3] See Autor, Katz, and Kearney, 2006, for documentation of the link between the expansion of information technology and the rise in skill demand.

demand for human capital skills and the supply of those skills through the native workforces of the region (UNDP, 2003). Furthermore, the World Bank's recent report on education reform in the Middle East notes that Middle Eastern countries have not been able to "capitalize on the progress made in increasing the level of human capital in the labor force over time" (World Bank, 2008, p. 296). Rising unemployment has meant that fewer people can be productive in the workforce. At the same time, the workforce in these countries is relatively unproductive, further exacerbating the region's slow returns to human capital investment (World Bank, 2008).

Demographic growth poses another challenge for education systems in the Arab region. Annual average growth rate for 2000–2010 is estimated at 1.2 percent for the world, 1.5 percent for developing countries, and 2.5 percent for the Arab states (UNESCO, 2000a). The population of 5- to 18-year-olds in the Arab states is projected to be 110 million by 2010. If the enrollment ratio in general education is 80 percent, the Arab states will have to ensure educational opportunities to 88 million students by 2010 (current figures hold this number at 59 million students). This places pressure on the education system in terms of expenditures, management, and finding qualified teachers for these children (UNESCO, 2000a).

There are additional challenges beyond skill mismatch and an expanding youth population. Many Arab states, particularly the wealthier Gulf nations, face a labor deficit caused by inadequate preparation of the national labor pool,[4] and many Gulf nations have a limited private sector and/or limited experience with entrepreneurship. In addition, females continue to participate in the labor market less than fully, and they experience occupational segregation, certain jobs being considered more appropriate for females than males. Other Arab states experience a high rate of outmigration because their labor markets cannot absorb recent graduates.

---

[4] We use the term *nationals* to mean citizens of a country. Expatriates, or non-nationals, are members of the immigrant populations residing in a country that are not citizens. In the Gulf countries, non-nationals are often low-skilled laborers or highly skilled employees who are in the country for a set period, much like "guest workers" in the United States and Europe.

Policymakers in the Arab world are therefore paying close attention to shortcomings in human resource development, skill mismatch in labor markets, and the associated need to enhance the quality of education. Deficiencies in these areas threaten to undermine progress toward creating the type of society—a knowledge and information society—needed to effectively address increasingly complex 21st century issues related to community well-being and development.

Research Questions

This monograph documents the measures that have been taken to address the human resource and labor market issues that four countries in the Arab region face as they enter the 21st century global economy. The four countries we selected—Lebanon, Oman, Qatar, and the UAE—provide examples of the diversity and similarity in the challenges faced by the region and the responses to those challenges. We asked the following questions:

- What are the human resource challenges that these countries face?
- What education, human capital, and labor market reforms have recently been implemented or are under way to address these challenges?
- What mechanisms and information are used to assess whether reforms are meeting their objectives, and is there evidence of success?

In the next sections, we introduce the analytic approach that guided our analysis of each country that we examined. We also describe how we collected the data and other information used in our study and note our rationale for selecting the four countries and the study's limitations. We conclude the chapter with a roadmap for the remainder of the monograph.

Analytic Approach

Our study assumed that a country's human resource base should have skills that match labor market needs and that countries seek to design a set of institutions and incentives to minimize any perceived mismatches that may exist. Thus, our goal was to identify the range of human resource challenges faced by our focal countries and to describe the reform measures each country has implemented to address those challenges. With this objective in mind, we arrived at a three-part analytic framework that follows our research questions: We first identified the most-pressing human resource issues for each country; we then catalogued the policy approaches to address the human resource problems; and, finally, we examined the availability of resources for evaluating the policies that have been put in place. At each stage of our approach, as discussed in the next section, we drew on the perspective of key informants in each country studied, as well as public reports and our analysis of various secondary data sources. We now turn to each component of our analytic approach.

Diagnosis and Articulation of the Problem: What Are the Human Resource Challenges That Each Country Faces?

Access to information on key education, training, and labor market indicators is a vital part of diagnosing and articulating the nature of any human resource challenges a country may be facing. Basic data on population (disaggregated by nationality, age, gender); primary, secondary, and post-secondary education outcomes; and labor market indicators, such as labor force participation and unemployment rates and the sectoral composition of employment, should be readily available to make an accurate diagnosis.

To understand the nature of the most-prominent human resource issues in our focal countries, we analyzed data available through in-country and international sources and examined reports and other sources of information to determine what has been diagnosed as the important human resource issues faced by each country. These analyses were supplemented by interviews with key decisionmakers in institutions responsible for education and labor outcomes to give us an understanding of their perception and articulation of the problem.

Approaches to Addressing the Problem: What Reforms Have Been Developed or Are Under Way?
To ascertain whether our study countries were addressing human resource challenges, we collected, through key informant interviews and various publicly available secondary sources, information on enacted or underway reform policies specifically designed to improve the human capital or skills of a country's population, or to facilitate the employment of human capital in diverse sectors of the economy. Table 1.1 provides the categories of reforms we considered, grouping the reforms into those related to education and training and those related to labor markets and the economy.

In terms of education and training reforms, we focused on those designed to increase participation in or raise the quality of primary and secondary schooling. We were also interested in reforms targeting higher education that had such objectives as raising participation rates in post-secondary or post-graduate schooling, increasing the knowledge and skills that students obtain, and shifting the

Table 1.1
Categories of Human Capital Reforms Covered in Study

Reform Categories and Subcategories
Education and training
Primary and secondary education
Post-secondary and post-graduate education
Training
Labor market and economy
Labor market reforms
Economic privatization
Economic diversification

mix of students in terms of fields of study or professional specialties. Reforms targeting training institutions were another area of focus, whether the programs concerned new labor market entrants or retraining of the current workforce. In each of these areas, reforms could be aimed at public-sector institutions, private-sector institutions, or both.

We also considered a set of reforms designed to promote the use of human resources through more-general reforms to the labor market or the economy. In the case of the labor market, these could encompass, for example, reforms affecting employment conditions in the public or private sectors, the provision of employee benefits by public or private employers, or the role of expatriates in the labor market. The reforms could be designed to affect the decisionmaking of individuals in or outside the labor force (e.g., increasing labor force participation rates or making certain sectors of the economy more or less attractive for employment) or of employers (e.g., making certain workers more or less attractive for employment). Broader economic reforms could also have implications for the use of human capital. In this domain, we focused on reforms designed to promote the private sector (particularly relevant in those economies with a large public sector) or greater economic diversification (an issue in those resource-rich countries that are highly dependent on income from a specific source, such as petroleum products). Reforms aimed at privatization and diversification typically have reform elements designed to address the labor needs of the private sector or the sectors targeted for expansion.

For the range of reforms shown in Table 1.1, we looked for ways in which reform efforts might complement each other or, alternatively, might be at cross purposes. At the same time, the categories of reforms we focused on covered only a portion of the broader economic, political, and social reforms implemented or in the planning stages in our four study countries or the Arab region more generally. Thus, for example, we did not focus on economic reforms affecting financial markets, other economic sectors (e.g., health care), trade, or government unless they had some bearing on human capital formation or use.

Availability of Resources for Policy Evaluation: What Mechanisms Are in Place for Evaluating Policy?

Accurate diagnosis and articulation of a problem depend on the availability of data and information from which an appropriate policy approach can be devised. In addition, a country must be able to track and report on progress in addressing identified problems. As part of the third component of our approach, we documented whether our four focal countries had put into place mechanisms to evaluate progress in achieving reform goals.

Effective policy-evaluation resources that track and report progress typically include regular population and labor force surveys that measure economic outcomes and social indicators, as well as careful administration of student assessments and collection of other information on education outcomes. Equally important is appropriate analysis of collected data, as well as clear and transparent reporting of results so that what is learned is ultimately useful to policymakers and other stakeholders. An effective system of data collection and policy evaluation provides policymakers with information about whether a given policy is working or not and, if not, what needs to be done so that it achieves its intended outcome. Again, drawing on information from interviews and secondary sources, we examined the extent to which these mechanisms were in place in each study country.

Approach to Data Collection and Interviews

As previously indicated, we used two sources of data to collect timely information about human resource challenges, reform efforts under way in our selected countries, and data available for policy evaluation. One source of information involved analysis of population, economic, education, and labor market data from country-level government organizations and from international databases available from the UNDP, UNESCO, the World Bank, and the International Monetary Fund

(IMF). These secondary data sources provide a context for understanding the human capital challenges that each of the countries faces.[5]

The second data source is information provided in interviews with knowledgeable officials in the government and private sector of each study country. For information on the human resource challenges faced by Qatar and reform efforts that are under way in that country, we analyzed notes from interviews conducted by RAND from 2001 through 2006 for studies assessing the primary and secondary education system (see Brewer et al., 2007), post-secondary education system (see Stasz et al., 2007), the labor market, civil service and training, and the country's national university.

Using the information provided by those studies on Qatar, we developed a semi-structured interview protocol for our interviews with key informants in the public and private sectors in our other three study countries. We conducted our interviews in Lebanon, Oman, and the UAE between January and August 2006. During our country visits, we conducted meetings with high-level officials across various sectors, including education, economy, civil service, manpower and vocational training, and data collection and planning. To understand how government initiatives were being received by the populace and whether reform efforts were meeting intended goals, we also met with leaders of private and quasi-private non-governmental organizations (NGOs) and research firms.

Table 1.2 lists, by country, the sectors in which we conducted interviews in Lebanon, Oman, and the UAE and on which we gathered information from studies on Qatar. Although we aimed for interviews in all sectors in each country, on many occasions we could not gain access to officials. In the case of "administrative reform and social affairs," only Lebanon has an office devoted to this sector. In the case of "manpower and vocational training," Qatar does not have a specific office devoted to this sector. Instead, the "civil ser-

---

[5] The secondary data sources on which we relied follow international standards in sampling methods and administration to targeted populations. When links to websites containing the datasets are available, we provide them for those readers who wish to consult the sources directly.

Table 1.2
Interviews Conducted, by Sector and Country

Sector	Lebanon	Oman	Qatar	UAE
Manpower and vocational training		√	N/A	√
Primary, secondary, and higher education	√	√	√	√
Civil service and labor		√	√	
Economy, finance, and planning	√	√	√	√
Administrative reform and social affairs	√	N/A	N/A	N/A
General government	√			
Private and mixed sector			√	√

NOTE: N/A = not applicable (ministry or sector does not exist).

vice and labor" sector develops policies related to manpower. Appendix A provides additional detail on the officials with whom we met or, in the case of Qatar, whose interview notes we analyzed.

Although interviews were tailored by sector, the questions required interviewees to reflect on the most significant challenges faced by the country with respect to human capital formation and development. We asked whether officials considered the education system of the country, the labor pool and workers' skills, or the economy and associated labor market as the greatest priority for the country and why. We also wanted to understand the key national policy priorities and role of the specific ministry or organization in formulating and addressing those priorities. We asked officials to tell us the important initiatives or reforms related to human capital or human resource development in the previous five years in the country. We questioned the motivation for reforms, the process for formulating and implementing reforms, and the challenges the country was facing in ensuring that reforms were successfully implemented. Finally, we asked what types of mechanisms were in place (e.g., data collection or evaluation efforts) to inform policymaking and whether there were any mechanisms to help policymakers better understand the success or failure of reform efforts. The generic interview protocol is provided in Appendix B.

We used the interview notes to provide an overview of the areas of human capital deficits in each country and the types of reforms under way, and to provide guidance on where to find published information. We then relied primarily on secondary data and published documents for much of the detailed analysis in the study. As a result, we do not directly reference or quote specific officials with whom we spoke in our chapters on the case studies. Instead, we use the interview information to describe the general nature of each country's reform efforts. When other materials provided a source of information about specific aspects of the reforms, those materials are directly cited. In the absence of a specific citation, the source is presumed to be information gathered during our interviews.

Rationale for Country Selection

Our study approach juxtaposes three Gulf countries—Oman, Qatar, and the UAE—and one non-Gulf country—Lebanon—to showcase similarities and differences in the reform strategies employed. Qatar and the UAE, with their similar geographic and cultural histories, share many demographic and economic characteristics. They also face similar workforce challenges because of their reliance on imported labor to fill skill gaps in their national labor pools. Oman shares strong political and cultural similarities with its fellow Arab Gulf Cooperation Council (GCC) members,[6] but its lesser dependence on natural resources for its wealth has caused its economic and socio-demographic development to differ from that of the other GCC members in important ways. Lebanon serves as a stark contrast to the Gulf countries because it is a major exporter of labor and is undergoing significant rebuilding after a prolonged civil war. We selected these countries to illustrate the differences in the challenges faced by what many outside the region consider to be a homogenous group of nations.

---

[6] The GCC was established in 1981 to foster relations among the countries in the Arabian Gulf. Its members are Bahrain, Kuwait, Oman, Qatar, Saudi Arabia, and the UAE.

In addition to taking into consideration the country-level characteristics in choosing our study countries, we factored in a number of logistic constraints. First, our data collection effort took place between January and August 2006. Because of this time constraint, we had limited time to arrange for visits, gain access to key informants, collect data, and follow leads on information within each country. Second, particularly for high-level government officials, we expected long delays in getting appointments, without which a personal connection or introduction would have been impossible to secure. We therefore made the purposeful decision to select countries that would allow for ease of access: countries close to the RAND office in Doha, Qatar, and within which we had collegial relationships. Qatar offered a unique opportunity in that RAND had assisted in the design and implementation of reforms to the kindergarten through grade 12 (K–12) education system and to Qatar University, its primary national university, from 2001 to 2006. We intended to include Jordan and Kuwait as part of the case studies, but ended up excluding them. In the case of Jordan, it became clear that we did not have the personal connections needed for ready access to key informants. In the case of Kuwait, after we had conducted an initial set of interviews, the political climate of the country changed: The emir dissolved the parliament, and many government ministries temporarily closed. Shortly thereafter, the emir died, whereupon our attempts to reschedule did not succeed in securing interviews because it was anticipated that the ministerial cabinet would change.

Limitations of the Study

It is important to keep in mind several limitations of our analysis. First, we provide in this monograph a portrait of policies and reform measures under way in each country, yet our study stopped short of formally evaluating whether the policies and reforms were meeting their intended goals. This is largely because many of the policies were in their nascent stages and it was therefore too early to assess the effects of the changes. A related issue is that the information needed to evaluate the effects of specific reforms was often not available. However, where possible, we point to evidence that may be suggestive of the early effects of specific reform efforts. Second, given the diversity of the countries in the Arab region in terms of history, political systems, economies, and demographic makeup, we did not seek to generalize the human resource challenges or reform efforts experienced by the four study countries to other countries in the Arab world. Nevertheless, by documenting how these four countries are responding to what are, in many cases, challenges that are shared by other countries in the region, we provide a catalogue of the range of education and labor market reforms that may serve as models for other countries and, eventually, lessons learned about what does and does not work.

Organization of This Document

Chapter Two describes the economic and sociopolitical histories of our four study countries. Chapters Three through Six focus, respectively, on the human capital reform initiatives in place or under way in those countries—Qatar first, followed by the UAE, Oman, and then Lebanon. The country chapters are organized according to our analytic framework; they each have five sections: relevant background on the country; human resource challenges; reforms under way to address those challenges; data available for policy evaluation; a summary of key findings. We begin with Qatar and the UAE because these two countries are the most similar in the group: They are resource rich, are governed by a ruling elite, have a large or relatively large public sector, and have a labor market dominated by non-nationals. Chapter Five then focuses on Oman, which is like Qatar and the UAE in that it is governed by a ruling elite, but has dwindling resources and a more diverse economy with less reliance on expatriate labor. Chapter Six's focus is on Lebanon, the country that contrasts most sharply with the other three countries: It is the only non-Gulf country of the four and has few natural resources, a participatory democracy, a large private sector, and minimal reliance on foreign labor. Chapter Seven then presents a synthesis perspective on the reforms under way in the four study countries and discusses implications for human capital reforms throughout the Arab region.

CHAPTER TWO
Economic and Sociopolitical Context for Reform in the Four Study Countries

We classified the countries in our study on the basis of four characteristics: source of national wealth, nature of sociopolitical system, diversity of economy, and composition of labor pool.[1] These four characteristics are intrinsically tied to each other. The countries that rely on natural resources for their wealth have similar political systems, have a large public sector that serves as the dominant employer in the country, and need to import expatriate (skilled and unskilled) labor to fill shortages in their local labor pools. Conversely, the countries that have a variety of sources of national wealth share a longer history of participatory government, have a balance between the public and private sectors, and rely less on expatriate labor. Figure 2.1 shows how the countries fit in our classification scheme.

Reliance on Natural Resources for National Wealth

As Figure 2.1 shows, two countries in our sample, Qatar and the UAE, are classified as resource rich, while the other two fall at the opposite extreme, that of having dwindling or poor natural resources from which to generate wealth. Qatar and the UAE rely largely on oil as

---

[1] Some of these characteristics are used in other sources to classify countries in the Arab world. For example, the World Bank divides countries in the Middle East and North Africa (MENA) region into those that are resource rich versus resource poor, and labor abundant versus labor scarce (World Bank, 2004). Three of our four study countries—Oman, Qatar, and the UAE—are classified as resource rich and labor scarce; our fourth country, Lebanon, is classified as resource poor and labor abundant.

Figure 2.1
Classification of Study Countries

Reliance on natural resources for national wealth	
Resource rich	Resource poor/dwindling
Qatar	Lebanon
UAE	Oman

Sociopolitical system	
Ruling elite	Full participatory democracy
Qatar	Lebanon
UAE	
Oman (some participation)	

Diversity of economy	
Dominated by single industry and large public sector	Balanced across multiple industries and large private sector
Qatar	Lebanon
Oman	
UAE	

Composition of labor pool	
Predominantly non-nationals	Predominantly nationals
Qatar	Lebanon
UAE	Oman

RAND MG786-2.1

their dominant source of national income, although that resource is diminishing in both Qatar (which increasingly relies on natural gas production) and the UAE (where oil is mainly concentrated in Abu Dhabi, and the other emirate states have only limited supplies). In Qatar, oil and gas account for more than 60 percent of gross domestic product (GDP), roughly 85 percent of export earnings, and 70 percent of government revenues (Qatar Planning Council, 2006a). According to 2005 figures from the Organization of the Petroleum Exporting Countries (OPEC), oil production in Qatar reached 7.6 million barrels per day (bbl/day), with proven oil reserves of 15.2 billion barrels estimated to continue for 23 years (OPEC, 2006). Qatar's natural gas production reached 43.5 billion standard cubic meters, and its reserves, which exceed 25 trillion cubic meters, are more than 5 percent of the world total and are the third largest in the world, behind Russia and Iran. Qatar is expected to become the world's top exporter of liquefied natural gas in the near future (OPEC, 2006). Of the countries in our study, the UAE has the largest reserves of oil, estimated at 98 billion barrels in 2005, or approximately 100 years at current production levels. The UAE's oil production is 2.378 million bbl/day, and its natural gas production is 46.6 billion cubic meters, with 6 trillion cubic meters of proven reserves. In 2004, oil and gas production alone accounted for a large portion (30 percent) of the UAE's GDP, giving Abu Dhabi (the emirate in which most of that production takes place) the strongest economy in the country. Yet the growing manufacturing and construction sectors in emirates such as Dubai are beginning to account for significant shares of economic activity (14 percent and 8 percent, respectively) (UAE Ministry of Information and Culture, 2006).[2]

Qatar and the UAE can be characterized as "oil states" in that the sale of oil, rather than the production capabilities of the state's population, is the generator of the state's wealth (Mohammed, 2003). This, plus the lack of domestic taxation, means that wealth does not tend to circulate in the economy (Beblawi and Luciani, 1987). Reliance on natural rather than human resources for the wealth of a country has had a major impact on the other three domains of our classification scheme. When oil was discovered in the Arab Gulf region, existing family rulers became the major recipients of the income; at the same time, the rulers directed large sums of that income toward socioeconomic development projects. Before long, the Gulf states supported their citizenry through public-sector employment or social welfare while relying on expatriates to fill any perceived shortages in the skilled and unskilled labor pools.

---

[2] Forty-four percent of the UAE's GDP is accounted for by the services sector, which includes government services. The total non-oil-related contribution toward the UAE's GDP in 2004 is listed at 230 billion dirhams, or 71 percent (UAE Ministry of Information and Culture, 2006).

Conversely, Lebanon and Oman are not able to rely predominantly on natural resources for their national wealth. Although the production and sale of oil contribute to Oman's national GDP, its economy is more diverse than those of the large oil states, Qatar and the UAE. The reason for this greater diversity is twofold: Oil was discovered relatively late in Oman (1964) compared with its Gulf neighbors (early 1930s), and Oman's oil reserves are quickly dwindling. Lebanon's GDP also does not rely on the production or sale of oil. Oil has never been a source of wealth for Lebanon; instead, Lebanon has relied on strong financial and service sectors, particularly before and after its 1975–1990 civil war.

Table 2.1 summarizes several key economic indicators for our study countries as of 2004.[3] Qatar and the UAE, both classified as "high income" countries by the World Bank, are the wealthiest countries in our study, with sizably larger gross national income (GNI) per capita figures in 2004 than Lebanon or Oman, which are both classified as "upper middle income."[4] Qatar and the UAE also had the fastest-growing economies, with 2004 real growth rates of 9.9 and 8.5 percent, respectively. Oman has the slowest-growing economy, at 3.1 percent real growth, and Lebanon falls in between, with a 6.3 percent real growth rate. Using a broader measure of development—the human development index, or HDI—that captures life expectancy and

---

[3] Table 2.1 and several others that follow in this chapter rely primarily on country-level data compiled by international agencies—e.g., the World Bank as part of its World development indicators (World Bank, 2007). In some cases, these data differ from statistics available from sources within our study countries, sources we drew on for our analyses in the country-specific chapters (Chapters Three through Six). However, we prefer to use the data from the international sources for this introductory discussion because they attempt to produce statistics that are as comparable across countries as possible, which often means adjustments have been made to official statistics prepared by country government agencies. When an indicator of interest for this chapter was not available from an international source, we report the relevant indicator from the country-specific source, when available, and note on the table any variation across countries in the year or definition of the indicator.

[4] Based on 2004 GNI per capita using the World Bank Atlas method, high-income countries exceed GNI per capita of $10,066, and upper-middle-income countries are in the range of $3,256 to $10,065. The World Bank does not report GNI per capita for Qatar for 2004 but estimates it as being in the high-income range.

Table 2.1
Key Economic Indicators of Study Countries, 2004

Country	GNI per Capita (U.S. $) [classification]	Real GDP Growth (percent/year)	GDP Contribution by Sector (percent distribution)	UNDP HDI [classification]
Lebanon	6,040 [upper middle income]	6.3	Industry: 22 Services: 71 Agriculture: 7	0.774 [medium]
Oman	9,070 [upper middle income]	3.1	Industry: 56 Services: 42 Agriculture: 2	0.810 [high]
Qatar	n.a. [high income]	9.9	Industry: 76 Services: 24 Agriculture: <1	0.844 [high]
UAE	23,770 [high income]	8.5	Industry: 55 Services: 42 Agriculture: 3	0.839 [high]

SOURCES: GNI per capita, real GDP growth, and GDP contribution by sector are from World Bank, 2007, for Lebanon, Oman, and UAE; and from Qatar Planning Council, 2005c, p. 17, and World Bank, 2007, Table 1.1, for Qatar. UNDP HDI figures are from UNDP, 2006, Table 1.

NOTES: n.a. = not available. GNI per capita was calculated using the World Bank Atlas method.

education (measured by adult literacy and gross school enrollment at the primary, secondary, and post-secondary levels) in addition to the standard of living (measured by GDP per capita), the UNDP ranks Qatar, the UAE, and Oman as "high" human development countries and Lebanon as a "medium" human development country.[5]

Sociopolitical System: The Role of Participatory Democracy

Figure 2.1 classifies three of our study countries—the three Gulf states—as dominated by a ruling elite, whereas Lebanon is the outlier because of its history (albeit a tumultuous one) of participatory

---

[5] For additional detail on the HDI, see UNDP, 2006.

democracy. Table 2.2 summarizes the governance models of our study countries along five dimensions that describe the political and legal structures in place, as well as the nature of the voting rights extended to citizens.

The political and legal infrastructures of the three Gulf nations have dramatically expanded as a result of oil revenues, and the expansion in oil revenues has enhanced the social and economic well-being of the people in these countries. Despite such advancements, however, ruling families retain ultimate decisionmaking authority. Executive and legislative powers in the three Gulf states are in the hands of the rulers and their appointed councils of ministers (Mohammed, 2003). As heads of state, however, rulers can wield a great deal of power and can intervene in the consultative branch at will (which is what happened in another Gulf country, Kuwait, when the parliament was dissolved in 2006). The three Gulf countries today are not

Table 2.2
Governance Models in Study Countries

	Lebanon	Oman	Qatar	UAE
Type of governance	Parliamentary republic	Monarchy	Constitutional emirate	Federation of emirates
Executive branch	President, Council of Ministers	Sultan	Emir	Federal Supreme Council
Legislative branch[a]	Unicameral parliament	None	None	None
Advisory bodies	None	State council, Consultative council	Shura Council	Federal National Council
Justice and legal system	Multireligious, civil	Islamic, civil	Islamic, civil	Islamic, civil
Voting rights	All citizens age 21 and above[b]	All citizens age 21 and above	All citizens age 18 and above	Limited

SOURCES: U.S. Department of State, 2007a through c and 2008.

[a] Has authority to write and pass legislation.

[b] Compulsory for adult males; authorized for females with an elementary education.

absolute monarchies; some participatory assemblies are allowed, and each country has some form of a constitution (as does Lebanon). Furthermore, enfranchisement seems an important goal to the rulers of Qatar and Oman, who recently passed laws to extend voting to all citizens, male and female. The president of the UAE's Federal Supreme Council also passed a law, in August 2006, to allow select members of the public to vote for 50 percent of the members of the Federal National Council, a political body that plays an advisory role to the Federal Supreme Council. Furthermore, the rulers in the three Gulf states do not have dictatorial powers. They are bound by shari'a (Islamic law), by age-old tribal customs and values, and by the process of shura (consultation).

To understand the link between a country's reliance on oil wealth and its political system, it is important to consider the genesis of the nation-state for Arab Gulf countries. Gulf countries as distinct nation-states initially formed as a strategic location for British trade ships en route to India. At the turn of the 20th century, many tribal leaders in the Gulf signed agreements that allowed Britain to oversee all foreign relations of the fledgling nation-states without interfering in their domestic politics. Under these agreements, Britain recognized the tribal leader as the representative of the people in that region. In turn, Britain offered the leaders protection from other countries or tribes in the region. No Gulf state was allowed to deal with another country, large or small; all foreign relations were conducted on their behalf by Britain. This protective relationship with Britain acted like a cocoon that preserved the tribes' social traditions and political systems, thus permitting the continued adherence to Arab tribal customs. It also contributed to the survival of their cultural institutions despite the dramatic impact of the great oil wealth of the past 50 years (Zahlan, 1998).

Once oil was discovered in the early 1930s, rulers received monthly retainer fees as part of the agreements with Britain and the oil companies. These monthly fees brought the rulers financial independence from the people: Taxation was no longer required. Eventually, the rulers disbursed large sums of the oil wealth for socioeconomic development projects. As the oil revenues increased, the former rudimentary methods of ruling inevitably became obsolete, and complex government bureaucracies were established (World Bank, 2004). The transformation of societies once heavily dependent on pearl production and trade to societies receiving the benefits of a social welfare state has, in some regards, resulted in a tacit acceptance of the political status quo (Zahlan, 1998).

Lebanon's political history differs greatly from that of the three Arab Gulf states in our study. Lebanon has a long history of ethnic and religious heterogeneity that has fed into a political system of plurality and participatory democracy. Lebanon's constitution, written in 1926, supports a balance of power among religious groups in the country, and an unwritten "National Pact" (*al Mithaq al Watani*) from 1943 stipulates that the president be a Maronite Christian, the prime minister a Sunni Muslim, and the speaker of parliament a Shiite Muslim (Collelo, 1989). After gaining its independence from France in 1943 (full withdrawal of French troops did not occur until 1946), Lebanon vacillated between periods of prosperity and peace and periods of political turmoil, the latter epitomized by its civil war from 1975 to 1990, after which came a number of political reform measures to ensure the sustainability of peace. Today, Lebanon is a parliamentarian republic with a sectarian-based electoral system. Direct elections must take place every four years for parliament members. In turn, parliament elects a president every six years, and the president and parliament together choose a prime minister.

Diversity of the Economy

Figure 2.1 differentiates our four study countries in terms of diversity of economy, by which we mean both the extent to which the economy depends on a single industry or sector as opposed to a more diversified mix and the extent to which employment is diversified between the public and private sectors. We define the public sector as those organizations that are exclusively government institutions, such as ministries and government councils. These are different from state-owned enterprises, which are fully owned by the state. In the oil-dependent countries in our study, oil and gas companies are state-owned enterprises.

Figure 2.1 classifies both public-sector institutions and state-owned enterprises as part of the public sector. The mixed sector consists of establishments owned by the government in partnership with a local national or foreign entity (examples include Qatar Airways in Qatar and United Emirates Airline in the UAE, both of which are 50 percent state owned and 50 percent privately owned). The private sector is defined as those establishments that are fully privately owned and operated.

As seen in Figure 2.1, we classified Qatar at the one extreme, with a large public sector and heavy reliance on the oil industry, and Lebanon at the other extreme, with a large private sector and a more diversified set of industries. Oman and the UAE lie between these two extremes.

Data presented in Table 2.1 confirm these distinctions between our study countries in terms of the sectoral composition of GDP. Of the countries in our sample, Qatar has the least diversified economy, with 76 percent of the GDP contributed by industry, notably oil and gas. Oman and Lebanon have more-diversified economies, with industry accounting for just 22 percent of Lebanon's GDP and 56 percent of Oman's. Over 70 percent of Lebanon's GDP comes from the services sector, which includes a wide variety of private enterprises. It is striking that the UAE, a country with a historically oil-dependent economy, shows signs of economic diversification, with the industry sector contributing 55 percent of its GDP and services contributing 42 percent.

Whether the government is a large employer or owner of key industries is another important indicator of the economy's diversity for our four countries. The governments of Qatar and the UAE are the largest employers in their countries, and employment of nationals is highly concentrated in the public sector. Lebanon has the smallest public sector, and Oman has a mixed economy, with both the private and the public sector employing Omani nationals. Lebanon has a strong entrepreneurial history and a small and limited public sector.

Because the governments of the three Gulf states in our study are not directly involved in the process of oil production (state-owned enterprises are responsible for production), these states retain the essential political characteristics of earlier, pre-oil days, when the pearling industry dominated the structure of society. The government's principal activity in the economy is to allocate, not generate, funds. Government departments responsible for administering welfare policies (e.g., ministries of education, health, water, and electricity) are not usually headed by members of the ruling families; nor are the ministries of commerce, which are responsible for implementing the commercial laws that protect nationals from expatriate competition.

The administrative sectors in these three countries employ a much higher proportion of the economically active population than do the administrative sectors in the non-oil-producing countries of the Arab world. About 50 percent of economically active nationals are in government service, where they enjoy many privileges—in salaries, qualifications, and fringe benefits—not necessarily available to non-nationals. All nationals in Oman, Qatar, and the UAE are provided with education free of charge from grade school to post-graduate study. All three countries also have scholarships available for nationals for study abroad. And utilities (gas, water, electricity, telephone, etc.) are subsidized for nationals. In addition to being excluded from these privileges, non-nationals can only do business with a national partner and, with few exceptions, cannot own more than 49 percent of any company.

In direct contrast to the large public sectors characteristic of these Gulf nations, the bulk of the Lebanese population is employed by the private rather than the government sector. Lebanon capitalizes on its multilingual population (Arabic, English, and French are all commonly used), its geographic location along the Mediterranean Sea, and its financial institutions to compensate for not having large amounts of natural resources to rely on.

Composition of the Labor Pool

Another feature that differentiates our four study countries (see Figure 2.1) is labor pool composition. As is true for most Arab Gulf countries, working people in Qatar and the UAE are predominantly non-nationals, or expatriates (this applies to the population as a whole, as well). As Tables 2.3 and 2.4 indicate, nationals of Qatar and the UAE are a

Table 2.3
Key Demographic Indicators of Study Countries, 2004

Country	Total Population (1,000s)	Population Growth (annual percent change)	Non-Nationals (percent)	Age 0–14 (percent)
Lebanon	3,540	1.0	6.6	29.1
Oman	2,534	0.9	23.9[a]	34.9
Qatar	777	5.8	80.8	22.3
U.A.E	4,320	6.7	78.1[b]	22.4

SOURCES: Total population, population growth, and share of those age 0–14 are from World Bank, 2007. Percent non-national figures are from Lebanon Central Administration for Statistics, 2005, Tables 6 and 7; Oman Ministry of National Economy, 2005b; Qatar Planning Council, 2005b, Tables 11 to 16; and UAE Ministry of Economy, *Statistics Abstract*, 2006, Table 1.

[a] Figure is for 2003.
[b] Figure is for 2005.

minority in their own countries. In Qatar, non-nationals make up 81 percent of the population of nearly 800,000 persons and 88 percent of the labor force. In the UAE, which comprises about 4.3 million persons, non-nationals are 78 percent of the population and 91 percent of the labor force. In both countries, the population is growing rapidly, between 6 and 8 percent per year as of 2004, although the share of the population under age 15, at 22 percent, is close to the average for all high-income countries (about 18 percent) (World Bank, 2007). Moreover, the official unemployment rate is very low, less than 5 percent in each case according to recent labor force surveys. Expatriate workers in these two countries are found primarily in the service industries, in either low- or high-skilled fields. Nationals, in contrast, work primarily in the public sector as bureaucrats. The increase in oil production, leading to growth in the welfare state and the existence of vast state bureaucracies, has unwittingly resulted in a distancing of the rulers and the development of a broad upper class of nationals, without a concomitant strengthening of a working class of nationals. In turn, the development of these two countries' infrastructures has often been designed,

Table 2.4
Key Labor Market Indicators of Study Countries, 2004

Country	Labor Force (1,000s)	Non-Nationals (percent)	Unemployment Rate (percent)
Lebanon	1,163	n.a.	8.1
Oman	873[a]	49.3[a]	13.0[b]
Qatar	444	88.1	3.9[c]
UAE	2,731	90.7	8.2 (M)[d] 19.7 (F)

SOURCES: Lebanon 2004 figures are from Lebanon Central Administration for Statistics, 2005, Tables 15 and 19; Oman 2003 figures are from Oman Ministry of National Economy, 2005b; Oman 2000 figure is from Oman Ministry of National Economy, 2004; Qatar 2004 figures are from Qatar Planning Council, 2005b, Table 13; Qatar 2001 figure is from Qatar Planning Council, 2002, Tables 5 and 36; UAE 2004 figures are from Centre for Labour Market Research and Information (CLMRI), 2005, Table 2.1 and p. 29.

NOTES: n.a. = not available. Labor force and unemployment rate take into account those age 15 and above.

[a] Figure is for 2003.
[b] Figure is for 2000.
[c] Figure is for 2001.
[d] UAE unemployment rate is reported separately for males (M) and females (F) and is for nationals only.

implemented, and undertaken not by nationals, but by a cadre of foreigners (Mohammed, 2003).

At the other end of Figure 2.1's spectrum are Oman and Lebanon, where nationals predominate in the labor pool and, likewise, in the population as a whole. Unlike its Arab Gulf neighbors, Oman, with a total population of 2.5 million, has a much lower representation of non-nationals in the population and labor force: 24 and 49 percent, respectively (see Tables 2.3 and 2.4). This is in part because of Oman's position in the first domain in Figure 2.1. Oman has a dwindling supply of oil and gas resources and thus cannot sustain a large public sector to employ its nationals (it cannot afford a large social welfare system). In consequence, the nationals turn to the private sector for employment. In contrast to Qatar and the UAE, Oman has a much lower rate of population growth (less than 1 percent in 2004), but a considerably higher share (almost 35 percent) of its population is under age 15. In addition, the unemployment rate is considerably higher, estimated at 13 percent.

Lebanon has an even lower share of non-nationals in its population. Although Lebanon has not administered a national census since 1932, recent estimates from a household survey indicate that expatriates make up only 7 percent of the population of 3.5 million people. There is no available figure for the non-national share of the labor force. As in Oman, population growth in Lebanon is about 1 percent per year as of 2004, and the share (29 percent) of the population under age 15 is almost as high as Oman's. With a national unemployment rate of 8 percent in 2004 (11 percent for those age 20 to 24 and 16 percent for those age 25 to 29), emigration to another country for work is often seen as a viable option for unemployed Lebanese youth.

Beyond the differences in the size and composition of the labor pools in our four study countries, there are differences in the investments made in the population's (and hence the labor force's) knowledge and skills, and the resulting patterns do not always accord with a country's level of wealth. Data in Table 2.5 show that literacy rates are at or near 100 percent for males and females age 15 to 24 in Oman and are nearly as high in the other three countries, although young males in the UAE have a literacy rate of just 88 percent. Considering gross enrollment ratios, Qatar and Lebanon demonstrate the highest rates at the primary level, and Qatar has the highest rate at the secondary level.[6] Enrollment at the post-secondary level is highest in Lebanon, whose rate far exceeds those of the other countries (although this indicator is not available for the UAE). Given the UAE's lower performance on literacy rates and enrollment ratios, it is not surprising that the UAE spends the least of the four study countries on public

---

[6] Gross enrollment ratios are determined by dividing the number of children enrolled at a given education level by the number of children of official school age for that education level (multiplied by 100). Given enrollment delays and grade repetition, gross enrollment ratios (especially at the primary level) may exceed 100. Net enrollment ratios are determined by dividing the number of children of official school age for a given education level that are enrolled at that level by the number of children of official school age for that level (again multiplied by 100). Thus, net enrollment ratios cannot exceed 100.

Table 2.5
Key Education Indicators of Study Countries

Country	2000–2004 Literacy Rate of Persons Age 15 to 24 (percent)		2004 Gross Enrollment Ratio			2002 Public Expenditure on Education (as percentage of GDP)
	Males	Females	Primary	Secondary	Post-Secondary	
Lebanon	97	93	106.8	88.7	47.6	2.6
Oman	100	97	87.3	86.4	12.9	4.6
Qatar	94	96	101.7	96.8	19.1	3.6[a]
UAE	88	95	83.8	66.4	n.a.	1.6

SOURCES: Literacy rates are from Population Reference Bureau, 2006; gross enrollment ratios and education expenditures are from World Bank, 2007, and UNESCO, 2006.
NOTE: n.a. = not available.
[a] Figure is for 1998.

education as a share of GDP despite its high level of income. In contrast, Oman spends 4.6 percent of its total GDP on education, the largest percentage of the study countries and a figure that is comparable to the average spending on education as a percent of GDP (5.0 percent) for the member states of the Organisation for Economic Co-operation and Development (OECD) in the same period (OECD, 2005).

The Case-Study Approach

Our case-study approach allows us to highlight issues that cut across our four countries and to draw lessons learned from the differences and similarities in policy responses to those issues while considering the unique political, historical, economic, and demographic features of each country. Given the nature of case-study research, we do not recommend generalizing to other countries in the Arab world. However, our analytic framework and methodology, both discussed in Chapter One, can be readily applied to examine the same issues in other nations of the Arab world.

CHAPTER THREE
Qatar

A peninsula off of Saudi Arabia extending into the Arabian Gulf, the state of Qatar has recently gained international attention for its wealth, which derives from the discovery of vast reserves of natural gas. Like Oman and the UAE, the other two Gulf countries in our study, Qatar presently depends on the exploitation of natural resources for its wealth, rather than on its human resources. This approach has produced great wealth in the short term but has not provided for a sustainable long-term economic development program. Similar to the situation in the other two Gulf countries, Qatar's national population has historically relied on a beneficent public sector for employment, which has led to a concomitant demand for expatriate labor in the private sector.

Qatar is facing challenges similar to those of Oman and the UAE: how to enhance the human capital of its nationals and how to promote their employment in the private sector to ensure the nation's economic stability. However, Qatar is starting the process for change later than its neighbors and has had to make sweeping changes at a faster pace. Until the present emir, Sheikh Hamad Bin Khalifa Al Thani, came to power in 1995, few economic or education reforms had occurred. Recently, however, Qatar's leadership has embarked on a number of education and labor market initiatives to enhance the employability of Qatari nationals in the modern technological, global economy. This chapter provides an overview of the measures recently taken to develop the human resources of Qatar's population by reforming the primary and secondary schooling system, increasing post-secondary education options, and instituting labor market initiatives to promote the employability of Qataris in the private sector.

We begin by providing relevant background on Qatar's political history, economy, population, education system, and labor force. We then use information provided in interviews with government officials and private-sector business leaders[1] and results obtained from analyses of secondary data to describe Qatar's national policy development and implementation process through the analytic framework discussed earlier, in Chapter One. We highlight the key human resource challenges faced by the country and describe the policy approaches for addressing the issues, with a focus on the education and labor market initiatives listed in Table 3.1. In addition, we comment on the availability of resources for policy evaluation, including the extent to which data are available for assessing any policy's progress. We conclude the chapter with a summary of the country's policy development progress to date.

Table 3.1
Human Capital Reforms Covered in Qatar Case Study

Reform Categories and Subcategories
Education and training
Primary and secondary education
Post-secondary and post-graduate education
Training
Labor market and economy
Labor market reforms
Economic privatization
Economic diversification

---

[1] We used data from interviews conducted as part of this study as well as data from prior RAND studies done to assist Qatari leadership's reform of the nation's K–12 education system, scholarship system for study abroad, labor market system, and Qatar University. A list of the organizations and government ministries in which we held our interviews is in Appendix A.

Overview of Qatar

Qatar is a relatively small country on the western coast of the Arabian Gulf, covering approximately 11,525 square kilometers, including a number of islands (Qatar Planning Council, 2005c). Figure 3.1 is a map of Qatar and its surroundings. In 2001, Qatar resolved longstanding border disputes with Bahrain and Saudi Arabia, solidifying its boundaries.

Qatar is divided into municipalities, with the Doha municipality serving as the nation's capital and commercial hub. Although Doha is the most heavily populated municipality, rapid residential growth is occurring in surrounding areas and municipalities, such as Ar Rayyan and Umm Salal Ali. Qatar's industrial base is spread across several municipalities, with petroleum and petroleum-based industries in Mesaieed (not shown in Figure 3.1; it is south of Umm Sa'id) and Dukhan, and natural gas in Ras Laffan (not shown; it is north of Al Khawr). Ras Laffan has become the most important industrial base for Qatar because it is from there that offshore gas production in the major gas field, the "North Field," is managed.

Arabic is the primary language in Qatar and the official language of the government, but English is widely spoken and commonly used in businesses, especially in the private sector, primarily because of the diversity of the population in Qatar. Recent figures estimate that about 40 percent of the population is Arab (20 percent is Qatari), 20 percent is Indian, 10 percent is Filipino, 13 percent is Nepali, 7 percent is Pakistani, 5 percent is Sri Lankan, and 5 percent is of some other ethnic background (for example, West European) (U.S. Department of State, 2008). Islam is the official religion, although significant populations of other religious groups reside in Qatar. Qatari nationals follow a traditional version of Sunni Islam, called Wahhabi Islam, that originated in neighboring Saudi Arabia. However, unlike in Saudi Arabia, females are permitted to drive if they obtain a license, are allowed to vote in local elections, and need not veil fully in public.

The remainder of this section briefly discusses Qatar's political history, economic development, population trends, education system, and labor market patterns.

Figure 3.1
Map of Qatar

SOURCE: U.S. Department of State, 2008.
RAND MG786-3.1

Political History

Qatar's political and economic history is intimately linked to that of surrounding countries. Similar to the other two Gulf countries in this study, it only recently became a sovereign state in the modern sense, and its economy depends heavily on the exploitation and exportation of oil and natural gas, which were discovered early in the 20th century.

A period of dominance by the Khalifa family of Bahrain over the territory now known as Qatar ended with Turkish occupation in 1872. The Ottoman Turks then evacuated the peninsula at the beginning of World War I. In 1916, Abdullah Bin Ali Al Thani, the leader of a prominent family, signed a treaty with Britain that brought the peninsula into the trucial system. This meant that in exchange for Britain's military protection, Qatar relinquished its autonomy in foreign affairs and other areas, such as the power to cede, mortgage, or otherwise dispose of part of its territories or to enter into any relationship with a foreign government other than Britain without its consent. In turn, Britain did not interfere with domestic affairs or infrastructure development. Because of this relationship with Britain, Qatar, like the other trucial states of the region, remained relatively isolated and relied predominantly on pearling and fishing as its main staples of income (Metz, 1994; Zahlan, 1998).

Britain had concluded similar agreements with Bahrain in 1880 and 1892, with the present-day UAE in 1892, and with Kuwait in 1899.[2] Before this time, a variety of families ruled the peninsula and a number of city-states, such as Doha and Al Khawr, were in existence. It was not until Britain recognized one ruler, the leader of the Al Thani family, as the sovereign of the region that the nation-state of Qatar came into existence. In 1968, Britain announced its intention to withdraw by 1971 from military commitments east of Suez, includ-

---

[2] The treaties also had provisions suppressing slavery, piracy, and gunrunning, but the British were not strict about enforcing those provisions. Instead, they were intent on protecting the trade route to and from India and on excluding other powers from the region (Zahlan, 1998, Al-Hafidh, 1973).

ing those in force with Qatar.[3] Qatar became an independent state on September 3, 1971.

Qatar has a long history of leadership shifts within the Al Thani family. On February 22, 1972, Sheikh Khalifa Bin Hamad took control from the reigning emir, Sheikh Ahmad Bin Ali, who was hunting with his falcons in Iran. Sheikh Khalifa had the tacit support of the Al Thani family and of Britain, and he had the political, financial, and military support of Saudi Arabia. In contrast to his predecessor's policies, he cut family allowances and increased spending on social programs, including housing, health, education, and pensions. He also filled many top government posts with close relatives (Zahlan, 1998). Sheikh Khalifa continued as emir till 1995, when, following a downturn in the country's economy in the 1980s and early 1990s, Sheikh Hamad Bin Khalifa, the heir apparent and minister of defense at the time, took over the running of the country from his father.

Economic Development

As is the case in other Arab Gulf countries, the exploitation and exportation of natural resources make up the bulk of Qatar's national wealth. Oil and gas account for more than 60 percent of Qatar's GDP, roughly 85 percent of export earnings, and 70 percent of government revenues (Qatar Planning Council, 2006a). It is estimated that proved oil reserves of 16 billion barrels will continue for more than 20 years (OPEC, 2006).

The discovery of oil in Qatar in 1939 promised greater prosperity for Qatar, but World War II interrupted oil exploitation, and oil production did not begin on a commercial scale until 1949. The war caused disruption of food supplies, prolonging a period of economic hardship in Qatar that had begun in the 1920s with the collapse of the pearl trade and had increased with the global depression of the early 1930s. The oil exports and payments for offshore rights that began

---

[3] For some while, the rulers of Bahrain, Qatar, and the Trucial Coast (now the UAE) contemplated forming a federation after the British withdrawal. A dispute arose between Qatar and Bahrain, however, because Qatar opposed Bahrain's attempts to become the senior partner in the federation.

in 1949 marked a turning point in Qatar—oil revenues dramatically transformed the economy and society, as well as Qatar's foreign relations. In 1961, Qatar joined OPEC; in 1970, Qatar became a member of the Organization of Arab Petroleum Exporting Countries (Al-Hafidh, 1973).

Public services developed haltingly during the 1950s: The first telephone exchange opened in 1953, the first desalination plant in 1954, and the first power plant in 1957. Qatar's infrastructure, foreign labor force, and bureaucracy continued to grow in the 1960s. There were even some early attempts to diversify Qatar's economic base, most notably the establishment of a cement factory, a national fishing company, and small-scale agriculture (Metz, 1994).

Qatar has had remarkable economic growth relative to its neighbors in the last decade, becoming one of the world's fastest-growing and highest per capita income countries. The 1980s and early 1990s were a period of slow economic growth and rapidly declining oil reserves—reserves were projected to last only about 15 years. In response to this bleak forecast, Qatar's leadership revitalized the country's economy through different diversification efforts: (1) expanding its petrochemical, steel, and fertilizer output; (2) expanding its tourism sector; (3) increasing the role of the private sector by privatizing public enterprises and creating a business-friendly regulatory environment; and (4) turning to the production of natural gas.[4] These efforts resulted in rapid economic growth—per capita GDP rose from an average of $14,000 in the 1990s to more than $25,000 in 2000 and over $28,000 in 2002 (Fasano, 2001; Fasano and Iqbal, 2003). Real GDP growth averaged about 10 percent per year in the second half of the 1990s, well above the 3.5 percent average of other GCC countries (Fasano, 2001; Fasano and Iqbal, 2003). Nominal GDP growth reached 33.3 percent from 2004 to 2005 (Qatar Planning Council, 2006b). As a result of this eco-

---

[4] As noted in Chapter One, Qatar's natural gas reserves are the third largest in the world, behind Russia and Iran. Proved reserves of natural gas exceed 25 trillion cubic meters, more than 5 percent of the world total. Qatar is projected to become the world's leading liquefied natural gas exporter (OPEC, 2006).

nomic development, Qatar, now classified as a high-income country by the World Bank, is one of the wealthiest nations in the world.[5]

The economic windfalls associated with the steady rise of oil prices in the past decade and the discovery of vast reserves of natural gas in Qatar have set the stage for large-scale development projects. When Sheikh Hamad Bin Khalifa Al Thani became the emir in 1995, infrastructure development accelerated. His ascension to the throne brought a cadre of like-minded reformers, including his wife Sheikha Mozah Bint Nasser Al Missned, to oversee a number of government institutions in the country. Since 1995, the country has undergone an unprecedented expansion of infrastructure, ranging from the laying out of new roads and highways to the establishment of new thematic "cities," or large self-supported sites, two examples of which are Ras Laffan, established to support gas production in the North Field, and Education City, established to facilitate large-scale education projects. In addition, residential development increased with the expanded influx of non-national workers.

Population Composition and Change

The increased economic and infrastructure activity that started in the mid-1990s has brought about an increase in Qatar's population, predominantly the non-national population. In 1970, the Qatari government, assisted by British experts, carried out a census that reported a population of 111,113, of whom 45,039 (approximately 40 percent) were identified as Qatari nationals (Metz, 1994). The oil boom of the 1970s brought a spike in population growth, as non-national workers flocked to new opportunities in the country. Figure 3.2 shows total population from 1960 to 2006 and its annual percent growth. According to the national census conducted in 2004, Qatar had 744,029 people, of whom 496,382 were males and 247,647 were females (Qatar Planning Council, 2006c).[6] Estimates for 2008 have Qatar's population at

---

[5] By one estimate, GDP per capita in Qatar now ranks third highest in the world, behind only those of Luxembourg and Norway (El-Quqa et al., 2005).

[6] These population figures from the Qatar census of 2004 (also reported in Table 3.2) differ from the population estimates available from the World Bank (see Figure 3.2).

Figure 3.2
Trends in Population Total and Growth Rate in Qatar, 1960 to 2006

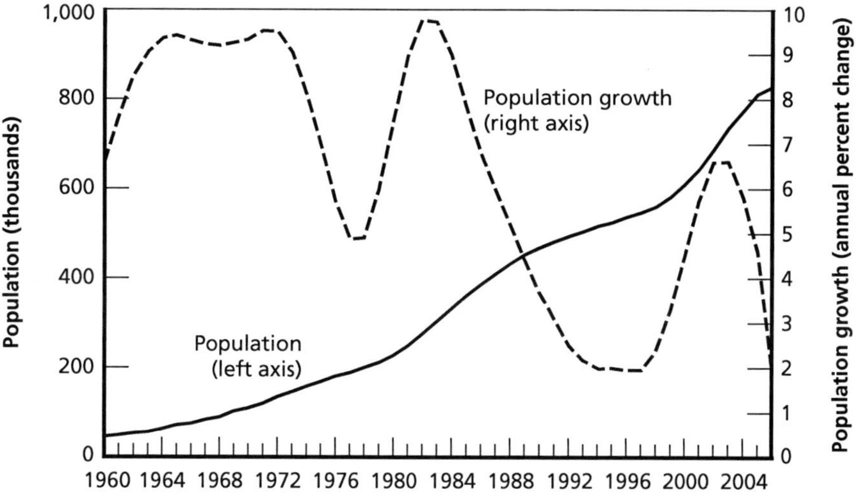

SOURCE: World Bank, 2007.
RAND MG786-3.2

1,448,446 (U.S. Department of State, 2008). According to World Bank indicators, the population growth rate in the 1990s steadied at about 2 percent, reached almost 6 percent in 2004, and has declined steadily since then, to about 2 percent in 2006. This uneven trend in population growth could stem from the highly regulated influx of immigrants into the country each year: The strict immigration quotas that Qatar's Ministry of Interior imposes for different countries of origin could be affecting the percent change of population growth each year.

Table 3.2 offers population counts from the 1986, 1997, and 2004 Qatar censuses by gender and three age ranges.[7] It is evident that the population in Qatar is largely male. The figures for 2004, shown in the table's bottom panel, indicate that the sex ratio (number of males per 100 females) in 2004 was 200.4. This is an increase from 1997's

---

[7] Public records of the 1986 and 1997 censuses do not demarcate by nationality. Public records of the 2004 census do provide some tabulations by nationality, which we report later in the chapter.

Table 3.2
Population in Qatar, by Age Group and Gender, 1986, 1997, and 2004

Survey and Age Group	Males		Females		Total (number)	Sex Ratio
	Number	Percent	Number	Percent		
1986 census						
Age 0–14	52,610	51.4	49,842	48.7	102,452	105.6
Age 15–64	192,980	73.4	69,784	26.6	262,764	276.5
Age 65 and up	2,189	58.1	1,581	41.9	3,770	138.5
Total	247,779	67.2	121,207	32.8	368,986	204.4
1997 census						
Age 0–14	70,696	51.3	67,009	48.7	137,705	105.5
Age 15–64	266,858	70.9	109,775	29.2	376,633	243.1
Age 65 and up	4,242	63.5	2,436	36.5	6,678	174.1
Total	341,796	65.6	179,220	34.4	521,016	190.7
2004 census						
Age 0–14	85,166	50.8	82,452	49.2	167,618	103.3
Age 15–64	405,542	71.5	161,826	28.5	567,368	250.6
Age 65 and up	5,674	62.7	3,369	37.3	9,043	168.4
Total	496,382	66.7	247,647	33.3	744,029	200.4

SOURCE: Qatar Planning Council, 2006c.
NOTES: Figures do not include "age unstated" category. Sex ratio is defined as the number of males per 100 females.

sex ratio of 190.7 but slightly lower than 1986's 204.5 (Qatar Planning Council, 2006c).

The largest difference in the number of males in Qatar relative to females is for those between the ages of 15 and 64 (e.g., the 2004 sex ratio for this group is 251), suggesting that most males in Qatar are not nationals. As described later, Qatar is similar to the UAE but unlike Oman in its heavy reliance on non-nationals to fill labor market needs. Data by nationality for the entire population in Qatar were not published as part of the 2004 tabulations, nor were they published in the 2001 or 2006 Qatar labor force surveys. Such tabulations are available for the working-age population, which in Qatar's case takes into account those age 15 and above. Below, in our discussion of the labor market challenges that Qatar faces, we describe participation in Qatar's labor force, focusing on nationality and highlighting Qatar's heavy reliance on non-nationals in the workforce.

Advances in Education

Before oil was discovered, there was no formal education system in Qatar. Instead, some children in villages and towns memorized passages from the Qur'an and learned to read and write in *kuttabs*, informal classes taught in mosques or homes by literate men and women knowledgeable about Islam. From the early days, the development of education in Qatar focused mainly on the male population (Metz, 1994; Brewer et al., 2007).

In 1956, the Ministry of Education in Qatar was established, ushering in an era of free education for both males and females. Public schooling was free, and from 1956 to 1962, Qatari students received a monthly stipend. Expatriate children whose parents were employed by the government were eligible for free government education. Through the 1960s, Qatar imported entire education packages from Egypt, Jordan, and Syria—curricula and books, education structures, and teachers (Metz, 1994; Jolo, 2004; Brewer et al., 2007).

Qatar's Ministry of Education schools are presently divided into three levels: primary (grades 1 through 6), preparatory (grades 7, 8, and 9), and secondary (grades 10, 11, and 12). Females and males attend separate schools, and their teachers are the same gender as they are. The one exception to this arrangement is the "model schools," which were developed to ease the transition for young males (those in the first four to six years of primary school) from home to school and to provide more employment opportunities for female teachers. In these schools, both the teaching staff and the administration are female. The first three model schools opened in 1978, and their success led to a five-year plan to implement this type of school systemwide (Brewer et al., 2007).

In addition to the publicly funded government schools, a significant number of private schools serve both Qataris and citizens of other countries who are residing in Qatar. These schools employ the curriculum of the country they are affiliated with and charge tuition. Tuition rates vary widely depending on type of school. Private "elite" schools, such as Qatar Academy, the American School of Doha (U.S. based), and Doha College, charge significantly more than the "community" schools, which specifically serve the large expatriate Arab, Near Eastern, and South Asian communities. A third type of private school, known as "private Arabic" schools, follows the Ministry of Education curriculum and is geared to Qataris and other Arabs who want to follow the Ministry of Education curriculum but in a private school setting.

Following independence from Britain in 1971, Qatar launched a new period of educational development to match the demands and challenges of independence. These reform efforts centered on Qatar developing its identity as a sovereign state: Curriculum was developed in-house and teacher-training programs were established to encourage Qataris to become teachers (Jolo, 2004). In 1973, Qatar's sole postsecondary education option was a teacher-training program with 150 students. In 1977, Qatar's only state-sponsored academically oriented university, Qatar University, was established. When it opened, Qatar University had four colleges—Education, Humanities and Social Sciences, Science, and Shari'a and Islamic Studies. In 1980, the College of Engineering was established, followed, in 1985, by the College of Administration and Economics. Qatar University presently offers six fields of study: humanities, education, sciences, shari'a and law, business administration and economics, and engineering. Before 2000, the College of Education offered a bachelor's degree in various subjects, including general education, and most Qatari public school teachers trained there. Since 2000, degrees in general education are no longer offered, although students can still pursue a bachelor's degree in arts or physical education or receive a diploma in early childhood education or special education.

With Qatar's investments in education, literacy rates increased, reaching, in 2004, 98.2 percent among Qataris age 15 to 19 (Qatar Planning Council, 2005b). Table 3.3 shows that despite inequality during the 1950s in terms of number of males and number of females attending grades 1 through 12, attendance was equalized for the genders by the late 1970s. Table 3.4 reports gross and net enrollment ratios for males and females as of 2004 at the preprimary, primary, secondary, and post-secondary levels. Although preschool is not required, over one-third of children attend preschool prior to starting primary school. Attendance is nearly universal at the primary level and only slightly lower at the secondary level. The gap between gross and net enrollment ratios indicates delayed progression through school, although UNESCO data indicate that grade repetition occurs for just 3 percent of students as of 1999 (the latest year for which data are available) (UNESCO, 2006). At all three of these levels, the gender parity in enrollment is evident. In contrast, there is a large gap in the enrollment ratios for young males and females at the post-secondary level, with over 30 percent of young females enrolled compared with just 10

Table 3.3
Enrollment in Grades 1–12 in Qatar Public Schools, by Academic Year and Gender

Academic Year	Males		Females		Total Number
	Number	Percent	Number	Percent	
1950–1951	240	100.0	0	0.0	240
1960–1961	4,607	65.3	2,450	34.7	7,057
1970–1971	11,883	56.6	9,096	43.4	20,979
1980–1981	21,908	51.4	20,702	48.6	42,610
1990–1991	32,099	50.5	31,497	49.5	63,598
2000–2001	35,184	48.2	37,824	51.8	73,008
2004–2005	36,746	47.6	40,328	52.4	77,074

SOURCES: Jolo, 2004, and Qatar Ministry of Education, 2005, Table 3.

Table 3.4
Gross and Net Enrollment Ratios in Qatar, by Education Level and Gender, 2005

School Level	Gross Enrollment Ratio		Net Enrollment Ratio	
	Males	Females	Males	Females
Preprimary	37.1	35.7	n.a.	n.a.
Primary	106.4	105.5	96.0	95.7
Secondary	101.1	98.8	91.0	89.2
Post-secondary	9.6	33.0	n.a.	n.a.

SOURCE: World Bank, 2007.
NOTE: n.a. = not available.

percent of young males. Indeed, in 2002, nearly three-fourths of Qatar University's 8,621 students were female (Brewer et al., 2007).

Labor Force Trends

Estimates prepared by the World Bank show the trend over time in the size of the labor force, which the World Bank defines as those persons age 15 to 64 who are economically active, meaning they are employed or they are unemployed and actively looking for work.[8] Together with estimates of the population of persons age 15 to 64 (the working-age population), these data provide a picture of the trend in the labor force participation rate, as well. These trends in working-age population, labor force, and labor force participation rate from 1960 to 2006 are shown in Figure 3.3.[9] According to these World Bank estimates, Qatar's population in 1980 was 229,242 inhabitants, and of these, about 152,510 (or 66.5 percent) were age 15 to 64, and 106,245 of these working-age individuals were in the labor force. For 2006, the

---

[8] In contrast to the World Bank, the Qatar Planning Council includes all employed or unemployed persons age 15 and above, rather than age 15 to 64, in its definition of the labor force.

[9] Below, we also rely on more-detailed labor force data from the Qatar censuses and labor force surveys. These estimates differ from those by the World Bank for the equivalent points in time.

Figure 3.3
Trends in Working-Age Population, Labor Force, and Labor Force Participation Rate in Qatar, 1960 to 2006

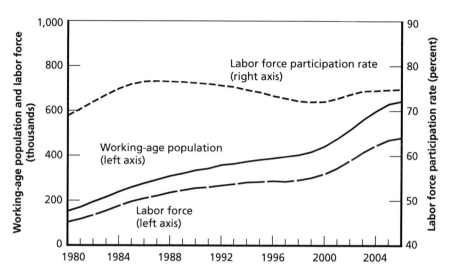

SOURCE: World Bank, 2007.
NOTE: Population and labor force take into account persons age 15–64.
RAND MG786-3.3

World Bank estimates show approximately 637,893 persons age 15 to 64 in Qatar, of whom 481,390 were in the labor force. In 1980, about 69 percent of Qatar's working-age population was in the labor force. This percentage grew to 77 percent between 1993 and 1997 and then dropped slightly, to 75 percent in 2006.[10]

Human Resource Challenges Faced by Qatar

Wealth from oil and gas revenue has allowed Qatar to develop its infrastructure quickly and to bring education and health benefits to the Qatari people. From the school enrollment ratios and the labor force participation rates detailed above, it seems that Qatar has been able to

---

[10] Again, this World Bank estimate of the labor force participation rate differs from the one we report below for 2004 based on the Qatar census.

provide nearly universal access to its education system and, given its current labor force participation rate of 75 percent, that a large portion of the working-age population is employed or able to actively look for employment.[11] However, most of the officials in the government and private sectors we interviewed noted that a number of human resource challenges overshadow the achievements made in access to education and labor force participation.

In this section, we highlight the most salient issues pointed to by our interviewees: a labor force dominated by foreign workers, the concentration of Qataris in public-sector employment, high unemployment rates among young Qataris, and an education system that is not producing workers with the skills that employers require. We discuss each of these challenges in turn using the most-recent population, education, employment, and labor market data available within the country.

Non-Qataris Compose the Bulk of the Labor Force

The growth in Qatar's working-age population since the 1980s (see Figure 3.3) can be attributed primarily to the immigration of expatriate workers and the opening of job opportunities for females. Qatar responded to both its rapid economic growth in recent decades and the relatively small population base it has available to exploit the country's vast natural resources by turning to non-nationals to meet its labor market needs. Data from the 2004 census, reported in Table 3.5, show that non-Qataris make up just over 80 percent of the working-age population. Among males, the share of non-nationals in this population is 87 percent; among females, it is 67 percent. Even in absolute terms, the numbers for males in the working-age population are striking: just under 52,000 Qatari males and nearly 354,000 non-Qatari males.

Since most non-nationals are in the country to work, they naturally make up the bulk of the labor force. As Table 3.6 shows, data from the 2004 Qatar census indicate that about 338,000 non-Qatari males age 15 to 64 and 51,000 non-Qatari females age 15 to 64 were in

---

[11] In comparison, the U.S. labor force participation rate for the population age 16 and above has hovered around 66 percent since 1998 (U.S. Department of Labor, 2008), and the U.S. elementary school net enrollment in 2006 was 92.8 percent for females and 91.4 percent for males (World Bank, 2007).

Table 3.5
Working-Age Population in Qatar, by Nationality and Gender, 2004

Nationality	Number			Percent Distribution		
	Males	Females	Total	Males	Females	Total
National	51,614	53,624	105,238	12.7	33.1	18.5
Non-national	353,928	108,202	462,130	87.3	66.9	81.5
Total	405,542	161,826	567,368	100.0	100.0	100.0

SOURCES: Qatar Planning Council, 2005b, Tables 11 to 16; and authors' calculations in accordance with World Bank definition of the labor force as age 15 to 64.

Table 3.6
Labor Force in Qatar, by Nationality and Gender, 2004

Nationality	Number			Percent Distribution		
	Males	Females	Total	Males	Females	Total
National	36,329	16,016	52,345	9.7	23.9	11.9
Non-national	337,776	50,946	388,722	90.3	76.1	88.1
Total	374,105	66,962	441,067	100.0	100.0	100.0

SOURCES: Qatar Planning Council, 2005b, Tables 11 to 16; and authors' calculations in accordance with World Bank definition of the labor force as age 15 to 64.

the labor force in 2004, representing 90 and 76 percent, respectively, of the males and females in the labor force. Overall, Qataris make up just 12 percent of the economically active population, with male nationals representing around 10 percent (36,329 persons) of the male labor force and female nationals representing about 24 percent (16,016 persons) of the female labor force.

Table 3.7, which uses the absolute figures on the size of the working-age population and the labor force from Tables 3.4 and 3.5, shows that the labor force participation rate is highest for non-Qatari males (96 percent) and considerably lower for Qatari males (73 percent). For females, the labor force participation rate is higher for non-Qataris (48 percent) than for Qataris (31 percent).

Table 3.7
Labor Force Participation Rates in Qatar, by Nationality and Gender, 2004

Nationality and Gender	Labor Force (number)	Working-Age Population (number)	Labor Force Participation Rate (percent)
National			
Male	36,329	51,614	73.4
Female	16,016	53,624	31.2
Total	52,345	105,238	51.8
Non-national			
Male	337,776	353,928	95.5
Female	50,946	108,202	47.5
Total	388,722	462,130	84.3
Total			
Male	374,105	405,542	92.8
Female	66,962	161,826	42.2
Total	441,067	567,368	78.4

SOURCES: Qatar Planning Council, 2005b, Tables 11 to 16; and authors' calculations in accordance with World Bank definition of the labor force as age 15 to 64.

Even though Qatari females have made economic advances in recent years, it is important to note that overall labor force participation for Qatari females remains relatively low. More than half of Qatari females are neither students nor in the labor force. And those who do enter the labor force have difficulty finding work (Stasz et al., 2007) because of occupational segregation, the basis of which is the social unacceptability of females working in certain fields or alongside males in certain contexts. For example, it is socially acceptable for females to work in the field of education, which is segregated by gender, so females are attracted to professions in this field. However, officials in the education sector with whom we spoke noted that there are not enough teaching jobs for qualified candidates who seek such positions, which means many Qatari females who graduate with a teaching certificate are unemployed (Brewer et al., 2007).

Qatari Employees Are Concentrated in Government Sector

Published labor force statistics based on population surveys, such as those derived from the Qatar's censuses and labor force surveys, are generally not disaggregated by nationality (exceptions being the data reported in Tables 3.5 to 3.7 above). Other labor market data, from establishment surveys in Qatar, are not inclusive of all employment, but do provide results by nationality and can therefore shed additional light on the labor force breakdown between nationals and non-nationals. For these establishment data, Qatar's employers are divided into four sectors based on ownership:

1. *Government sector:* ministries and other exclusively government institutions.
2. *State-owned enterprises:* entities fully owned by the state, some operating independent budgets, and some receiving their budgets directly from the government (e.g., Qatar General Petroleum Corporation, also known as Qatar Petroleum).
3. *Mixed sector:* establishments owned by the government in partnership with a local national or foreign entity (e.g., Qatar Airways, which is 50 percent state owned and 50 percent privately owned).
4. *Private sector:* establishments fully privately owned and operated.[12] (A Qatari must own 51 percent of any private business.)

Tables 3.8 and 3.9, which are based on establishment survey data, offer a snapshot of how Qatari and non-Qatari employees are distributed across these different sectors. It is evident from Table 3.8 that Qataris are well represented in the government sector and underrepresented in the private and mixed sectors. Almost all (99 percent) of the workers in the private sector are non-nationals, whereas almost 50 percent of employees in the government sector are Qataris. Drawing on

---

[12] These are limited to financial institutions and hotels.

Table 3.8
Distribution of Labor Force in Qatar, by Nationality and Sector, 2004

	Public Sector						Private Sector[a]	
	Government		State-Owned Enterprises		Mixed Sector			
Nationality	No.	%	No.	%	No.	%	No.	%
Total	78,307	100.0	24,684	100.0	12,459	100.0	322,111	100.0
Nationals	38,936	49.7	6,661	26.9	2,457	19.7	2,228	0.7
Non-nationals	39,371	50.3	18,023	73.1	10,002	80.3	319,883	99.3

SOURCES: Qatar Planning Council, 2005a, Table 17; and authors' calculations.
NOTE: Trainees are not included.
[a] Private sector includes employees in international/diplomatic occupations and in private households.

the data in Table 3.8 for Qataris only, 91 percent of working Qataris are employed in the government and state-owned enterprises—together, the broad public sector—77 percent in the government sector alone.

Table 3.9 provides another breakdown of employment by nationality, here distinguishing the different sectors of economic activity (i.e., the equivalent of industry classifications). Within this classification, the largest industry category for Qatari employment is public administration and defense: 55 percent of Qataris work in these fields. The second largest industry category is education: 19 percent of Qataris are teachers, administrators, or other employees in the education sector. For non-Qataris, the largest employment categories are construction (30 percent), wholesale and retail trade (14 percent), and domestic servants (14 percent).

These patterns reflect the fact that for most Qataris, employment in the public sector has historically been more attractive than working in the private sector. Interviewees in the private sector and in the government sector noted a number of reasons for this:

- *Greater total compensation.* Qataris in the public sector are offered a salary based on level of education, plus a number of benefits—

Table 3.9
Percent Distribution of Persons Employed in Qatar, by Economic Activity and Nationality, 2004

	Number of Employees		Percent Distribution	
Economic Activity	Nationals	Non-Nationals	Nationals	Non-Nationals
Agriculture, hunting, and forestry	5	10,195	0.0	2.6
Fishing	4	1,821	0.0	0.5
Mining and quarrying	3,847	14,150	7.7	3.7
Manufacturing	721	39,317	1.4	10.2
Electricity, gas, and water supply	1,443	2,921	2.9	0.8
Construction	334	116,715	0.7	30.2
Wholesale and retail trade; repair of motor vehicles, motorcycles, and personal and household goods	749	53,689	1.5	13.9
Hotels and restaurants	39	10,241	0.1	2.7
Transport, storage, and communications	1,078	14,140	2.1	3.7
Financial intermediation	797	3,969	1.6	1.0
Real estate, renting, and business activities	336	11,522	0.7	3.0
Public administration	27,518	25,920	54.8	6.7
Education	9,606	10,271	19.1	2.7
Health and social work	2,250	9,304	4.5	2.4
Other community, social, and personal service activities	1,376	8,754	2.7	2.3
Domestic services	143	53,215	0.3	13.8
Total	50,246	386,144	100.0	100.0

SOURCES: Qatar Planning Council, 2005b, Tables 38 and 45; and authors' calculations.

NOTES: Activity category of "regional and international organizations and bodies" is not included. Trainees are not included. Numbers may not add to total because of rounding.

e.g., a retirement pension and an interest-free mortgage to build a house on a government-provided plot of land.
- *Job security.* Qataris who lose their government job retain their salary and benefits until a comparable government job is found.
- *Shorter working hours.* Government offices are generally open from 8 a.m. until 1 p.m. and have six weeks of holiday each year, as well as numerous breaks throughout the year for national and religious holidays.
- *More prestige.* Historically, positions in government have carried more visibility and prestige than comparable jobs in the private sector.

Furthermore, according to our interviewees, many Qataris lack the skills demanded by non-governmental employers, which often forces employers to look to non-Qataris to fill job openings. These skills include knowledge about information technology or other computer skills, finance and accounting, marketing and public relations, English language skills, and engineering. In addition, many private-sector employers noted that expatriate workers are more cost-effective than Qatari workers for three reasons. First, Qataris expect to be paid what the government would pay them and to work the government's shorter working hours. Second, Qataris often need extensive English-language or specific on-the-job training to be effective in positions with private employers. Large companies are known to provide in-house English training or pay for a Qatari's education abroad. And, third, Qataris sometimes "job hop," leaving a company that has invested in their training to work for another company once training has been completed. Expatriate workers, in contrast, may not leave their job or the country without the expressed consent of their employer.

Unemployment Rates Are High Among Young, First-Time Workers

Given the challenges in matching workers to jobs in Qatar, particularly in the private sector, there is growing recognition that many young workers in Qatar will undergo a spell of unemployment in making the transition from school to work. Unemployment figures from the 2001 labor force survey provide some insight into the unemployment patterns, particularly for young workers.[13] As can be seen in Table 3.10, while the unemployment rate was just over 2 percent overall for males in 2001, it was about 30 percent for males age 15 to 19 and about 9 percent for males age 20 to 24. For females overall, the unemployment rate, at nearly 13 percent, was almost six times the overall rate for males, and the rate for females in the two youngest age groups was 79 and 47 percent, respectively. Even among females age 25 to 29, the rate was nearly 30 percent.

More-detailed tabulations from the 2001 and 2006 labor force surveys (not shown) reveal that almost all those unemployed in the three youngest age groups were new labor market entrants (i.e., persons not previously employed) and were disproportionately represented by Qataris (Qatar Planning Council, 2007). For unemployed Qataris, the 2001 labor force survey included questions about their willingness to take a job in the private and mixed sectors of the economy and, for those who were unwilling, questions about their reasons.

Table 3.11 shows the results for unemployed male and female Qataris and confirms the biases against private-sector employment noted above. Overall, 20 percent of unemployed Qatari males and nearly 66 percent of unemployed Qatari females were not willing, as of 2001, to accept employment in the private and mixed sectors. In addition to the male-female split on this question of willingness, the explanations given differed substantially for males and females. Among unemployed Qatari males who would not accept a private- or mixed-sector job, the most common explanation was that wages were low (50 percent), followed by undesirable hours of work (31 percent), days of work (20 percent), and low social status (19 percent). For unemployed Qatari females, the most prominent concern was a mixed-gender work environment (76 percent), followed by low social status (53 percent). Only 18 percent of unemployed Qatari females reported that

---

[13] The 2004 census collected labor market information similar to that in the 2001 labor force survey, but its published tabulations do not include unemployment figures. The 2001 survey provides unemployment figures but not the tabulations needed to calculate unemployment rates for groups of workers defined by nationality. As a result, we focus on the unemployment rate disaggregated only by age and gender.

Table 3.10
Number of Unemployed and Unemployment Rate in Qatar, by Age Group and Gender, 2001

Age Group	Unemployed (number)		Labor Force (number)		Unemployment Rate (percent)	
	Males	Females	Males	Females	Males	Females
15–19	1,032	499	3,415	633	30.2	78.8
20–24	2,323	1,852	25,518	3,984	9.1	46.5
25–29	1,281	1,778	45,528	6,360	2.8	28.0
30–34	643	1,056	47,154	13,396	1.4	7.9
35–39	170	694	43,127	11,530	0.4	6.0
40–44	256	356	42,156	8,024	0.6	4.4
45–49	143	124	31,991	4,368	0.4	2.8
50–54	165	120	18,670	1,442	0.9	8.3
55–59	62	0	9,356	430	0.7	0.0
60 and up	63	0	5,592	233	1.1	0.0
Total	6,138	6,479	272,507	50,400	2.3	12.9

SOURCES: Qatar Planning Council, 2002, Tables 7-1, 7-2, and 37; and authors' calculations.

low wages were the reason for their unwillingness to accept private- or mixed-sector work.

These data on unemployment suggest that Qatar faces a significant challenge in ensuring that its graduates of secondary and post-secondary education are able to quickly transition into the labor market without spending long periods searching for work. Moreover, there appear to be various barriers that reduce the willingness of unemployed Qataris to accept employment in the private and mixed sector, barriers that appear to vary substantially among Qatari males and females.

Table 3.11
Unwillingness of Unemployed Qataris to Work in the Private and Mixed Sectors and Reasons for Unwillingness, by Gender, 2001

Response	Percentage of Unemployed Giving Response	
	Males	Females
Not willing to work in private/mixed sector[a]	20.2	65.5
Work related		
Low wage	50.4	18.1
Hours of work	31.1	15.7
Timing of work	7.9	10.2
Days of work	20.0	2.5
Lack of retirement benefits	11.4	1.8
Personal reasons		
English language	6.2	2.9
Social status	18.5	52.8
Long distance between residence and workplace	8.6	4.3
Mixed-gender work environment	n.a.	75.9
Other reasons	26.6	18.0

SOURCES: Qatar Planning Council, 2002, Tables 46 and 47; and authors' calculations.
NOTE: n.a. = not available.

[a] Only those respondents indicating unwillingness were asked for their reasons; multiple responses were allowed.

Qataris Are Not Obtaining the Types of Education Needed to Compete in Qatar's Economy

Given the challenges in the school-to-work transition and the relatively low representation of Qataris in private-sector employment, it is relevant to ask whether Qataris are well prepared by the country's education system to enter the 21st century workplace. Of interest is the performance of the education system in Qatar—both primary and secondary schools and higher education institutions—as well as the educational attainment of the Qatari population. Of the countries included in our study, Qatar has some of the richest data on this topic, and the information reveals significant shortfalls in the preparation that students receive for future employment.

If we look to what is being studied in the secondary schools, it is evident that students in Qatar's public education system are not preparing themselves to directly enter Qatar's private and semi-private sectors or to enter post-secondary institutions with a solid foundation in such fields as mathematics and science. Table 3.12 shows the number of graduates of Qatar's publicly funded Ministry of Education schools from academic years 1980–1981 to 2004–2005 by gender and field of study. Students in their last two years in Ministry of Education secondary schools must select one of three fields—literature, literature and mathematics, or mathematics and sciences; we collapsed the results for the first two of these fields into one, "literature," for the table.

It is apparent from Table 3.12 that since the 1980s, the majority of graduates of Qatar's Ministry of Education schools have been opting to study literature and the humanities rather than the science and mathematics subjects most needed in a labor market heavily reliant on the production of oil and gas. The trend of males being more likely to graduate with a major in literature and females being more likely to graduate with a major in the sciences (except in 1980–1981) stopped after 1995–1996. Since then, both males and females have been more likely to graduate with a major in literature than in the sciences. In the most recent year of data (2004–2005), almost 70 percent of graduating females and 62 percent of graduating males majored in literature.

As is clear, Qatari students are not concentrating their studies in the important fields, such as mathematics and the sciences. Even if they were, however, that would not guarantee their successful preparation for the labor force. To determine that, it is necessary to know whether the knowledge they gain of such subjects is on a par with international standards for primary and secondary education.

As we discuss more fully below, Qatar is one of the first countries in the Arab world to institute comprehensive national student assessments to determine how students are performing against educational standards in specific grades and subjects. These exams—known as the Qatar Comprehensive Educational Assessment (QCEA)—cover

Table 3.12
Fields of Study of Qatari Secondary School Graduates, by Gender, 1980–1981 to 2004–2005

Gender and Field of Study	1980–1981		1985–1986		1990–1991		1995–1996		2000–2001		2004–2005	
	Number	Percent	Number	Percent	Number	Percent	Number	Percent	Number	Percent	Number	Percent
Male												
Literature	488	65.6	861	70.8	1,156	72.2	1,221	57.5	991	56.7	1,583	61.5
Science	256	34.4	355	29.2	446	27.8	903	42.5	757	43.3	991	38.5
Total	744	100.0	1,216	100.0	1,602	100.0	2,124	100.0	1,748	100.0	2,574	100.0
Female												
Literature	376	50.9	330	43.3	505	46.1	784	46.2	1,571	63.8	2,021	69.4
Science	362	49.1	432	56.7	591	53.9	914	53.8	892	36.2	893	30.6
Total	738	100.0	762	100.0	1,096	100.0	1,698	100.0	2,463	100.0	2,914	100.0
All												
Literature	864	58.3	1,191	60.2	1,661	61.6	2,005	52.5	2,562	60.8	3,604	65.7
Science	618	41.7	787	39.8	1,037	38.4	1,817	47.5	1,649	39.2	1,884	34.3
Total	1,482	100.0	1,978	100.0	2,698	100.0	3,822	100.0	4,211	100.0	5,488	100.0

SOURCES: Jolo, 2004, and Qatar Ministry of Education, 2005, p. 208.

Arabic language, English as a foreign language, science, and mathematics. The results of the first administration of the exams, in April 2004, were benchmarked to international standards, thereby providing insights into the quality of graduates produced by Qatar's public education system prior to reforms that commenced in September 2004 (discussed below). Figure 3.4 displays the April 2004 QCEA results (as the percentage of correct test score items on the multiple-choice component of the assessment) for students in Qatar's Ministry of Education schools and private Arabic schools by grade and subject. These data indicate that students are not graduating from secondary school with a knowledge base consistent with international standards. Specifically, students in grades 11 and 12 on average correctly answered only 35 percent of the mathematics questions and approximately 40 percent of the science and the English questions.[14]

Another concern, besides the unpreparedness of secondary school graduates for entry into employment or post-secondary science and engineering fields of study, is, according to employers in the private sector, that there are not enough Qatari science and engineering graduates of Qatar University to fill Qatar's labor market needs. Graduates in the humanities are in abundance, however. Figure 3.5 confirms this concern, showing the number of Qatari graduates from Qatar University for academic years 1998–1999 to 2004–2005 by three broad fields: humanities and social sciences; business and economics; and sciences, mathematics, engineering, and technology. It is clear that within this time frame, most Qatari students graduated with a degree not in mathematics, science, engineering, or technology, but in humanities or social sciences. Table 3.13, which is based on data compiled on first university degrees by the U.S. National Science Foundation (NSF), shows a similar pattern of degrees being granted primarily outside the sciences and engineering. Out of 1,330 degrees total, just 281 were in the sciences

---

[14] These results should be interpreted with caution. The statistics are raw, unequated student scores, so no between-grade or cross-subject comparisons should be made. However, these scores do offer an understanding of general student performance vis-à-vis what the international community deems important to know and be able to do in the four subjects. Students were instructed to select the correct answer out of four options. Students who guessed thus had a 25 percent chance of being correct.

Figure 3.4
Student Results on Multiple Choice Component of QCEA, 2004

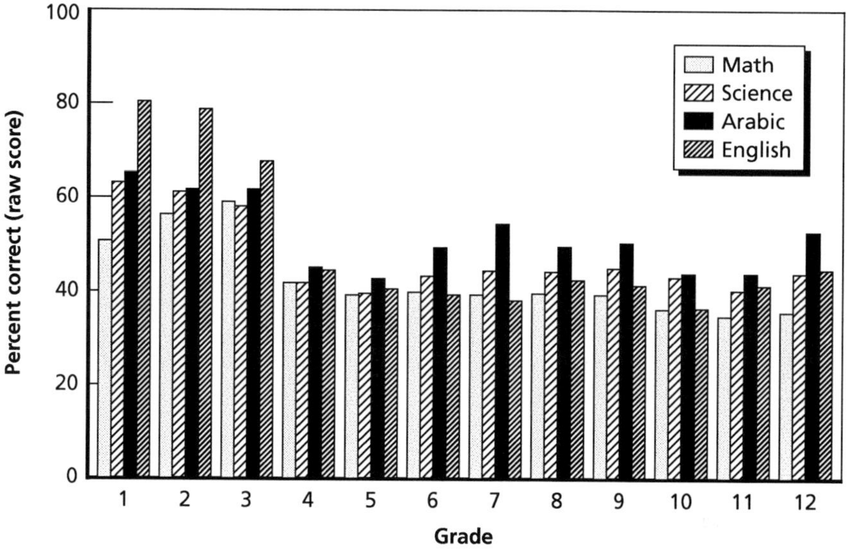

SOURCE: Qatar Supreme Education Council, 2005a, pp. 20–23.
RAND MG786-3.4

and engineering fields in 2002, the most recent year for which these data were available. This means that 281 graduates obtained a degree in the sciences or engineering that year. If we express this number of graduates as a share of the 24-year-old population, we find that just 3 percent of the 2002 graduates received university degrees in these critical fields.[15] It is interesting to note from Table 3.13 that on a population basis, males and females are receiving science and engineering degrees at the same rate even though females are more than twice as likely to receive a university degree. Officials from Qatar University noted that fewer than 50 percent of Qataris graduate within five years of

---

[15] By way of comparison, according to the same source, the annual number of natural science and engineering degrees in the United States, expressed as a share of the 24-year-old population, reaches 5.7 percent, nearly double the rate for Qatar. At the same time, the rate in the United States is viewed as being too low given the demands of a technology-oriented economy.

Figure 3.5
Qatari Graduates from Qatar University in Humanities, Business, and Sciences, 1998–1999 to 2004–2005

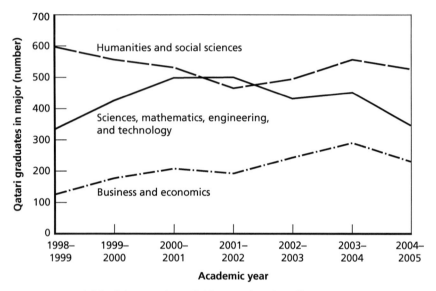

SOURCE: Unpublished data made available to authors by officials at Qatar University.
RAND MG786-3.5

enrolling, showing that there is a lack of commitment to the pursuit of a post-secondary degree among many students.

Of particular concern to many officials in the education and labor market sectors, as well as to leaders in the private sector with whom we spoke, is the fact that Qatari males are not pursuing advanced degrees and are opting to enter the labor force directly after their secondary education. Table 3.14, which shows the number of Qatari males and females in the workforce by educational attainment, indicates that a full two-thirds of Qatari males (68 percent) do not have a post-secondary education. According to our interviewees, a large attraction for Qatari males is employment by the government or with the police or military force, where a post-secondary degree is not required. In contrast, over 70 percent of Qatari females in the workforce have at least some post-secondary education, with 65 percent overall having a bachelor's degree. Consequently, when comparing average education levels

Table 3.13
Breakdown of First University Degrees Granted in Qatar, 2002

	Degrees Granted (number)		
	Males	Females	Total
All fields	365	965	1,330
Science and engineering fields	128	153	281
Physical/biological sciences	10	44	54
Computer sciences	34	64	98
Agricultural sciences	n.a.	n.a.	n.a.
Engineering	76	0	76
Social/behavioral sciences	8	45	53
Non-science and non-engineering fields	237	812	1,049
No. of persons in 24-year-old population	4,000	4,000	8,000
	Ratio of Persons Getting Degree to Population of 24-year-olds (percent)		
	Males	Females	Total
First university degree	9.1	24.1	16.6
Natural sciences or engineering degree	3.0	2.7	2.9
Social/behavioral sciences degree	0.2	1.1	0.7

SOURCE: NSF, 2006, Tables 2-37 and 2-39.
NOTE: n.a. = not available.

of Qatari workers, females stand at 14.1 years and males at 10.7 years (and 11.8 years overall) (Qatar Planning Council, 2005a).

Approaches to Reform in Qatar

The previous section highlighted the significant human resource issues to be faced by Qatar in the coming decades that interviews with officials in the public and private sectors pointed to and that our analyses of existing data corroborated. Figure 3.6 summarizes these issues schematically.

Table 3.14
Educational Attainment of Employed Qataris, by Education Level and Gender, 2004

Education Level	Males		Females		Total	
	Number	Percent	Number	Percent	Number	Percent
Secondary and below						
Illiterate	1,059	3.0	235	1.6	1,294	2.6
Reads and writes	2,950	8.4	288	1.9	3,238	6.4
Primary	5,080	14.5	468	3.1	5,548	11.0
Preparatory	7,051	20.1	949	6.3	8,000	15.9
Secondary	7,942	22.6	2,431	16.0	10,373	20.6
Subtotal	24,082	68.6	4,371	28.8	28,453	56.6
Post-secondary and above						
Diploma	1,250	3.6	524	3.5	1,774	3.5
Bachelor's	8,702	24.8	9,884	65.2	18,586	37.0
Higher diploma	296	0.8	91	0.6	387	0.8
Master's	551	1.6	173	1.1	724	1.4
Doctorate	229	0.7	114	0.8	343	0.7
Subtotal	11,028	31.4	10,786	71.2	21,814	43.4
Total	35,110	100.0	15,157	100.0	50,267	100.0

SOURCES: Qatar Planning Council, 2005b, Tables 18 and 19; and authors' calculations.
NOTES: Figures exclude "unspecified" for education level. Numbers may not add to total because of rounding.

The first box in Figure 3.6 notes the heavy reliance on expatriate workers in the country and the fact that the public sector is the primary employer of Qatari nationals. This situation occurred primarily because of Qatar's economic and political history. As detailed earlier, Gulf nations that were in trucial agreements with Britain had relatively small population bases and little infrastructure in place to deal with the sudden human resource needs of oil production. In Qatar, no comprehensive education system was in place, and the few people who were educated received a religious education that for the most part

Figure 3.6
Schematic of Challenges Faced by Qatar: Need to Address an Underqualified and Unprepared National Workforce

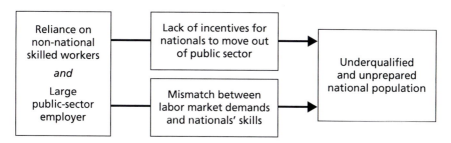

excluded females from participating. Therefore, from an early stage, non-national workers filled the gap in Qatari nationals' skills. In addition, low-skilled expatriate labor has been necessary to the country's infrastructure development through the years.

The distribution of revenue from oil has brought about a lack of incentives for Qataris to work outside the public sector. In the early stages of oil production, oil companies gave their proceeds directly to the emir as a condition of extracting oil within the country. The emir then distributed much of the proceeds to Qataris in the form of subsidies for petrol, water, and electricity; free primary, secondary, and postsecondary education; access to free health care; and generous employment benefits for those working in the public sector, including a salary based on years of schooling, a plot of land, and an interest-free mortgage to build a house on that land. The system of distributing wealth among nationals is also used in the two other Arab Gulf nations in our study, Oman and the UAE, but it is not in place throughout the Arab Gulf (e.g., in Saudi Arabia).

This system offers advantages—for example, it provides a country's leadership with a certain amount of security and legitimacy while providing its citizenry with stable employment. However, because of the benefits Qataris derive by working in the public sector and because the day-to-day operations in the oil and gas industry are taken care of primarily by expatriates, Qatar's leaders have faced challenges in their attempts to encourage Qataris to study subjects of use in the oil industry (such as mathematics, science, engineering, and technology) or to obtain skills important in today's global knowledge economy (such as proficiency in English, computer and information technology, and enhanced critical thinking and problem solving). The lack of incentives and the associated skills mismatch have resulted in a Qatari labor force that lacks the qualifications and preparation needed for the 21st century work world (Stasz et al., 2007). High rates of unemployment, especially among young workers, are symptomatic of the mismatch between Qataris' expectations about the job market and employers' demands.

Qatar's leadership recognizes the burden being placed on the economy by its citizenry's reliance on the public sector for employment: An unqualified workforce means potentially greater unemployment and further reliance on the government for financial assistance and support. Steps are being taken to address the challenges associated with developing the human resources of Qatar nationals so that Qataris will be employable in major industries, including the private and semi-private sectors. Interviews with employers in the petroleum and gas industries and in Qatar Foundation note that Qatar's leadership has two primary goals: (1) to make the country a competitive player in the global economy by raising the quality of the human capital of nationals and (2) to reduce the reliance on expatriate labor (Qatar Petroleum, 2008). Our analyses of recent reforms show that Qatar's leadership is endeavoring to meet these objectives in four ways:

1. Reforming the primary and secondary education system
2. Reforming the post-secondary education system
3. Training Qatari secondary school graduates
4. Promoting the employment of Qataris in the industrial, petroleum, and private sectors.

Qatar's leadership seeks to address the burgeoning numbers of Qataris headed for employment in the government sector by reforming the nation's primary, secondary, and post-secondary education system and enhancing its population's skills through government training efforts; and by encouraging the employment of Qataris in the private sector through nationalization efforts and a number of labor market initiatives. We discuss each of these avenues in turn.

Qatar Introduces a Comprehensive Primary and Secondary Education Reform

As noted earlier in this chapter, Qatar has been quite successful at extending education to all children, including girls and students living outside the capital city of Doha. However, Qatar's primary and secondary education systems have not been preparing students for employment in the global economy or for pursuing post-secondary education opportunities. Only recently were extensive reforms to the quality of education that Qatari students receive undertaken.

In November 2002, Qatar embarked on a systemic reform to its primary and secondary education systems to tackle perceived deficits in the quality of education offered to students. RAND assisted in the design and implementation of the reform from 2002 through 2005. In 2001, RAND conducted a study that found that many of Qatar's students were retained in their same grade each year and that most secondary school graduates were unprepared to enter selective post-secondary institutions or science- and technology-related jobs. The inability of the education system to meet the nation's human resource needs stemmed from a number of inherent and systemic problems, including the absence of a coherent vision of education goals; a hierarchical organizational structure within the Ministry of Education; an outdated curriculum that focused on rote memorization; lack of innovation in the classroom; no authority to make decisions at the school level; no systematic appraisal of student outcomes (Brewer et al., 2007).

In an effort to address the problems of the Ministry of Education system and improve the rigor and quality of education in the country, Qatar adopted a reform that featured a transparent and flexible standards-based education system. The goals of this reform are to promote the autonomy of education providers (teachers and school administrators), provide a variety of government-funded schooling options for parents to choose from, enhance the critical thinking and problem-solving skills of the student body, and hold all school leaders, teachers, parents, and students accountable for the success of students (Brewer et al., 2007).

In 2002, Emiri Decree 37 established the Qatar Supreme Education Council to direct the nation's education policy and to oversee the reform alongside two independent government offices, the Evaluation Institute and the Education Institute (described in more detail below, along with a third institute that was established in 2005).

The reform has four main features:

1. Curriculum standards, developed according to international benchmarks, in modern standard Arabic (FusHa), English as a foreign language, mathematics, and science
2. A standards-based assessment system levied on students in all government-sponsored schools in grades 1 through 12[16]
3. A school evaluation and data management system
4. The development of schools that are publicly funded but have relative administrative autonomy from the Supreme Education Council or Ministry of Education.

The new schools, called "Independent" schools, are publicly funded but independently operated and exist alongside current Ministry of Education schools. Twelve Independent schools opened in 2004, 21 in 2005, 13 in 2006, and 19 in August 2007—together they represent approximately 29 percent of the total 227 publicly funded schools in Qatar teaching over 50 percent of Qatar's school children (Qatar Ministry of Education, 2005). All government-funded schools will be Independent schools by 2012 (Qatar Supreme Education Council, 2006a). A new education organization, the Education Institute, oversees the operation of the Independent schools, developed the new curriculum standards that the Independent schools follow, and provides professional development to teachers and administrators. The Ministry of Education continues to oversee the remaining 150 primary, preparatory, and secondary schools. While the Independent schools maintain

---

[16] As of 2006, assessments were administered to students in grades 4 through 11. As of 2007, assessments were administered only to students in those grades in the newly established schools.

operational autonomy subject to the terms of the contract signed with the Supreme Education Council, the Ministry of Education continues to directly operate the traditional government schools.

Important to the reform is the school evaluation system that is based on surveys administered to students in publicly funded schools and their parents, teachers, and school administrators, and on a comprehensive standards-based assessment system, the QCEA, administered to all students in government-sponsored schools each year.[17] The first wave of surveys and assessments was administered in March and April 2004 (see some of the assessment results in Figure 3.4, above). Starting with the 2005 administration, results have been published in school report cards each year to promote parental choice in schooling for their children; the first set of school report cards was disseminated in April 2006. According to members of the Institutes, the goal is for parents to use the information provided in the report cards to select the school they wish their children to attend. Schools will therefore have to compete for students. The Independent schools allow for open choice, although space is presently limited because of oversubscription (Qatar Supreme Education Council, 2007a); attendance in Ministry of Education schools, in contrast, is based primarily on a student's proximity to the school, and parents are not allowed to send their children to a school outside the neighborhood boundary.

In addition to the national assessment system, Qatar is participating in three international assessments: the 2007 TIMSS (Trends in International Mathematics and Science Study), the 2006 PIRLS (Progress in International Reading Literacy Study), and the 2006 PISA (Programme for International Student Assessment). The Evaluation Institute develops and administers the surveys and assessments and publishes the school report cards.

By design, Qatar's primary and secondary education reforms are comprehensive and aim to change the education system as a whole rather than focusing solely on a few pieces of that system, such as cur-

---

[17] Government-sponsored schools include Ministry of Education schools; the newly developed, Independent schools; and the private Arabic schools that follow the Ministry of Education curriculum but are privately funded.

riculum or teacher training. By electing to pursue a comprehensive education reform rather than target one component of the education system, Qatar is attempting not only to improve students' skills and learning, but also to encourage parental choice and render the education system less centralized, thereby fostering a culture of innovation and change within the schools themselves (Brewer et al., 2007). The reform includes

- School organizational change that allows for school-level administrative autonomy
- Curriculum change
- The use of national assessments that allow cross-grade and through-time comparisons of student achievement vis-à-vis internationally benchmarked standards
- An accountability system for schools that is based on parental choice
- Teacher and administrator training programs
- The integration of information technology in teaching and learning
- Participation in international assessments to gauge students' achievement through time compared with that of students in other countries.

It has only been a few years since the inception of the reform, so it is difficult to ascertain whether the goals have been met or the presence of the Independent schools has generated change in the Ministry of Education. However, results from the 2006 administrations of two of the international tests, PISA and PIRLS, show that student scores in Qatar lag those of students in almost all participating non-Arab countries and are higher than those of students in most of the other participating Arab countries (Qatar Supreme Education Council, 2008). Furthermore, results from the 2007 administration of QCEA suggest that only a small portion of students in Independent schools can be categorized as "meeting" the curriculum standards, upon which the QCEA is based. On average, 4.5 percent of Independent school students in grades 4 through 11 are meeting the Arabic language standards, 7.5

percent are meeting the English standards, 3 percent are meeting the mathematics standards, and less than 1 percent are meeting the science standards (Qatar Supreme Education Council, 2007b).

Post-Secondary Education Reforms Are Also Considered a Priority
At the same time that Qatar's leadership overhauled its primary and secondary education systems, it also expanded and reformed its post-secondary education opportunities. Qatar has instituted reforms to its national university, opened a number of branch campuses of post-secondary institutions that offer a variety of undergraduate degrees needed in Qatar's economy, and systematized Qatar's scholarship services for students who wish to study abroad.

Qatar University Reforms. In 2003, the administration of Qatar University embarked on a mission to reform the academic and institutional structures of the university and to strengthen key governance and management operations, such as external oversight, academic governance, and management. The reforms under way in Qatar University focus on decentralization of the university's administrative and academic structures to encourage organizational autonomy and make practices more transparent. Further reform efforts are in place to improve the quality of academic and campus life through

- A new admissions process and requirements
- Higher academic standards for retention and graduation
- A new core curriculum that reinforces skills-based learning outcomes
- A decentralized university-wide academic planning process
- Systematic program and departmental evaluations
- Increased opportunities and financial support for research
- Improvements to student support services, registration, and advising practices
- New opportunities for student-led activities.

Reforms aimed to enhance the skills of Qatar University graduates in order to meet the needs of the labor market include

- Admitting females to civil engineering, computer engineering, chemical engineering, and industrial systems programs (as of the 2003–2004 academic year)
- Offering a core curriculum in mathematics, science, and Qatari culture and history
- Enhancing admission standards across fields of study
- Encouraging the practice of scholarly endeavors by both faculty and students.

Branch Campuses of Overseas Universities. To expand educational offerings for post-secondary students in Qatar and in the Gulf region more generally, Qatar has looked to overseas institutions of higher education to bring their programs to Qatar. Starting in 1998, Qatar Foundation sponsored a number of North American university branch campuses in Education City on a new site in Doha.[18]

Table 3.15 summarizes the five institutions that have opened to date. These schools cover the fields of engineering, computer science and business, fashion design, international relations and diplomacy, and medicine. The programs bring curriculum and faculty from their home institutions to their Doha campus to provide the same post-secondary and graduate programs that are offered in the United States. In the case of Weill Cornell Medical College, the Education City campus represents the first time a U.S. medical school has offered its courses and programs overseas. In the coming years, other programs and institutions are expected to be attracted to Education City to establish branch campuses. Unlike sites in other countries, these campuses do not operate on a self-supporting basis; they are subsidized by Qatar Foundation. As a result, the universities can operate in the region without regard to whether market tuition rates will support their programs.

In addition to the institutions listed in Table 3.15, there is one vocational college in Qatar, the College of North Atlantic–Qatar (CNA-Q), established in 2002. It is a Canadian-based technical college that offers training courses for a variety of trades: business studies, engineering technology, information technology, and health sciences.

---

[18] Education City was officially inaugurated in 2003, but the first campus opened in 1998.

Table 3.15
Institutes of Higher Education on Qatar's Education City Campus

Institution (Year Established)	Description
Virginia Commonwealth University School of the Arts–Qatar (1998)	Offers female students a comprehensive four-year curriculum leading to a bachelor of fine arts degree in communication design, fashion design, or interior design.
Weill Cornell Medical College–Qatar (2001)	Offers a co-educational two-year pre-medical program in the sciences basic to medicine, with additional seminars in the humanities (English and medical ethics), and a separate four-year medical program that replicates the curriculum offered at Weill Cornell in New York. All teaching is by Cornell faculty, and academic standards are very high. At the completion of their studies, graduates receive the doctor of medicine degree from Cornell University. There is a separate admission process for each program. The first class entered in the 2003–2004 academic year.
Carnegie Mellon University in Qatar (2003)	Offers undergraduate degrees in business and computer science. Curriculum offered to students in Qatar is the same one offered to students at the U.S. campus.
Texas A&M University–Qatar (2003)	Offers undergraduate degrees in chemical, electrical, mechanical, and petroleum engineering. The curriculum offered to students in Qatar is identical to that offered at the main campus in College Station, Texas. Plans are in effect to offer graduate programs and to establish two interdisciplinary research centers to address the production and use of natural resources and environmental sustainability issues.
Georgetown University School of Foreign Service in Qatar (2005)	Offers a four-year program leading to a bachelor's degree in foreign service.

Students graduate with a two-year technical degree. There is also the CHN (Christelijke Hogeschool Nederland) University of the Netherlands, which offers undergraduate programs in hospitality and tourism management.

Higher Education Institute. In March 2005, under the auspices of the Supreme Education Council, the Higher Education Institute (HEI) was established to manage Qatar's post-secondary school scholarship system. HEI administers scholarships and identifies top universities, degree programs, and short-term professional development courses in

Qatar and around the world for HEI scholarship applicants. HEI also determines target specialties for scholarship recipients. Currently, the highest priority is given to medicine, engineering, finance, and economics because they are the high-demand fields in the labor market. The scholarship program thereby serves as an incentive mechanism to increase the number of students studying essential fields.

HEI administers the previous (pre-HEI) scholarship program that is still in effect for those students that received scholarships prior to the HEI's establishment. The HEI also administers five new scholarship programs—Emiri Scholarship, National Scholarship, Employee Scholarship, Diploma Scholarship, and Pre-College Grant programs—the first three of which include both undergraduate and graduate study options. (Details on the scholarship programs are in Appendix C.) Applicants to the scholarship programs must be Qatari citizens, have a predetermined minimum score on a relevant English language test (for universities in English-speaking countries only), meet certain criteria for past academic performance, and agree to work in an area of importance to Qatar upon graduation for a time equal to the length of the scholarship (except in the case of the Pre-College Grant) (Qatar Supreme Education Council, 2006b).

Several other scholarship programs are under consideration and may be implemented in the near future: Loan-Based Scholarships are intended for non-Qataris accepted at institutions deemed prestigious by HEI, as well as approved programs at Education City and Qatar University; Professional Development Grants are meant to assist individuals admitted to short-term study programs to help improve or develop new job skills for career advancement or job transition. Other financial assistance may be available as well to help Qataris participate in internationally recognized academic and professional development opportunities, such as the Fulbright program or special internships (Qatar Supreme Education Council, 2005b).

Efforts to Train Qatari Secondary School Graduates
Employers noted that once recent secondary and post-secondary Qatari graduates are employed, they need extensive training in English, information technology, and computer skills and lack "soft" skills, such as

positive attitudes toward work and a willingness to learn on the job (Stasz et al., 2007). Studies as early as 1973 have argued that "a sophisticated system of manpower planning, complemented by a highly coordinated system of training was required by [Qatar] to promote the skills needed for its people to succeed in the oil and gas economy" (Al-Hafidh, 1973, p. 14). However, no concerted effort to enact a coordinated training system for Qataris has yet developed. A recent IMF study (Fasano, 2001, p. 384) found that Qatar needs to enhance the employability of its local labor force without hindering competitiveness and recommended a number of measures to accomplish this:

- Provide appropriate training.
- Curtail the government's role as the employer of first resort.
- Improve job placement services and the links between training and the labor market.
- Strengthen the links between higher education and the labor market.

Qatar is beginning to improve its training efforts. For many years, training programs have been initiated by individual corporations, such as Qatar Petroleum, or by the Qatar Ministry of Civil Service Affairs and Housing (MoCSAH). These programs are geared to re-train or train Qataris in a particular skill set to fill existing jobs. In addition, there are about 100 smaller-scale private training institutes that offer short courses in clerical, information technology, and English language training. However, because there is no accreditation program for these training institutes, the quality of their programs is unknown. Efforts are under way to certify post-secondary training institutes. Officials at the Supreme Council's HEI reported that they are carrying out an inventory of these institutions and are developing quality assurance mechanisms and a self-assessment document. Each center will be independently assessed and certified for some period. Those failing to qualify will be given feedback on what they need to do to improve and become certified.

Since 1999, Qatar has encouraged training of its citizens through the MoCSAH. Article 1 of Law 9, promulgated in 1999, stipulates that the Organization and Manpower Planning Department of the MoCSAH develop a National Training Plan to be implemented by the Institute of Administration Development (IAD). Training at the IAD is limited to ministries and government agencies and does not provide for training activities related to the private sector's needs. The IAD provides short-term training courses for Qatari government employees. Officials at the MoCSAH note that the IAD started with 22 programs in 1997 and currently has 160 tailor-made programs covering such topics as management, finance, information technology, English language, banking, insurance, and tourism. From 1997 to 2005, the IAD trained 11,000 students, of whom 4,500 were female. The most popular training programs it offers are management programs, followed by finance and information technology programs. The IAD receives requests from government institutions, usually through their human resource departments, to train their employees in specific skills. Before taking up positions, new jobholders may spend up to six months at the IAD. Individuals already working in the government can also apply for training programs, if their ministry agrees. However, final approval has to come from the MoCSAH. The IAD awards certificates at the end of each training program. Taking IAD training courses is an important factor for promotion, and most employees return to the IAD for additional training courses. The program is recognized regionally, by Egypt's Arab Administrative Development Organization, and internationally, by Canada's Public Administration Institute.

The MoCSAH also runs the Training Center, established in 2000, which prepares Qatari high school graduates for entry-level private-sector jobs and helps the government meet Qatarization goals (see discussion below). The Training Center targets Qatari nationals who have not been employed and who would normally not be able to work in particular sectors because their performance in school was poor or their study area is not in demand.[19] The Center helps such individuals gain vocational qualifications and other skills needed to join the private sector. The length of instruction is 1.5 to 2 years, and

---

[19] A small fraction of students are college graduates. For example, a number of primary school teachers have enrolled to improve their abilities in classroom management.

the program has two phases: (1) a foundational year in which students take extensive courses in English language, computing, and foundation skills; (2) preparation to obtain a Business and Technology Education Council Intermediate Certificate in Principles of Work Level 1 or Level 2. Trainees receive internationally recognized awards.

The Training Center collects information about job vacancies and works in conjunction with sponsors from the private and public sectors. Sponsors provide trainees with financial incentives/stipends, mentoring services on specific jobs, and a suitable workplace for gaining work experience; trainees cannot graduate without work experience. The Training Center provides progress reports to sponsors on a regular basis. After the program is finished, the employer decides whether to hire the trainee.

As of November 2005, the Training Center had trained 616 Qatari females and 435 Qatari males. At the time, however, enrollments were heavily skewed toward female Qataris: Roughly 90 percent of the 2005 trainees were female. The Center is encouraging more males to attend its program to increase their self-confidence by involving them in the Special Services Preparation Program, which includes Disaster Management, First Aid, Personal Safety, and Social Responsibilities programs.

Privatization and Economy Diversification Efforts

In addition to improving the quality of the Qatari education and training system, Qatar's leadership has taken steps to diversify the economy to broaden its base of economic activity beyond oil and gas, both through expansion of the private sector and through policies to expand research and development. It has also instituted several labor market reforms and taken measures to promote the employment of Qataris through Qatarization policies.

Promotion of the Private Sector. Qatar recently allowed 100 percent foreign ownership in the agriculture, industry, health, education, and tourism sectors. Previous laws stipulated that foreigners could not own more than 49 percent of a business. The maximum corporate tax has been reduced from 35 to 30 percent (Fasano and Iqbal, 2003). Moreover, Qatar partially privatized Qtel (the only telecommunications company in the country) and the electricity and water sector in 1998 by selling most of the government's power plants to a privately held company.

Promotion of Research and Development. The Qatar Foundation for Education, Science, and Community Development (called Qatar Foundation), established in 1995 with Her Highness Sheikha Mozah as chair of its board of directors, is a private, non-profit organization. Its mission is to raise both the competency of individuals and the quality of life in Qatar through investments in human capital, innovative technology, state-of-the-art facilities, and partnerships with elite international organizations. To achieve its mission, Qatar Foundation has set up a number of affiliated organizations in the fields of education, health, and community development (Brewer et al., 2007). For example, Qatar Foundation runs the Social Development Center, which provides low-income females with family development courses and training in such commercial skills as industrial dressmaking and traditional Qatari handicrafts. In addition, Qatar Foundation initiated Education City and is developing the Qatar Science and Technology Park (QSTP), a free zone that allows tenants to independently own and operate a local entity that is not subject to tax, duty, or capital controls.

The goal for the QSTP is to attract companies with a focus on gas and petrochemicals, health care, information and communication technologies, water technologies, the environment, and aircraft operations so that Qatar will become an internationally recognized hub for research and commercialization. Qatar provides the infrastructure and services to tenant organizations involved in the development and application of technology. QSTP creates a supportive environment for corporate technology-development activities by offering ready-to-occupy premises suitable for labs and offices; services that cover basic business needs, as well as expert advice; and access to the faculty, graduates, and facilities of universities at Qatar's Education City.

Promotion of Females in the Labor Market. Table 3.16 shows, separately for males and females, the trend since 1986 in the labor force participation rate (also known as the rate of economic activity), which, for these data, Qatar's Planning Council defines as the percentage of

Table 3.16
Labor Force Participation Rates in Qatar,
by Gender, 1986 to 2004

Year	Males	Females
1986	93.0	27.5
1997	91.0	35.2
2001	90.2	37.6
2004	91.7	40.6

SOURCES: Qatar Supreme Council for Family Affairs, 2004, Table 6.1; Qatar Planning Council, 2002, Table 5; and Qatar Planning Council, 2005b, Table 13.

the economically active population age 15 and above in the labor force. In general, between 1986 and 2004, female participation in Qatar's labor force increased noticeably. In 1986, about 28 percent of females age 15 or over were in the labor force; by 2004, this had increased to nearly 41 percent.

Officials in the education, labor, and private sectors with whom we spoke attribute the increase in female participation in Qatar's labor market, especially among nationals, to societal forces such as greater acceptance of working females; females' increased educational attainment through the years; the leadership of Sheikha Mozah and the influence of female role models in high-level government positions, such as the Minister of Education and the President of Qatar University, both appointed in 2003; and employed Qatari females and business owners.

In addition, interviewees noted that greater political will on the part of Qatari leadership has contributed to recent increases in females' labor market participation. Since 1998, Qatar has shown the political will to promote the economic activity of females by enacting laws that promote their participation in the workforce.[20] These include

---

[20] The government's Qatarization policies, described in more depth below, have also had a major impact on females' employment opportunities since they encourage private-sector employers to hire Qataris, regardless of gender.

- The Civil Service Act (Law 1 of 2001) and Council of Ministers Order 13 of 2001, which regulates implementation of the Act. This law equalizes the rights and duties of males and females in the workplace and also grants females rights that assist them in their efforts to balance family and job responsibilities.
- Law 24 of 2002 (the Pensions Law) provides females with retirement benefits and makes special provisions that allow working females to combine their earnings and pension entitlement with those of a deceased spouse.
- A new labor law in 2004 (Law 14) replaced an older, 1962 law that had been in force for over 40 years. The new labor law provides equality in working rights to males and females, including pay, training opportunities, and job advancement. This labor law also provides workers with new rights: Contracts must be in writing, workers' financial rights have priority over all properties of the employer and all debts on the employer including the government's, lawsuits by workers are treated as urgent and are litigated at no cost to the employee, and there are now penalties for noncompliant employers. The law also includes provisions for labor unions and employer associations.

Qatari females still tend to find employment in the education sector, yet they are increasingly engaging in entrepreneurial enterprises. Data obtained from the Qatar Chamber of Commerce show that the number of female entrepreneurs active in their businesses by 2005 accounted for about 17 percent of the total and that females have almost all licenses to operate certain businesses, such as beauty salons. Qatari females have also entered new professions, becoming doctors, police officers, and customs agents, occupations typically dominated by males (Bahry and Marr, 2005).

Qatarization. In 2002, Qatar formally ended the policy of automatic employment in the public sector for Qatari secondary and university graduates. The government now assists job seekers through the MoCSAH's Training Center (described above). It also enacted a number of five-year plans to promote the employment of "quality" Qatari nationals in the private and mixed sectors. According to Qatari

Labor Law 3 of 1962, a vacant position must be first offered to a Qatari national; then, if it cannot be filled, it can be offered to a non-Qatari Arab, followed by a non-Arab foreigner. In the early 1970s, a decision was made to Qatarize administrative posts in the government sector. By the 1990s, the proportion of top school administrative positions held by Qataris reached 96 percent (Qatar Ministry of Education, 1996). In May 1997, the Emir decreed that private-sector businesses had to ensure that at least 20 percent of their employees were Qatari nationals (Winckler, 2000).

The most recent five-year plan (2000–2005) had a target of 50 percent of jobs in the energy and industry sectors for Qataris (Qatar Petroleum, 2008). According to recent estimates, more than 1,300 Qataris are employed in the energy and industry sector, close to 28 percent of the sector total.[21] Many other Qataris are in training and are about to enter the workforce. Qatarization goals have also been implemented in the Independent school system for teachers and staff to encourage schools to hire and train Qatari nationals.

Efforts to Collect Demographic, Economic, Labor Market, and Education Data Are Expanding

For more than two decades, Qatar has been gathering and disseminating demographic, economic, labor market, and education data in support of government planning and policies. These data provide a basis for understanding the human capital and labor market challenges faced by the country, as well as information for monitoring the country's progress following the implementation of reforms. As we detail in this section, these information resources include data collected and published by the Qatar Planning Council, a new source of education data collected by the Qatar Supreme Education Council, and other recent activities to extend the types and quality of data collected.

---

[21] For details on the Qatarization plan for the energy and industry sectors, see Qatar Petroleum, 2008.

Principal Data Provider: The Qatar Planning Council[22]

To adequately determine the country's economic and labor market needs, Qatar established the Planning Council in 1998. The Council is the main government body focusing on economic and social plans and policies in the state of Qatar; it also coordinates and cooperates with other GCC states in support of its activities.

The Statistical Department of the Planning Council, which began operating in 1980 as the Central Statistical Organization, is the official source of data on Qatar.[23] It supplies all government ministries with statistical data from administrative sources, vital statistics, censuses, and surveys. The Statistical Department's objectives include publishing annual and other periodic economic and social statistics; providing data and information about Qatar for local, regional, and international organizations; collecting economic and social data from censuses and sample surveys; providing technical support, supervision, and auditing of surveys or censuses collected by other government or private-sector entities; and maintaining and enhancing the technical capacity and information systems for data collection and reporting.

The data collected and published by the Statistical Department include

- An annual establishment survey of economic activity in industry, building and construction, wholesale and retail trade, banking and insurance, and government
- A national census that was first administered in 1986
- A population and housing census that was fielded in 1997 and 2004

---

[22] Information in this section is drawn from the Qatar Planning Council's official website (Qatar Planning Council, 2008).

[23] The name change occurred when the Central Statistical Organization became part of the Planning Council upon the Council's establishment in 1998. In June 2007, the Statistics Authority replaced the Planning Council's Statistical Department. The Qatar Statistics Authority is the official national statistical agency and is independent of the Planning Council. It serves the same general purposes that the Statistical Department did but has a broader vision: "to be recognized by national and international users as the trusted official source of high-quality, demand-driven statistical information" (Qatar Planning Council, 2008).

- A household-based survey to measure family income and expenditures that was conducted in 1982, 1988, and 2001
- A household-based labor force survey that was conducted in 2001 and in 2006.

Future plans call for the next population and housing census in 2010, in coordination with the other GCC countries.

New Source of Education Statistics
Since the 1980s, the Ministry of Education has collected data on enrollment and test achievement for all students in the publicly funded Ministry of Education schools and enrollment data for students in private Arabic schools. It also began collecting student enrollment data from the Independent schools in the 2004–2005 academic year. Basic demographic data on students, such as age, nationality, and religion, are also collected. These data are adequate for providing educators and policymakers with important information about numbers of students in each school, number of classrooms, and student-to-teacher ratios, but they are inadequate for helping policymakers to understand how well the education system is doing as a whole.

As part of the primary and secondary education reform efforts, Qatar created the Qatar National Education Data System (QNEDS), which is housed in the Evaluation Institute. Data in QNEDS are from the student, parent, teacher, and administrator surveys, as well as from the QCEA administered each year by the Evaluation Institute. QNEDS improves on statistics collected by the Ministry of Education in a number of ways—for example, QNEDS allows tracking of individual students through time, analysis of siblings, and comparisons across grades or schools. Furthermore, the surveys administered by the Evaluation Institute ask questions about the schooling experience and expectations of stakeholders, allowing for a wealth of analyses. Whereas data from the Ministry of Education are only available to the public in hard-copy tabulations, QNEDS data are directly accessible. With a response rate of about 90 percent—over 80,000 students and 7,800 teacher responses annually—since the first administration of the surveys and assessments in 2004, QNEDS is a vital component of the education reform effort and the first of its kind in the region.

Other Activities to Extend Statistical Resources

In January 2006, Qatar joined the IMF's General Data Dissemination System (GDDS) (IMF, 2006). Established in 1997, the GDDS provides a framework to assist IMF member countries in developing their statistical systems with the objective of producing comprehensive and accurate statistics for policymaking and analysis. Other Middle East countries that participate are Jordan, Kuwait, Lebanon, and Oman (IMF, undated).[24]

In April 2006, the Planning Council announced its plans to build sustainable labor market policies for Qatar through the "Qatar Labor Market Strategy National Action Plan," a comprehensive program of activities developed in concert with the World Bank. The plan focuses on four major outcomes:

1. Labor-related information management and collection
2. Training and work support
3. Labor market policy and institutional development
4. Public service employment and productivity.

For each of these areas, a number of projects are planned, such as development of a national qualifications framework, better-coordinated collection and management of labor-related data, assessment of the need for a committee on workforce development, provision of training in manpower planning, and examination of education issues, such as why Qatari males are disproportionately underrepresented in higher education (*Peninsula*, 2006).

---

[24] The GDDS is a framework to develop national statistical systems in producing economic and socio-demographic data (IMF, undated). The GDDS diagnoses data quality strengths and weaknesses compared with international practices and catalogues technical assistance needed, thereby guiding national policymakers on how to address these issues to improve the data collection methodology and dissemination practices. It serves as a vehicle for countries to progress toward using the Special Data Dissemination Standard (SDDS).

Summary

Qatar is one of the world's wealthiest nations. Endowed with tremendous reserves of natural gas but a small population of nationals, it has relied in recent decades on a large influx of foreign workers to exploit its natural resources. Employment of nationals has been concentrated in the government, where they enjoy generous benefits and attractive working conditions and thus have little incentive to work in the private sector. Our analyses of data from the Ministry of Education, Supreme Education Council, Qatar University, and Qatar's labor force survey show that graduates of Qatar's K–12 public education system score far below international standards in core subjects and that there are too few graduates in the science, engineering, and technology fields, which are the fields particularly in demand in the private sector. Unemployment is particularly high among young persons, especially male nationals.

According to our interviewees in the private and public sectors of the country, Qatar's leadership recognizes that to promote economic stability, it must encourage the employment of Qatari nationals in the mixed and private sectors. Although Qatar will remain one of the richest nations in the world in the coming decades, it will not be able to compete in the knowledge economy of the 21st century if its public sector remains the largest employer of Qatari nationals. Until Qatar's young nationals receive the education and training needed to equip them with the appropriate skills for the market, the pool of Qatari human resources entering the market will be unqualified. This could threaten Qatar's long-term economic viability. One way to mitigate this issue is to increase the flow of foreign labor into the country, but attempts to restrict in-migration and the push for Qatarization suggest that the leadership wants to increasingly rely on its own people to address future human resource needs.

Qatar is poised to be a major leader in human capital development in the region. The country has embarked on one of the most comprehensive reform efforts in the region, one that encompasses reforms in education and training and in the labor market and economy (see Table 3.17) and that has been called the region's "most ambitious, far-reaching, and focused" reform effort to date (Frank, 2006). Qatar is

Table 3.17
Summary of Education and Labor Market Reforms Under Way in Qatar

Reform Categories and Subcategories
Education and training
Primary and secondary education
Establishment of coordinating bodies
School organizational change
Standards-based accountability
Restructured curriculum
National student assessment and evaluation
Participation in international student assessments
Professional development for teachers and administrators
Integration of information technology in learning environment
Post-secondary and post-graduate education
Reform of administrative, curricular, and academic standards of national university
Establishment of foreign or private higher education institutions
Scholarship programs (for low-income students or in targeted fields and institutions)
Training system
Establishment of technical/vocational college
Public-private partnerships to train nationals
Independent certification of post-secondary training institutions
Labor market and economy
Labor market reforms
Establishment of goals for employment of nationals in private sector
Elimination of automatic employment of nationals in public sector
Equalization of worker rights or access to benefits in public and private sectors
Other economic reforms
Allowance of foreign ownership of companies in selected sectors
Establishment of free zones exempt from government requirements

implementing its education reforms and working toward labor market reforms at a faster pace than other countries in the region, partly because it only began these changes five years ago.

Training in Qatar is still piecemeal, however, and incentives for Qataris to take jobs in the private sector remain inadequate. Also, inadequate data on labor market indicators make matching Qatari nationals to jobs in the private sector difficult. All of these factors thwart Qatarization goals. In sum, Qatar has a long road ahead but has a focused effort in place to ameliorate the inadequacies in the skills of its national population. The fruits of its reform efforts may not be realized for another generation, after students experiencing the K–12 education reform have completed the new standards in mathematics and science. For future students, the systemization of data collection efforts that began in 2006 with Qatar's participation in the IMF's GDDS will provide a feedback mechanism for making the reforms under way even more effective.

CHAPTER FOUR

The United Arab Emirates

Of the four countries examined in our study, the UAE has the largest oil reserves, estimated at 98 billion barrels, or approximately 100 years at current production levels (OPEC, 2005).[1] The boom in oil production over the past few decades has brought about great infrastructure developments, necessitating a large influx of expatriate labor to fill deficiencies in the skills of the citizen population. Indeed, the UAE's population rose dramatically as large waves of migrants—mostly from other Arab and South Asian nations—arrived seeking work opportunities. More recently, there has been a steady influx of African, European, and North American migrants. Together, non-nationals make up about 80 percent of the UAE population (UAE Ministry of Economy, *Statistics Abstract*, 2006).

The UAE is facing a number of economic and demographic challenges to its future stability. Similar to Qatar and Oman, its government sector has become the largest employer of the citizen population (referred to in the UAE as Emiratis). The citizen population experiences a relatively low labor force participation rate, and this is especially the case for female nationals. In addition, the UAE is experiencing a population boom among its youth. Recent figures estimate that 38 percent of nationals are less than 15 years of age. Recognizing these issues, UAE leadership has focused on increasing the labor force participation rate of nationals and ensuring that the growing youth popu-

---

[1] 2004 OPEC estimates put UAE oil reserves at 97.8 billion barrels. UAE exports of crude oil and refined products were estimated in 2004 at nearly 2.7 million bbl/day, or almost 978 million barrels during the year (OPEC, 2005).

lation is prepared for work outside the government sector. In particular, the government of the UAE has tried to address both the surge in the growth of non-national laborers in the country and the low labor force participation rates of nationals through policies that promote the development of training opportunities and post-secondary education programs and, more recently, through primary and secondary education reform efforts. The primary goals of these initiatives are to enhance the skills of Emiratis and promote their employment in the private sector. These education, training, and labor market initiatives were a central focus of our study.

We begin this chapter by providing important background on the political, economic, demographic, education, and labor market conditions in the UAE. We then use the analytic framework we developed (see Chapter One) to document and organize the education and labor market initiatives under way. We first diagnose and articulate the problem, identifying and delineating the most-salient human resource challenges that the country faces. We base this analysis on an overview of education and labor market indicators available through international databases and reports published by local governmental and non-governmental sources. We then document the initiatives under way to address the human resource problem; these initiatives are listed in Table 4.1.

Our documentation is based on an analysis of information from reports, public websites, and interviews with government officials in the education and labor market sectors. We cover initiatives that seek to expand the human capital of the national population and increase its participation in the growing private sector, focusing on education (K–12, post-secondary, and training) and labor market (economic diversification, privatization, and employment policy levers) reforms. To the extent that information was available, we measure changes against policy goals. Finally, we examine the resources available in the UAE for policy evaluation and development.

We also discuss opportunities for improving data collection and analysis systems to enhance the formulation and implementation of education and labor market policies. We conclude the chapter with a summary of the reforms under way and our overall findings.

Table 4.1
Human Capital Reforms Covered in UAE Case Study

Reform Categories and Subcategories
Education and training
Primary and secondary education
Post-secondary and post-graduate education
Training
Labor market and economy
Labor market reforms
Economic privatization
Economic diversification

Overview of the UAE

Established in 1971, the UAE is presently a federation of seven emirates (formerly known as Trucial States): Dubai, Sharjah, Ajman, Umm al Qaywayn, Al Fujayrah, Ra's al Khaymah, and Abu Dhabi (the capital).[2] Figure 4.1 is a map of the UAE and neighboring countries. The UAE stretches across approximately 83,600 square kilometers, with the emirate of Abu Dhabi occupying the largest share (87 percent). The Sultanate of Oman borders the UAE on the north and east, and Saudi Arabia borders it on the south and west. The UAE has a long stretch of coastline along the Arabian Gulf (also called the Persian Gulf, as is the case in Figure 4.1), and the city of Dubai was an important port of call along the trade route from South Asia to the northern part of the Arabian Gulf. The Musandam Peninsula, which lies at the northernmost tip of the country, is territorially part of the Sultanate of Oman, but the people of this area share cultural and historical ties with the UAE. This peninsula has served as a strategic location because it juts out into the Strait of Hormuz, which is the access point from the Indian Ocean

---

[2] The federation was officially established as six emirates. Ra's al Khaymah joined in 1972.

**Figure 4.1
Map of the United Arab Emirates**

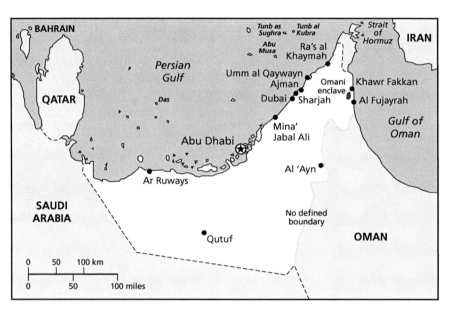

SOURCE: U.S. Department of State, 2007c.
RAND MG786-4.1

and Gulf of Oman into the Arabian Gulf. The trade routes along the Arabian Gulf have shaped the UAE's strong historical and cultural ties to the other Arab nations of the Gulf, as well as Iran, and to the nations of the South Asian subcontinent (Metz, 1994; UAE Ministry of Information and Culture, 2006).

The vast majority of Emiratis are Muslims who follow the Maliki tradition of the Sunni sect of Islam. In certain pockets of the country, other, related schools of thought are closely followed: The Wahhabi school is adhered to by residents of the Al Buryami Oasis (the Al 'Ayn region of Abu Dhabi), and the Shafli school is adhered to by residents of the Al Batinah coast. The majority of the non-national population is also Muslim, both Sunni and Shiite; and there are smaller but significant numbers of Hindus and Christians living and working in the country. Arabic is the official language of the UAE, but English is widely spoken, particularly in Abu Dhabi, Dubai, and Sharjah, where most of the commercial activity takes place. Over 80 percent of UAE residents live and work in those three emirates (U.S. Department of State, 2007c; Metz, 1994; Zahlan, 1998).

In the remainder of this section, we briefly discuss the UAE's political history, economic growth, population patterns, education system, and labor market trends.

Political History

The individual emirates in the UAE share a similar historical trajectory with the other nations of the Gulf (Metz, 1994). The foundations for agreements between the Trucial States and Britain started in the 1800s when the British, seeking to secure safe passage for their trade route to India, signed agreements with the rulers of Bahrain and the Trucial States to cease engaging in the warfare that was posing a threat to British vessels. The British cemented their presence in the area after they defeated the large fleet of ships built by the *Qawasim*, the local rulers of Sharjah and Ra's al Khaymah, under the pretext that they were engaging in piracy. The British first called the area the Pirate Coast but then changed the name to the Trucial States to reflect the truce agreements that were signed with the local rulers of the emirates. Britain continued to exert its influence by signing more treaties and effectively kept the Ottomans from exerting much influence over the area. The most important of these series of treaties and agreements culminated in 1892, when the rulers of the emirates pledged to deal exclusively with the British on all matters related to economic and foreign relations (Zahlan, 1998; UAE Ministry of Information and Culture, 2006). This arrangement remained in place until 1971, when the British withdrew military commitments from the region and the UAE federation was established.

By 1971, the Al Nuhayyan ruling family of Abu Dhabi had cemented its leadership position, beginning with Sheikh Zayid Bin Khalifa (1855–1909), who was also referred to as Zayid the Great, and culminating with his grandson Sheikh Zayid Bin Sultan (1966–2005), who was known as the father of the federation. A period of instability followed directly upon the death of Sheikh Zayid the Great as his sons rivaled one another for rule. The situation stabilized in 1928 when Sheikh Shakhbut Bin Sultan assumed power. After a period of relative calm and just as the economic boom from oil began, Sheikh Shakhbut stepped down, in 1966, in favor of his brother, Sheikh Zayid Bin Sultan, who had emerged within the ruling family as a visionary and the candidate most capable of leading Abu Dhabi during a time in which drastic changes were about to take place. Following Sheikh Zayid's ascension to rule, Abu Dhabi, under the Al Nuhayyans, and Dubai, under the Al Maktoums, underwent a period of rapid development that spread across the other Trucial States (Zahlan, 1998; UAE Ministry of Information and Culture, 2006).

Sheikh Zayid Bin Sultan ruled Abu Dhabi for 39 years. He was the first president of the Federal Supreme Council, which he formed, and was responsible for engineering the unification of the UAE. Sheikh Zayid is credited with presiding over a period of stability and tremendous economic growth in the UAE and is widely revered by his people (UAE Ministry of Information and Culture, 2006). His son Sheikh Khalifa Bin Zayid Al Nuhayyan now rules Abu Dhabi. The current ruler of Dubai, Sheikh Mohammed Bin Rashid Al Maktoum, became ruler after his brother Sheikh Maktoum Bin Rashid Al Maktoum passed away in early 2006 (UAE Ministry of Information and Culture, 2006; Al Baik and Al Nowais, 2006).

In the UAE federation, central authority rests in Abu Dhabi, but each emirate is governed by the head of its local ruling family. Along with Abu Dahbi's Al Nuhayyans and Dubai's Al Maktoums, the other ruling families are Al Nuamis of Ajman, Al Sharqis of Al Fujayrah, Al Qasimis of Ra's al Khaymah and Sharjah, and Al Muallas of Umm al Qaywayn. All of these families have ruled their respective emirates since well before the federation was formed (Metz, 1994; Zahlan, 1998).

Under the current federation, the highest central authority in the UAE is the Federal Supreme Council. It is the executive and legislative entity that directly oversees the national affairs of the state. According to the UAE constitution, the federal government is afforded jurisdiction over foreign relations, defense, security, immigration, communications, health, labor affairs, and education. The federation is also united under a common currency, the UAE dirham.[3] Local governments, to varying degrees, retain jurisdiction over remaining government services and are expected to assume a greater role sometimes in other instances—for example, the greater role in education that resulted from a recent push for an increasingly decentralized school management system (UAE Ministry of Education, 2006c). The members of the Federal Supreme Council are the rulers of the seven emirates. The ruler of Abu Dhabi is the president, the ruler of Dubai is the vice president, and both are elected to five-year terms. The Federal National Council, a 40-member advisory body to the Federal Supreme Council, reviews proposed laws by the Council of Ministers or cabinet members who head up the various government functions and then recommends amendments to the laws, passage, or rejection. Ultimate authority regarding laws, however, rests with the Federal Supreme Council (Metz, 1994; Al Mazroo'i, 2005). Members of the Federal National Council have been appointed by the rulers of the emirate states since its inception; seats are allocated based on population. The first limited public election (50 percent of the seats) of the Federal National Council took place in December 2006 (Ahmad, 2006).

Economic Growth

Prior to the discovery of oil and the unification of the emirate states, the area now occupied by the UAE was relatively desolate and sparsely populated. Up until full-scale oil production came into effect in the 1960s, the economies of the coastal emirate states depended heavily on pearling, although mass cultivation of cultured pearls in Japan in the mid-1900s had already begun to erode the viability and competitiveness of the Arabian Gulf's natural pearling industry (Metz, 1994). Today, largely as a result of its oil wealth and its efforts to diversify into finance and services, the UAE has become an important player in the world economy. Formally, the UAE takes part in setting economic policies as a member of the World Trade Organization (WTO) and OPEC. It takes part in regional and international politics as a member of the UN, GCC, and Arab League.

---

[3] In February 2008, 1 UAE dirham was equal to U.S. $0.27.

The UAE has undergone substantial economic growth over a relatively short period. The country's GDP rose dramatically over the course of just 30 years. Figure 3.2 displays the growth of the UAE GDP beginning in 1973 (the first year in the World Bank data series), two years after the federation was formed. After faltering in the mid-1980s, GDP growth recovered and has remained steady since the late 1980s. From 1993 to 2005, GDP more than doubled in real terms, going from $47 billion to $104 billion in 2000 U.S. dollars. This growth stems in large part from the production and sale of oil. As seen in Figure 4.2, the real GDP growth rate experienced much more volatility during the 1970s and 1980s but has since stabilized, varying between 5 and 10 percent per year from 1995 to 2005.

Approximately 94 percent of the UAE's oil reserves are in the emirate of Abu Dhabi. The remaining oil reserves are in Dubai (4 percent), Sharjah (1.5 percent), Ra's al Khaymah (0.1 percent), and shared among the other three emirates, Ajman, Umm al Qawayn, and Al Fujayrah. Over 90 percent of the UAE's gas reserves are owned by

Figure 4.2
Trends in GDP and GDP Growth in the UAE, 1973 to 2005

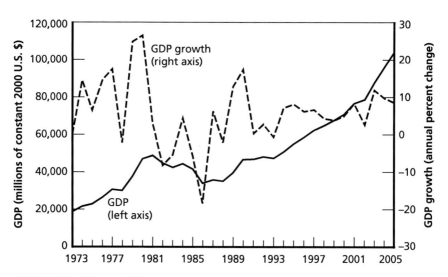

SOURCE: World Bank, 2007.
RAND MG786-4.2

Abu Dhabi, as well, with the remaining reserves in Sharjah (5 percent), Dubai (2 percent), and Ra's al Khaymah (0.6 percent). Consequently, the greatest economic growth has occurred mainly in Abu Dhabi, Dubai, and Sharjah. However, to offset the lack of resources in the other emirates, Abu Dhabi has traditionally been a major contributor to the Trucial States Development Fund, which helps subsidize many infrastructure development projects in the non-oil-producing emirates (UAE Ministry of Information and Culture, 2006).

While much of the growth in GDP can be attributed to oil and natural gas production, significant growth in the services sector has also been an important factor, especially in Dubai. In 2004, value-added to GDP was 55.1 percent from industry, 2.7 percent from agriculture, and 42.2 percent from services largely accounted for by the emirate of Dubai (World Bank, 2007; UAE Ministry of Information and Culture, 2006).

While GDP continues to grow, GDP per capita has stabilized at around $21,000 (constant 2000 U.S. dollars) after a steady decline beginning in the early 1980s, as shown in Figure 4.3. This decline in GDP per capita from the early-1970s to mid-1980s largely resulted from the dramatic influx of foreign workers into the country (i.e., from a proportionately large increase in the denominator of the GDP per capita measure). Figure 4.3 also illustrates the volatile swings in the growth rate of GDP per capita during the 1970s and 1980s and the subsequent stabilization from 1995 to 2005, when the annual rate of change varied between –5 percent and 5 percent per year.

Population Composition and Change

The economic boom from oil that began more than 30 years ago created many employment opportunities as the nation's infrastructure improved and the oil industry grew. As Figure 4.4 shows, the population of the UAE grew in the period following the discovery of oil, going from an estimated 500,000 in 1975 to 4.6 million in 2006.[4] In

---

[4] Note that there is an important difference between the population figure reported by the World Bank for 2005—4.53 million—and the estimate based on the 2005 UAE census—3.77 million (see Table 4.2, below).

Figure 4.3
Trends in GDP per Capita and GDP per Capita Growth in the UAE, 1973 to 2005

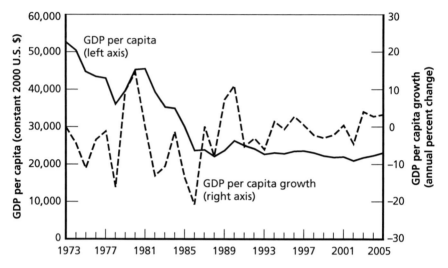

SOURCE: World Bank, 2007.
NOTE: Per capita GDP based on total population, which includes non-nationals.
RAND MG786-4.3

2004, the annual average population growth rate was estimated at 7 percent, one of the highest in the region.[5] The precipitous increase in the population over the past few decades is mainly attributed to the in-migration of foreign workers, who traditionally have been brought in to fill jobs that the national human resource base could not fill. Estimates show that from 1975 to 2004, the national population grew by 700,000, going from approximately 200,000 to 900,000. At the same time, the population of non-nationals grew by nearly 3 million, going from 360,000 to 3.4 million (CLMRI, 2005).

---

[5] This trend has not held in more-recent years: World Bank indicators reported an estimated population growth rate of 5 percent in 2005 and only 2 percent in 2006. This downward move may be the result of modifications to UAE immigration policies that control the flow of foreign workers into the country, a flow that largely accounted for the high population growth rates of previous years.

Figure 4.4
Trends in Population Total and Growth Rate in the UAE, 1960 to 2006

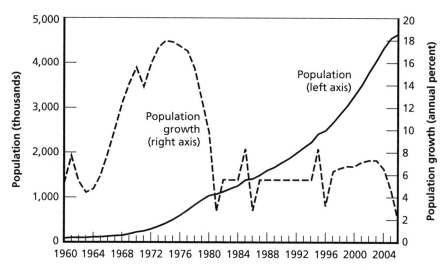

SOURCE: World Bank, 2007.
RAND MG786-4.4

Table 4.2 shows recent preliminary estimates from the 2005 UAE population census by age and nationality, as well as the more limited tabulations from the 1995 census. Among the total UAE population, as of 2005, the largest share (79 percent) was age 15 to 64, and 20 percent was under age 15. Among nationals in that year, nearly 38 percent were under age 15; among non-nationals, only 15 percent were. Just under 3 percent of Emiratis were above age 64, compared with less than 1 percent of non-nationals. Very few, if any, non-nationals spend their retirement years in the UAE. This is true of non-nationals in the other two Gulf nations in our study, as well, because employment contracts typically are not renewed as non-nationals near or reach retirement, and most of them return to their home country. Policymakers are concerned that when the large group of nationals under age 15 reach workforce-entry age, the market may not be able to readily absorb them, placing upward pressure on the unemployment rate (Al-Shamsi, 2005; UAE Ministry of Information and Culture, 2006).

Table 4.2
Population in the UAE, by Nationality and Age Group, 1995 and 2005

Nationality and Age Group	Population					
	1995			2005		
		Percent Distribution			Percent Distribution	
	Number	By Nationality	By Age Group	Number	By Nationality	By Age Group
National	n.a.	n.a.	n.a.	825,495	21.9	100.0
Age 0–14	n.a.		n.a.	313,872		38.0
Age 15–64	n.a.		n.a.	488,592		59.2
Age 65 and up	n.a.		n.a.	21,728		2.6
Age not stated	n.a.		n.a.	1,303		0.2
Non-national	n.a.	n.a.	n.a.	3,280,932	79.9	100.0
Age 0–14	n.a.		n.a.	486,706		14.8
Age 15–64	n.a.		n.a.	2,780,324		84.7
Age 65 and up	n.a.		n.a.	11,801		0.4
Age not stated	n.a.		n.a.	2,101		0.1
Total	2,411,041	100.0	100.0	4,106,427	100.0	100.0
Age 0–14	634,394		26.3	800,578		19.5
Age 15–64	1,751,096		72.6	3,268,916		79.6
Age 65 and up	25,386		1.0	33,529		0.8
Age not stated	165		0.0	3,404		0.1

SOURCES: 1995 data are from UAE Ministry of Economy, 2000, Chapter 2, Table 2-1; 2005 data are from UAE Ministry of Economy, 2006, Chapter 2, Table 2-9.

NOTES: n.a. = not available. To obtain population totals and be consistent with preliminary figures reported by the 2005 UAE census, the group not stating its age was included. As reported in the 2005 census preliminary results, 335,615 non-resident individuals in the UAE at census time were not included in the 2005 figures. Numbers may not add to total because of rounding.

The UAE has the highest proportion of expatriates of all the Gulf countries. According to the 2005 estimates shown in Table 4.2, non-nationals were approximately 80 percent of the UAE population.[6] Data for 2001 for Qatar indicate that non-nationals made up about 73 percent of its population, followed by Kuwait, at 62 percent. The remaining Gulf States—Saudi Arabia, Bahrain, and Oman—also have significant numbers of expatriates (they make up approximately one-third of the population) but relatively fewer than do Qatar, Kuwait, and the UAE (Al-Fakhri, 2004).

Education Advances and Gender Differences
The UAE's education system began in much the same way as those of the other Gulf nations in our study, Qatar and Oman. Early education began with children studying together on the grounds of the village mosque, reciting passages of the Qur'an while typically guided by individuals versed in the sacred text. Formal education started to take shape between 1907 and 1953, when prominent pearl traders began establishing schools in their local towns. The oldest school in the UAE was opened in Sharjah in 1907, followed by a school in Dubai in 1912. The predecessor of the Ministry of Education, the Dai'rat Al Maarif, was established in 1936 in Dubai to oversee the burgeoning schooling system in the emirate. The UAE's modern version of government schools began in academic year 1953–1954 with the opening of Al Qasimiyah School in Sharjah. In 1971, after the formation of the federation, the Ministry of Education and Youth (also referred to just as the Ministry of Education) was established to replace Dai'rat Al Maarif in Dubai, and government schools began to open under its supervision throughout the UAE (UAE Ministry of Education, 2006a). Many of the teachers, especially in the boys' schools, came from other Arab nations because few Emiratis were trained as teachers in that early period (Metz, 1994).

In 1977, in Al 'Ayn, Abu Dhabi emirate, UAE University became the first major post-secondary institution to open its doors in the coun-

---

[6] The expatriate share for the UAE in 2001 was an estimated 77 percent, just below the figure in Table 4.2.

try, offering a liberal arts and sciences program in literature, sciences, education, and political science, and a program in business administration. Within five years, shari'a (or Islamic jurisprudence), agriculture, and engineering were added (Metz, 1994). Every year, UAE University enrolls an entering class comprising 90 percent nationals and 10 percent non-nationals and offers all of them free tuition along with room and board. Another major government post-secondary institution is the Higher Colleges of Technology (HCT), which was established in 1988 and currently enrolls approximately 16,000 students across 15 branch campuses throughout the UAE in separate facilities for males and females (UAE HCT, 2008a). HCT provides programs in technical specialty fields as an alternative to the more liberal arts education offered at UAE University. The third government-funded post-secondary degree-granting institution, Zayed University, was established in 1998; it has campuses in Dubai and Abu Dhabi and admits only female students at this time. Unlike UAE University, which admits non-nationals, HCT and Zayed University admit only Emiratis (UAE HCT, 2008a; Zayed University, 2007b). Together, the three federal-level higher education institutions—UAE University, Zayed University, and HCT—enroll the greatest share of nationals, although there are 23 private and local emirate-based higher education institutions also providing post-secondary education programs (UAE Ministry of Information and Culture, 2006).

As is the case in the other Gulf nations in our study, government primary and secondary schools in the UAE are gender specific. Typically, children attend kindergarten when they are age 3.5 to 5.5 (UAE Ministry of Education, 2006b). Kindergarten is followed by the primary level (age 6 to 11), the preparatory level (age 12 to 14), and then the secondary level (age 15 to 17) (His Highness Sheikh Mohammed Bin Rashid Al Maktoum, 2008).[7] Table 4.3 reports gross and net enrollment ratios by education level as of 2005. These data reveal that enrollment at the preprimary level is comparable for males

---

[7] Beginning in 2002–2003, the primary and preparatory stages were renamed the 1st and 2nd stages, respectively (UAE Ministry of Economy, *Statistics Abstract*, 2002, 2003, 2004, and 2005).

Table 4.3
Gross and Net Enrollment Ratios in the UAE, by Education Level and Gender, 2005

Education Level	Gross Enrollment Ratio		Net Enrollment Ratio	
	Males	Females	Males	Females
Preprimary	65.0	64.0	n.a.	n.a.
Primary	84.5	82.0	71.4	69.6
Secondary	62.3	65.6	55.8	59.2
Post-secondary[a]	12.2	39.5	n.a.	n.a.

SOURCE: World Bank, 2007.
NOTE: n.a. = not available.
[a] Post-secondary ratios were not available for 2005; those shown are for 2003.

and females and, at 65 and 64 percent, one of the highest rates in the region. More striking is the less-than-universal rate of gross enrollment at the primary level for both males and females—85 and 82 percent—and the even lower level when net enrollment ratios are considered. This indicates that students are not progressing through school on time, although the estimated rate of grade repetition is just 2 percent at the primary level (UNESCO, 2006). It is also worth noting that the male-to-female enrollment ratio—whether measured as the gross or net ratio—slightly favors males at the primary level but females at the secondary level. More conspicuous is the enrollment differential at the post-secondary level that is evident in Table 4.3: Females outnumber males by more than three to one. Indeed, during the 2004–2005 academic year, females (nationals and non-nationals) represented almost 78 percent of the students enrolled at UAE University (12,077 female students versus 3,453 male students) (UAE University, 2007b).

Table 4.4 reveals that a relatively large portion of Emirati students are enrolled in private schools in the early grades (Vijayan, 2006). In 2005–2006, the combined share of males and females enrolled in kindergarten was about equal in government and private schools, with about 47 percent of students overall enrolled in private schools. By the primary level, the share in private schools had dropped to

Table 4.4
Enrollment of Emiratis in Government and Private Education Systems, by Gender and Education Level, 2005–2006

School Type and Student Gender	Education Level							
	Kindergarten		Primary (Grades 1–5)		Preparatory (Grades 6–9)		Secondary (Grades 10–12)	
	Number	%	Number	%	Number	%	Number	%
Government								
Male	9,665	26.0	39,751	36.6	33,787	42.4	19,784	39.1
Female	10,042	27.0	42,096	38.7	34,525	43.3	25,401	50.2
Private								
Male	9,403	25.3	15,483	14.2	6,905	8.7	3,194	6.3
Female	8,073	21.7	11,366	10.5	4,438	5.6	2,185	4.3
Total	37,183	100	108,696	100	79,655	100	50,564	99.9

SOURCE: UAE Ministry of Economy, *Statistics Abstract*, 2006, Chapter 13, Table 13-4.

NOTES: Since 2002–2003, primary and preparatory stages of government schools have been designated as 1st and 2nd stages. These are generally comparable to 1st, 2nd, and secondary stages in private schools, data on which were extracted from the cited source. For consistency, we use the terms *primary*, *preparatory*, and *secondary*.

approximately 25 percent for males and females combined. The combined private school share then declined further, to approximately 14 and 11 percent, respectively, at the preparatory and secondary levels.

Table 4.4 also reveals, consistent with the data in Table 4.3, that the total share of females enrolled in school increases during the secondary years. Up through the preparatory stage, males slightly outnumber females, making up 51 percent of students in government and private schools. By the time students reach the secondary or high school stage, however, 55 percent of all students are females in government and private schools, the difference primarily being in government schools. The reduction in the share of males, particularly in government schools, indicates that males are more likely to discontinue their schooling past the preparatory years.

The greater share of females compared with males in higher education, noted above in Table 4.3, is further illustrated in Tables 4.5 and 4.6 in terms of enrollment and graduation rates from the three main public institutions of higher learning, as well as the private and local institutions (aggregated as a group). Table 4.5 shows that while the majority of enrollees in the single largest institution, UAE University, are nationals, Emirati males only account for 19 percent of the student body while Emirati females account for 71 percent. The remaining 10 percent is non-nationals, both males and females. In the residual higher education sector, which mostly enrolls non-nationals (68 percent), Emirati males account for only 14 percent of the student body, compared with 18 percent for Emirati females. It should be noted that most Emiratis who study abroad are males, so the data shown do not consider all students who are pursuing post-secondary education. Ahmed (2003) asserts that precise data on these individuals are not available but estimates that approximately 2,500 Emiratis total are studying abroad in higher education institutions (pp. 3 and 6).[8] Nonetheless, despite the lack of data and information on this group, the number of nationals studying overseas is not likely to be high enough to eliminate the large disparity between the number of Emirati males and females pursuing post-secondary education.

Table 4.6 shows that the graduation numbers for Emiratis follow much the same patterns as the enrollment numbers.[9] Of the 2,640 Emirati graduates of UAE University in academic year 2001–2002, 85 percent were females. Of the HCT Emirati graduates, 56 percent were females; of the Emirati graduates from the private and local, or emirate-based, institutions, 64 percent were females.

---

[8] Note that the report indicates both that approximately 2,500 students study abroad and that 2,557 study in the United States alone. This is an illustration of the impreciseness of the data.

[9] We do not include graduates from Zayed University in Table 4.6, because the first graduation of students did not occur until Fall 2002.

Table 4.5
Enrollment in Higher Education Institutions in the UAE, by Nationality and Gender, 2001–2002

	Enrollees							
	Nationals				Non-Nationals (male and female)		Total	
	Male		Female					
Institution	Number	Percent	Number	Percent	Number	Percent	Number	Percent
UAE University	2,848	19	11,068	71	1,584	10	15,500	100
Zayed University	n.a.	n.a.	2,225	100	n.a.	n.a.	2,225	100
HCT	4,663	38	7,572	62	n.a.	n.a.	12,235	100
Private and local institutions	3,811	14	5,291	18	19,598	68	28,700	100

SOURCES: Ahmed, 2003, Table 1; and authors' calculations.
NOTE: n.a. = not available.

Table 4.6
Emirati Graduates from Higher Education Institutions in the UAE, by Gender, 2001–2002

	Graduates					
	Male		Female		Total	
Institution	Number	Percent	Number	Percent	Number	Percent
UAE University	405	15	2,235	85	2,640	100
HCT	1,114	44	1,422	56	2,536	100
Private and local institutions	239	36	424	64	663	100

SOURCES: Ahmed, 2003, Table 2; and authors' calculations.

Labor Force Trends

We now turn to labor force trends, examining national labor force indicators. Figure 4.5 displays the growth in the working-age population and labor force since 1980 according to World Bank data.[10] During this period, the working-age population in the UAE is estimated to have grown from 745,000 to 3.6 million persons, and the country's labor force grew five times in size, from approximately 560,000 to 2.8 million persons. According to these figures, the labor force participation rate (both nationals and non-nationals together) remained steady, at approximately 77 percent from 1998 to 2006.

Figure 4.5
Trends in Working-Age Population, Total Labor Force, and Labor Force Participation Rate in the UAE, 1980 to 2006

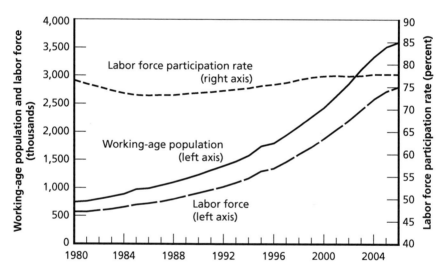

SOURCE: World Bank, 2007.
NOTE: Population and labor force take into account persons age 15–64.
RAND MG786-4.5

---

[10] The World Bank defines the labor force as those persons age 15 to 64 who are economically active, meaning they are employed or they are unemployed and actively looking for work. The UAE's Ministry of Economy includes all those age 15 and above in its definition of the labor force.

We can also compare male and female labor force participation rates. As Table 4.7 shows, there are substantial differences between the rates for males and females. The total labor force participation rate for males (both nationals and non-nationals) remained relatively constant, at 92 to 95 percent, from 1980 to 2006. For females, however, the rate grew steadily, from 16 percent in 1980 to approximately 40 percent in 2006. Overall, these data show that about 78 percent of the working-age population in the UAE is in the labor force. As we discuss in the next section, these patterns in labor force participation rates differ substantially for nationals and non-nationals.

Having reviewed the basic political, economic, and social indicators of the UAE, we next identify and describe the human resource challenges that the country faces. We look to secondary sources available in international and locally based publications, as well as government websites, and analyze how the problem has been framed. This provides the context for our examination of the education and labor market initiatives that the country has pursued to address these challenges.

Human Resource Challenges Faced by the UAE

In many respects, the UAE and the two other Gulf nations in our study face similar human resource issues. The UAE underwent tremendous economic expansion in a matter of decades and responded to its

Table 4.7
Labor Force Participation Rates in the UAE, by Gender, 1980 to 2006

Year	Labor Force Participation Rate (percent)		
	Males	Females	Total
1980	94.9	16.3	76.3
1985	94.6	21.3	73.2
1995	92.4	31.9	75.3
2006	92.0	39.8	77.9

SOURCE: World Bank, 2007.

need for labor by importing large numbers of non-nationals. In fact, the relatively high rate of population growth experienced by the UAE over three decades is largely accounted for by in-migration of foreigners. Understanding the importance of education to development of its own citizenry's human capital, the UAE expanded the basic education opportunities for males and females and made great strides toward universal schooling. However, data reveal that the rate of progress through the basic education stages for male nationals tends to drop in the secondary years. This trend is further exacerbated in the post-secondary years, with the result that the vast majority of in-country university enrollees and graduates are female. We also found through the data we explored that despite increases in labor force participation among nationals in the past 30 years, rates of participation remain relatively low, particularly for females.

In this section, we first discuss the two human resource issues that, according to our interviewees and our documentation review, the UAE government has recently focused on: the country's reliance on foreign labor and the relatively low rate of labor force participation among Emirati females. We then discuss the mismatch between the fields of study of secondary and post-secondary graduates and the demands of the UAE economy, as well as the lack of coordination in the training system.[11]

---

[11] Other human resource challenges that have gained prominence for Arab states, such as high youth unemployment rates and the concentration of national workers in the public sector, are difficult to verify in the UAE because of data limitations. We therefore could not explore these issues for the UAE as much as we could for Qatar and Oman. For example, the UAE does not report the results of official survey data on unemployment rates among nationals (CLMRI, 2005). The Ministry of Economy's 2006 *Statistics Abstract* (UAE Ministry of Economy, *Statistics Abstract*, 2006) provides information on unemployment numbers disaggregated by gender, but not by nationality. Another potential source of information on unemployment among Emiratis would be Tanmia (the National Human Resource and Development and Employment Authority), which registers job seekers. However, this organization does not provide data on unemployment that are consistent with international standards.

Expatriates Dominate the Workforce and Emiratis Participate at Low Rates

Much of the population and labor force growth in the UAE in recent decades resulted from the large number of non-national workers in the country. As noted above, much of the overall population is non-nationals, and this is even more the case for the working-age population (see Table 4.1). Thus, it is not surprising that the labor force consists primarily of non-nationals, as is evident in Table 4.8. Despite efforts to increase the share of nationals in the labor force, little has changed in the last decade. Table 4.8 shows that only 8 percent of the 2005 workforce in the UAE was Emirati, which is very similar to the percentage in 1995.

The small share of the labor force that consists of nationals reflects in part their low share in the working-age population. But it is also a reflection of the relatively low rates of labor force participation among Emirati males and females. Table 4.9 shows the labor force participation rate by gender and nationality for the most recent census year, 2005. Approximately 69 percent of Emerati males participated in the labor force in 2005, compared with 19 percent of Emirati females. In other words, only one of every five Emirati working-age females is in the labor force, despite their high levels of educational attainment (see discussion, above). Emirati females also face a considerably higher

Table 4.8
Distribution of Labor Force in the UAE, by Nationality, 1995 and 2005

	Labor Force			
	1995		2005a	
Nationality	Number	Percent	Number	Percent
National	121,291	9.0	214,320	8.4
Non-national	1,214,603	91.0	2,345,348	91.6
Total	1,335,894	100.0	2,559,668	100.0

SOURCES: CLMRI, 2005, Table 2.1; UAE Ministry of Economy, 2007, for 2005 figures; and authors' calculations.

a Estimated.

Table 4.9
Labor Force Participation Rates in the UAE, by Gender and Nationality, 2005

Gender	Labor Force Participation Rate (percent)		
	Nationals	Non-Nationals	Total
Male	68.9	96.3	93.5
Female	19.1	45.6	38.4

SOURCE: UAE Ministry of Economy, 2007.

unemployment rate than their male counterparts do. Despite the lack of consistent data on unemployment rates, the 2004 unemployment rate for female nationals was estimated at 19.7 percent, which compares with 8.2 percent for male nationals (CLMRI, 2005). In contrast, as shown in Table 4.9, 2005 labor force participation rates for non-nationals were 96 percent for males and 46 percent for females.[12]

Table 4.10 shows that, just as was the case in the other two Gulf countries we examined, low rates of female participation in the workforce contribute to the fact that females in the UAE represent a relatively small fraction of the overall workforce—just 13.8 percent as of 2006. This is one of the lowest shares among the Gulf nations,[13] and it has changed little since 1995, when it was at 12 percent. However, Table 4.11 indicates that among the small population of nationals, the female share of the workforce has grown. In 1995, females were just 13 percent of nationals in the workforce; but by 2005, that share

---

[12] The UAE's Ministry of Economy calculates the labor force participation rate as the share of individuals age 15 and over (compared to the World Bank's age 15 to 64) who are economically active. The unemployment rate is measured as the share of economically active individuals not currently employed but actively seeking work.

[13] According to the *2004 Gulf Yearbook* (Al-Shamsi, 2005), the share of females (both nationals and non-nationals) in the labor force across all Gulf nations is 19 percent. The share of females in the labor force varies considerably across the Gulf nations, however: Bahrain is at 21 percent, Saudi Arabia at 19 percent, Oman at 20 percent, Qatar at 17 percent, and Kuwait at 24 percent. This source places the UAE at 13 percent, which is close to World Bank estimates.

Table 4.10
Gender Distribution in the UAE Labor Force, 1995 and 2006

	Labor Force (percent distribution)	
Gender	1995	2006
Male	88.1	86.2
Female	11.9	13.8

SOURCE: World Bank, 2007.

Table 4.11
Gender Distribution in the UAE Labor Force, by Nationality, 1995 and 2005

	Labor Force (percent distribution)			
	1995		2005	
Nationality	Males	Females	Males	Females
National	87.0	13.0	78.2	21.8
Non-national	88.5	11.5	87.3	12.7
Total	88.3	11.7	86.5	13.5

SOURCES: CLMRI, 2005, Table 2.1, for 1995 figures; UAE Ministry of Economy, 2007, for 2005 figures; and authors' calculations.

had grown to 22 percent. Similarly, females constitute a rising, albeit smaller, share of the non-national labor force.

Like many of the Gulf governments, the UAE government has been actively recruiting female nationals for the workforce. A 2005 UAE report (CLMRI, 2005) on development of national human resources argues for stepped-up efforts to increase job placement rates for Emirati females, including placement in careers previously open only to males. The report states that more Emirati females are currently seeking jobs than have successfully found placement in a job. The UAE government has taken steps to reduce the gap in labor force participation between males and females—for instance, in the mid-1990s, it passed laws extending maternity leave and adopted international labor conventions mandating equal opportunities and fair treatment for males and females in the workforce. The late Sheikh Zayed, early on, through public speeches, pushed for greater participation of females in the workforce, and he appointed the first UAE female minister, Sheikha Lubna Bint Khaled Al Qasimi of the Ministry of Economy.[14] The UAE constitution itself stipulates equality for all citizens, and labor laws prohibit wage discrimination on the basis of gender (UAE Ministry of Information and Culture, 2006).

Nonetheless, the greatest barriers to participation of Emirati females in the workforce remain social and cultural factors. These can include social and family obligations that prevent workforce participation, the refusal of male family members to grant females permission to seek work, and perceived social and cultural factors that discourage females from joining the workforce. These issues tend to be even more pronounced for work participation outside the government sector, limiting the number of females who seek employment in the private sector (World Bank, 2006). Recently, Tanmia (the UAE National Human Resource and Development and Employment Authority), a federal-level agency with responsibility for training nationals and placing them in jobs, as well as for monitoring progress made throughout the UAE toward achieving nationalization goals, undertook a public relations campaign to encourage females to join the private sector. It has sponsored career fairs and symposia and has even reached out to the community in an effort to remove some of the cultural constraints keeping females from taking positions outside the government sector (Hanafi, 2006; UAE Tanmia, 2008).

The General Women's Union, an organization active in campaigning to increase women's economic and political roles and whose membership includes prominent individuals from the UAE community, has as its mission the encouragement of women's greater participation in the workforce. This organization has engaged in community outreach to increase public awareness of issues related to women, children, and the family and has facilitated education and training pro-

---

[14] This ministry is also referred to as the Ministry of Economy and Planning. Note that a new cabinet was appointed in February 2008. Sheikha Lubna Al Qasimi became the minister of foreign trade, and two other women were appointed as ministers of state (Salama, Elewa, and Za'za', 2008).

grams to equip females with basic work skills that may assist them in finding a job. These efforts and the efforts of the government have been somewhat successful in increasing the participation of females in the workforce. Females are now entering some professions, albeit in modest numbers, that were previously open only to males. Small breakthroughs in civil aviation, the military, firefighting, and other civil service jobs are changing the community's perceptions of traditional female roles. More recently, females have assumed prominent posts in the health and banking sectors, as well as in new initiatives currently under way, such as Dubai's Media and Studio Cities. Businesswomen councils affiliated with the UAE Chamber of Commerce have also been active in breaking down barriers that have kept females from fully participating in the workforce (UAE Ministry of Information and Culture, 2006).

The Education and Training System Is Not Preparing Emiratis to Meet the Needs of Employers

Officials in the government and private sector suggested that an insufficient number of Emirati graduates of secondary school and university possess the skills needed to meet the growing demands of the country. The nation requires graduates in such technical fields as science and engineering to supply the booming oil, gas, and construction sectors; it also needs graduates in information technology and business for the growing financial services sector. The officials also commented on the lack of strong critical thinking, research, and communications skills among graduates of the UAE education system. What we learned in our interviews also led support to our findings from examining secondary data sources on the workforce. One government official noted that a large number of Emirati males who graduate from secondary school choose to join the military or police force instead of seeking a university education.[15]

Data on fields of study among secondary school graduates provide further insight into whether students are concentrating in fields rel-

---

[15] Stasz et al. (2007) also found that male Qataris tend to favor the military and police as careers after graduating from secondary school.

evant to labor market needs. Table 4.12 shows the majors of secondary school graduates of UAE government schools since 1999. These data reveal that graduates in the arts outnumbered those in the sciences by 1.4 to 1 as of academic year 2005–2006. Moreover, as of that same year, Emiratis made up 77 percent of the graduates majoring in the arts and just 49 percent of graduates majoring in the sciences. An important point here is that secondary school graduates who major in the arts tend to require retraining to fill jobs in the most rapidly growing sectors, such as information technology and services; and in 2006, 67 percent and 71 percent of female and male Emirati graduates, respectively, majored in the arts. (CLMRI, 2005; UAE Ministry of Economy, *Statistics Abstract*, 2006).

At the post-secondary level, there are a number of related challenges. The gap between what is required in terms of skills in the market and the kind of training that graduates are receiving is particularly acute when we examine trends in the majors of graduates at

Table 4.12
Secondary School Graduates of Government Schools in the UAE, by Major, 1998–1999 to 2005–2006

	Arts Graduates		Science Graduates	
Academic Year	Total	Percent National	Total	Percent Non-National
1998–1999	7,895	n.a	7,232	n.a
1999–2000	9,175	n.a	7,325	n.a
2000–2001	10,150	n.a	7,936	n.a
2001–2002	10,429	n.a	7,811	n.a
2002–2003	11,474	77.3	7,999	49.0
2003–2004	10,727	77.6	7,965	49.6
2004–2005	10,943	79.2	7,798	51.7
2005–2006	11,208	76.9	7,950	49.3

SOURCES: UAE Ministry of Economy, *Statistics Abstract*, 2003, 2004, 2005, 2006, Chapter 13.
NOTE: n.a = not available.

UAE University. Figure 4.6 shows the number of graduates in the five largest colleges of the university between 1998–1999 and 2004–2005. It is evident that by far, the vast majority of students graduate from the College of Humanities and Social Sciences. Despite a demand for graduates in the technical fields, what can be seen is a five-year drop, beginning with 2000–2001, in the number of graduates from the College of Science, College of Engineering, and College of Medicine and Health Sciences (shown summed together as Sciences and Engineering). The College of Education is third in number of graduates, followed by the colleges of Business and Economics and Shari'a and Law.

Figure 4.6
Graduates of UAE University, by College, 1998–1999 to 2004–2005

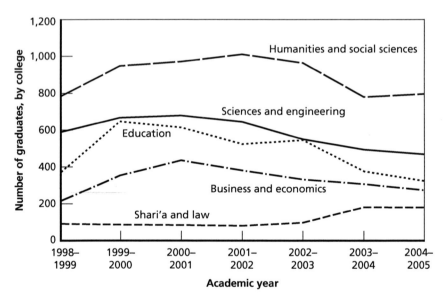

SOURCE: UAE University, 2006b: Vol. 2002/2003, Table 1-1-3, Vol. 2003/2004, p. 7, and Vol. 2004/2005, p. 7.
NOTES: Sciences, Engineering, and Medicine and Health Sciences were combined into the Sciences and Engineering category even though they are different faculties/colleges. Colleges not shown include Food Systems and Tutorial External Studies. Medical Laboratory Technologies and Information Technology colleges were not included because they had only recently been opened. UAE University also offered post-graduate studies during the period shown, but beginning in 2003–2004, graduates obtained either a master's degree or a diploma.
RAND MG786-4.6

The only college showing an upward trend in number of graduates is the College of Shari'a and Law, although the numbers stabilized in the last two years depicted.

In addition, we learned in interviews with UAE University officials that it is becoming more difficult even for nationals to gain admission because more applicants compete for fewer available seats each year. University enrollment has declined, from a peak of 16,985 in 2001–2002 to 15,530 in 2004–2005 (UAE University, 2007b). The downward trend in absolute number of graduates in several of the university colleges shown in Figure 4.6 partly reflects declining enrollment overall. Increasing competition for admission into UAE University could ultimately reflect rising academic standards and higher quality graduates. Our interviews revealed that students who do not gain admission to UAE University pursue studies in the country's growing number of private higher education institutions. As previously noted, we also learned in our interviews that a large number of male nationals who do not go on to post-secondary study gravitate toward careers in the military or police.

Ultimately, the issues associated with the preparation of Emiratis for the labor market affect their employment potential, particularly in the private sector (Al Fakhri, 2004). One recent study found that in addition to pointing to deficits in technical skills, employers point to weaknesses in the areas of "communication, interpersonal skills, customer relations, and work ethics" among college graduates (Ahmed, 2003, p. 14). These basic indicators and what we learned in our interviews suggest that continued undersupply of new Emirati workforce entrants with technical or business backgrounds, especially in an economy heavily dependent on oil, gas, information technology, and financial services, will further lead employers to look to hire foreign workers with the required skills.

Efforts to Train Emiratis Have Been Piecemeal
A 2002 report from Tanmia's CLMRI notes that because of the reliance on skilled workers from abroad, "the United Arab Emirates does not have a training-led employment culture" (Abdelkarim and Haan, 2002, p.13). Training has been in conjunction with the introduction of

new technology, not for longer-term sustained development of human resources and capacity. With no coordinated efforts to provide training and a lack of information on private training providers, training programs have often been duplicative and of dubious quality. Indeed, their quality has been called into question by the very companies and organizations whose employees are targeted for training. These private institutions typically offer courses or programs in English and information technology. Despite being good options for gaining and improving on skills in demand in the private sector, however, these courses and programs tend to vary considerably in quality. Abdelkarim and Haan (2002) also argue that public investments in training should go to efforts that teach technical, industrial, and soft skills, such as communication and customer relations. Until recently, the public sector did little to provide systematic training opportunities as a way to foster economic productivity and meet the market's skill needs. While some public training institutions have been established, such as the Institute of Administrative Development and the General Information Authority, government support for training has not been able to close the gap between labor market need and the supply of skilled human resources to fill that need. Recent education and training initiatives, discussed further below, indicate that the government has recently examined in some detail the need to promote a concerted and coordinated training effort, one that is linked to the nation's long-term human skill needs (Abdelkarim and Haan, 2002).

Emiratis Prefer Working in the Government Sector
Although data on the distribution of Emirati workers in the public and private sectors are not readily available, it is well known that the bulk of working nationals are in the public sector. Estimates suggest that the share of Emiratis in the private sector has remained relatively constant, at less than 2 percent, for over approximately the last decade (CLMRI, 2005). For Emiratis, work in the private sector has traditionally not been as attractive as work in the government sector, partly because the government sector offers better benefits, prestige and status, flexible working conditions and shorter working hours, and greater job security. For example, despite the higher salaries offered in the private sector,

nationals still rank employee benefits and job security as the two most important issues in considering a career and employer. A recent survey revealed that while virtually all graduates (97 percent) of Abu Dhabi Women's HCT indicated that they planned to join the workforce, only 12 percent indicated a willingness to work in the private sector, primarily because the government would give them better benefits, job security, and shorter working hours (UAE federal e-government portal, 2006c). Also, in a 2004 survey of banks, the long workweek (some private companies implement a six-day workweek) and strict working hours were cited as contributors to the banking sector's inability to meet its expected quota for employing nationals (CLMRI, 2005).

Implications of Overdependence on a Non-National Workforce

Like the other Gulf states in the study, the UAE faces the issue of a large foreign national labor force with the potential to pose significant long-term economic, political, and social consequences. Al Fakhri (2004) examines the main reasons behind the predominately non-national labor force of a country such as the UAE and the heavy reliance on non-national workers at the expense of equipping the national population with the skills required to enter the workforce. While the focus on education reform is gaining momentum in the UAE, the historical deficit in education investment continues, exacerbating the poor outcomes of the education system.[16] Table 4.13 summarizes the historical, economic, societal, and political/legal factors that contributed to the unabated growth of the non-national labor force as the primary human resource base of the UAE.

---

[16] We can examine this issue using World Bank (2007) compiled indicators on percentage of GDP per capita expenditures on primary and secondary education. Data for the UAE are available back to 1999. In 2004, the UAE (at 7.1 percent) spent a smaller share of GPD per capita on primary education than did Oman (16.3 percent), Kuwait (16.3 percent), and high-income OECD nations (19.3 percent). The same is true for secondary education: The UAE spent 9.3 percent, ranking below Oman (15.5 percent), Kuwait (18.4 percent), and high-income OECD countries (26.4 percent). The figures for the UAE have not varied considerably since 1999. We should note that it is likely that the World Bank uses total population numbers to calculate the per capita figures and thus includes the UAE's large non-national population.

Table 4.13
Underlying Factors Driving Growth in Non-National Labor Force in the UAE

Underlying Factor	Explanation
History	Gulf countries, including the UAE, have had historical and economic ties with nations of the Indian subcontinent, facilitating the migration of non-national workers to the Gulf region.
Economy and the market	Natural economic flow of labor to where wages are higher. Rapid growth of the government sector, requiring non-nationals to supplement the national workforce. Growth in labor-intensive production systems, requiring large numbers of semi-skilled workers. Reliance of the growing private sector on a non-national workforce.
Social and educational	Low participation of females in the workforce. Low-quality basic and higher education systems that have not met the employment needs of the most rapidly growing services and industrial sectors. Redistributive welfare-state government policies, undermining the appeal of non-government jobs among nationals. Government subsidization of post-secondary education pursuits, often for extended periods abroad, regardless of field of study or demand for skills.
Political and legal structure	Control of labor flow to encourage rapid growth in target sectors. Limited enforcement and monitoring of labor laws and regulations, and lack of coordination between federal and local authorities in enforcing labor laws. Political and legal systems that have not evolved to address human capital deficits in coordination with rapid economic growth. Intra-regional competition in establishing free trade zones, further increasing the flow of foreign labor into the region.[a]
Data and Information	Lack of comprehensive, consistent, and timely information and data on labor force and population indicators to aid in policymaking.

SOURCES: Adapted from Al-Fakhri, 2004, pp. 72–74, and Budd, 2002.

[a] Jebel Ali, the recent large-scale, ambitious project embarked on by the emirate of Dubai, is an example of regional competition aimed at attracting international companies to set up facilities for engagement in production and manufacturing (Sfakianakis, 2005, p. 79).

Of greatest current concern to policymakers and regional observers in the UAE is the risk from security breaches, in such vital production sectors as oil and gas, and also in hotels, malls, and other services and tourism facilities. Despite strict measures taken by the UAE government in the processing of foreign entrants, the extent to which the overwhelming presence of non-national workers in the UAE—particularly the large low-skilled, low-wage-earning, mostly male portion—poses a risk to the nation's security is unknown (Al-Fakhri, 2004). Recently, strikes in Dubai raised additional questions about human rights and fair labor practices, as well as about the potentially wide-ranging economic impact of future labor unrest if a longer-term solution to workers' grievances is not reached (Kerr, 2007).

In addition, despite rapid development and commercialization in the UAE, the Emirati population remains predominately religiously conservative and close knit, and thus the large foreign presence, across all skill types, has introduced significant social stresses. It is believed that Gulf societies, including that of the UAE, are experiencing a widening societal fragmentation, and these nations' governments will only continue to face difficulties and complications in planning for the provision of public services, such as health and education. Regional observers argue that this fragmentation ultimately compromises the well-being of both nationals and non-nationals (Al-Fakhri, 2004). It should be noted, however, that by and large, the UAE experienced sustained peace and stability throughout the period in which it saw tremendous growth in the non-national population.

We have now identified and described the human resource challenges that the UAE faces. We found that the nation has had to rely heavily on non-national workers for the human capital necessary to fuel its economic growth. While this reliance stems from an inherently small national population that cannot meet all the country's labor market needs, there are employers reporting that it partly stems from a deficit in skills among nationals. We also examined data that revealed low labor force participation among nationals, especially females, and a labor force participation rate among males that has remained unchanged for 30 years. Furthermore, the share of nationals (males and females) in the workforce is one of the lowest in the region and has not increased in over 10 years. Data on secondary and post-secondary graduation rates from UAE University further reveal that there has been a steady decline in post-secondary graduates majoring in technical fields (sciences and engineering) despite a growing demand for individuals with specializations in these fields.

Approaches to Reform in the UAE

We have thus far described the UAE context and highlighted the main challenges that the nation faces in developing its own national human resource base. Figure 4.7 illustrates these issues and provides a schematic guide for our discussion of the strategies the country has pursued to address these issues.

The first box in Figure 4.7 places the UAE's rapid pursuit of economic growth and diversification together with the mismatch between the labor market demands associated with that growth and the skill supply in the Emirati human resource base. The fastest growth has been in the private sector, which relies almost exclusively on non-nationals, both because of skill deficits in the national population and the national population's traditional favoring of public- over private-sector employment. In this section, we examine the education and labor market reforms that the UAE has pursued to address the human resource challenges described. We also discuss potentially conflicting national policies that seek to promote economic diversification and privatization, important goals of the UAE's economic strategy, and simultaneously increase the share of nationals in the workforce. We describe how providing an environment favorable for growth in the private sector often conflicts with implementing regulations that require businesses to hire nationals (see rightmost box in Figure 4.7). The UAE's success in diver-

Figure 4.7
Schematic of Challenges Faced by the UAE: Need to Balance Nationalization Efforts with Policies Promoting Economic Growth

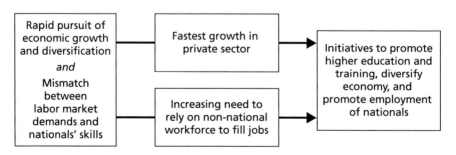

sifying its economic base while enhancing the national population's skills to help sustain its diversification efforts will depend on striking the appropriate balance between the strategies pursued to reach these two goals. We examine the strategies that the country has pursued, some of which complement each other and some of which conflict, thus hindering progress toward developing a national human resource base.

Public-sector officials with whom we spoke were well aware of the long-term economic, social, and political consequences of a growing national population not adequately prepared to contribute to the nation's productivity and a heavy dependence on non-national labor. Although the UAE is not faced with the prospect of dwindling natural resources the way Oman is (see discussion in the next chapter), the concentration of its natural resources in the Abu Dhabi emirate keeps the nation looking to diversification as a means of sustaining the economies of all the emirates. The UAE is still facing the reality of a citizenry unprepared for productive work in the new, knowledge economy, which makes the task of reducing the nation's reliance on foreign labor more difficult, especially for those economies, such as Dubai's, that are increasingly based on sectors requiring skills in services, finance, and information technology. As noted above, some progress has been made in increasing the share of Emiratis in the workforce, particularly Emirati females; but male participation rates in the growing private sector remain very low (UAE Ministry of Information and Culture, 2006).

The main issue that the UAE faces today is still the relative noncompetitiveness in skills of nationals versus non-nationals. The UAE's relatively large demand for labor in relation to its working-age population of nationals will continue to keep the nation reliant on non-nationals to some degree. Our findings through interviews and secondary data sources suggest that the main concern of policymakers today is that the nation's reliance on a foreign workforce has undermined the incentives for nationals to pursue education and training to meet labor demands, and the nation is seeking to address this concern through labor market reforms and investments in various education and training reforms that are currently under way. The UAE government has sought to address the underlying human capital deficit in the national population and the reliance on non-national labor using a number of major policy levers. These reforms are primarily in the following two areas:

1. Expansion of opportunities for higher education and training, especially in targeted fields
2. Emiratisation, or nationalization of the workforce, especially in the private sector.

The UAE has been expanding its focus to include reform of the nation's primary and secondary education system. Some efforts have been made to address concerns about the quality of education provided in government schools. The formation of the Abu Dhabi and Dubai Education Councils in 2005 to specifically target primary and secondary education suggests that major reforms are on the way (Novakovic, 2005; Abdul Aziz, 2006; Al Shaiba, 2006). The Abu Dhabi Education Council aims to introduce a stronger role for the private sector in public education through a program called Public-Private Partnership for Public School Management. Contracting with local and regional private education organizations to manage a selected group of schools in the Abu Dhabi emirate began in the 2006–2007 academic year (Abdul Aziz, 2006; Khaleej Times Online, 2006a). The Abu Dhabi Education Council also supports the development of an education database, ostensibly to assist in evaluating new initiatives, such as the public-private partnership, and proposing new education policies (Abu Dhabi Education Council, 2007; Abdul Aziz, 2006). The Dubai Education Council lists as important goals the development of standards linked to global best practices and greater involvement of all stakeholders concerned with education (Dubai Education Council, 2007). Affiliated with the Dubai Education Council is the Dubai Knowledge and Human Development Authority, which is tasked to ensure education outcomes are aligned with labor market needs. It oversees reform initiatives related to the K–12 education system and closely coordinates with efforts to develop the post-secondary education sector (Knowledge and Human Development Authority, 2008). Recently, a Dubai School Inspections Bureau was established within the Authority to develop school performance standards and monitor adherence of schools to these standards; it recently began devising plans for its functions and scope of work (Salama, Elewa, and Za'za', 2008). These different government bodies were established to link governmental, private, special needs, and vocational training and education systems. Because these initiatives have only recently been launched, their impacts cannot yet be assessed.

While the Abu Dhabi and Dubai Education councils were established to encourage new education initiatives designed to improve the quality of the UAE's education system, they cite support of the Ministry of Education as an important component of their missions (Abu Dhabi Education Council, 2007; Dubai Education Council, 2007). In fact, the Minister of Education is also the director general of the Abu Dhabi Education Council. In an interview posted on the Ministry of Education's website, he discussed the need to modernize the nation's education system so that it keeps up with the pace of development taking place in the UAE's economic sector (UAE Ministry of Education, 2006c; Khaleej Times Online, 2006b). The gap between the human resource needs of the marketplace and the preparedness of the nation's graduates has become the focus of the Ministry's current efforts. By 2006–2007, the Ministry had replaced the grade 12 secondary school exit exam with an assessment system beginning in grade 4 and extending to grade 12. The Ministry is also presiding over a gradual shift to a more decentralized system in which the individual emirates manage their own education affairs while the federal Ministry of Education provides oversight, guidance, and support. The Minister of Education also stated that the Ministry will oversee a major reform effort involving expertise from around the world to assist in setting a long-term strategy for improving the UAE's education system (UAE Ministry of Education, 2006c). The Ministry of Education has developed a set of strategic objectives that include a focus on "modernization" of the curriculum, provision of a more comprehensive instructional and leadership training system, upgrade of school facilities, and greater parental involvement in the education system (UAE Ministry of Education, 2008a, 2008b). Many of these efforts at reforming primary and secondary education were unveiled at the beginning of 2007–2008 in a select number of Ministry schools termed "Al Ghad schools" (Schools of Tomorrow). A bilingual (Arabic and English) curriculum is being phased in at these schools, and education advisers are beginning to provide support and training for principals and teachers in approaches to fostering student-centered learning, integration of information technology, and strategies for enhancing community involvement. The Ministry has indicated that it plans to expand these programs to other government schools as they begin to show signs of success in the schools in which they are currently being implemented (UAE Ministry of Education, 2008c).

Because comprehensive primary and secondary reform is only in the early stages in the UAE, our focus in the remainder of this section is on higher education, workforce training, and Emiratisation reform efforts. We also briefly discuss efforts to promote the private business sector and diversify the economy away from reliance on the production and sale of oil. This combination of efforts has given the UAE a unique position in the Gulf as a leader in trade, banking, and tourism. Improvements are still needed, however, if the country is to develop a productive Emirati workforce.

Post-Secondary Education and Training Reforms

One strategy for addressing the skill gap in the UAE has been the use of initiatives designed to raise academic standards in existing higher education institutions (such as UAE University) and initiatives designed to broaden opportunities for post-secondary education and training for nationals and non-nationals (Al-Fakhri, 2004). The second type of initiatives includes establishing Dubai's Knowledge Village and Academic City (described in more detail below), both of which are intended to encourage the development of research and knowledge capital to further promote homegrown enhancement of human resources. These initiatives also include establishing, in 1999, Abu Dhabi's Centre of Excellence for Applied Research and Training (CERT), which aims to promote technology advancement by providing facilities in which experts can conduct research. Because the largest economies in the UAE are in Abu Dhabi and Dubai (with most jobs in the gas and oil sectors in Abu Dhabi, and most jobs in the finance and banking sectors in Dubai), it is natural that the largest efforts to promote the skill development of Emiratis are concentrated in these two emirates. Other emirates are embarking on smaller-scale education and workforce training initiatives.

These efforts in the UAE to improve post-secondary education and training have been under way for a relatively longer time than have efforts aimed at primary and secondary education. Because of the direct links to the job market and the nation's economic growth, higher education and training received attention from policymakers earlier, whereas the attention to reform at the primary and secondary levels is more recent. This timing is in contrast to that in Qatar and Oman, the other two Gulf nations in our study, where reform of the primary and secondary education systems has been under way for a number of years. Even so, it is too early to assess whether any of the UAE's current efforts will mitigate the human resource challenges at hand.

Higher Education Initiatives. As noted earlier, UAE University, the dominant institution of higher education in the UAE, has seen its enrollment decline over time. Our interviews revealed that students who would have enrolled in UAE University are likely to have been drawn into other higher education institutions (including private colleges and universities) or to have sought job-specific training through the numerous newly established training centers. For those who do attend UAE University, efforts are being made to upgrade existing programs. For example, although some individual programs at UAE University are accredited by U.S. higher education accreditation agencies, the university as a whole is still undergoing an accreditation process (UAE University, 2006b).[17]

We learned through an interview with an official at UAE University that there has been a recent focus on efforts to link UAE University programs with practical experience for students, with specific attention to providing hands-on experience in the business and technology fields. In particular, UAE University instituted an internship program for students in the College of Engineering to work in companies both within and outside the UAE. Students have been placed

---

[17] The accrediting agency is the United States Southern Association of Colleges and Schools. For more information, see UAE University, 2007a.

in international companies in Great Britain, France, Sweden, Finland, and Italy. Within the UAE, the university has established partnerships with technology parks and placed students in the military in engineering internships. International companies have also recruited students from UAE University into internship programs for a number of years; agreements between the international companies and the university sometimes include cost sharing (UAE Ministry of Information and Culture, 2006).

However, one of a few studies conducted on work placement across a wide variety of sectors in the UAE found that a significant share of the internship programs surveyed in the study (about half) did not result in actual work placement for UAE University graduates, despite the fact that the organizations surveyed reported viewing the programs as a viable mechanism for recruitment. Reasons given by employers included lack of vacancies; trainee inability to perform the job; lack of loyalty to the company; and unrealistic expectations related to working hours, job title, and compensation (Ahmed, 2003).[18] The results from this study, although limited to internship programs, are an impetus for conducting more examinations of this kind to understand both employers' and employees' expectations and views toward work.

The two other public higher education institutions in the UAE—HCT and Zayed University—have played increasingly important roles in equipping Emirati students with skills for the workplace. HCT was established to address the need to train students in technical skills highly demanded in the oil sector and related technology-dependent industries. In addition to providing this training, HCT offers foundation programs encompassing courses in English, mathematics, and other basic subjects to support the transition to programs within the university (especially for students from UAE public schools, where the primary language of instruction is Arabic). Instruction in HCT pro-

---

[18] These findings are generally consistent with those of a study conducted on post-secondary options for secondary school graduates in Qatar (Stasz et al., 2007). In that study, employers reported some of the same barriers to hiring Qataris, including unrealistic expectations about job titles and lack of loyalty to the organization. Additionally, working hours in the private sector tend to be longer than in the public sector, giving graduates another important reason to prefer government jobs.

grams is in English to prepare graduates to work in an international environment (UAE HCT, 2008a, 2008b, 2008c). Zayed University, established in 1998, offers programs typical of an international liberal arts university, with additional emphasis on research and outreach focused on developing and supporting public and private institutions serving national policy goals (Zayed University, 2007a; Dubai Education Council, 2007). As is the case with HCT, Zayed University (and UAE University, as well) uses English as the primary language of instruction in the business and engineering disciplines.

Beyond the efforts discussed above that focus on the school-to-work transition, UAE University has established mechanisms to encourage faculty members to engage in research that would contribute in a general sense to human resource development (UAE University, 2007c). The University awards grants internally to promote research in certain areas and encourages faculty to forge links with the private and public sectors by providing research and expert services. University management of external research occurs through the Center for Externally Funded Research, where faculty members are provided with support and advice when applying for or after being awarded external grants. UAE University is launching a number of other tools to support faculty research endeavors, such as the Electronic Research Management and Support System, the goal of which is to broadly "serve research and development activities at the University" (UAE University, 2007b). UAE University also hosts a number of specialized centers such as the Roadway, Transportation, and Traffic Safety Research Center, and the Central Laboratories Unit, where environmental, agricultural, and industrial testing and analyses are conducted (UAE University, 2007c).[19] Through these different efforts, UAE University seeks to develop its reputation as an institution of higher learning and research and to play an important role in the development of research capital and the human resources needed to sustain it.

---

[19] Other centers are the Date Palm Research and Development Programme, to cultivate this highly prized tree in the region, and the Modeling Simulation Lab, which hosts computers capable of high-powered mathematical computations.

Other Education, Training, and Research Initiatives. A number of efforts are under way to promote the links between higher education institutions, training programs, and industry. The Dubai and Abu Dhabi Education Councils were tasked with unifying training initiatives across the emirates and consolidating various institutions' efforts to address the shortcomings of the education system. Membership on both councils was designed to involve the public and private sectors in order to more effectively address the need to develop a global workforce that can meet local, regional, and international needs. Along with improving primary and secondary education, the two councils' mandates are also to look into consolidating the provision of certain common vocational education and training needs across the industrial and commercial sectors to more effectively and efficiently meet market needs for human resources (Cooper, 2005; Dubai Education Council, 2007; Abu Dhabi Education Council, 2007).

Another initiative aimed at promoting the advancement of national human capital is Knowledge Village, in Dubai. Knowledge Village is the physical site where "soft infrastructure," such as business, legal, and information technology services, is provided, all in a "free zone" where organizations are generally exempt from certain labor and administrative regulations. These provisions were made to encourage the establishment of company branch offices, as well as campuses of international higher education and training institutions, that would then provide their services in Dubai (Dubai Knowledge Village, 2004b).[20] Organizations in Knowledge Village are expected to recruit from the UAE and provide training in knowledge-based skills, with the goal of ultimately developing the capacity to supply the necessary human capital from within the resident population. This approach is

---

[20] Institutions that establish branch offices in free zones are typically exempt from certain incorporation requirements (such as identifying an Emirati sponsor to own a 51 percent share), as well as Emiratisation and other, local labor requirements. Free zones have been established in several of the emirates, but by far most of them are in Dubai, where 10 currently operate and there are plans to build seven more. Dubai's free zones cover sectors ranging from information technology, to education and training, to manufacturing of everything from retail products and textiles to car parts. The other emirates, with the exception of Abu Dhabi, have also established free zones (UAE Ministry of Information and Culture, 2006).

consistent with Dubai's efforts at diversifying its economy beyond oil and gas production. Because institutions in Knowledge Village are in a free zone, the UAE government fast-tracks visa approvals, permits home ownership by foreigners, is less strict about the requirements to hire nationals (discussed below), and reduces the restrictions on quotas placed on the importation of workers of certain nationalities (UAE Ministry of Information and Culture, 2006). Foreign institutions that come to Knowledge Village must operate on a fully private basis without subsidies. They have to take financial risk in opening their operations at Knowledge Village, since there is no guarantee that income from fees will cover their costs.

Knowledge Village touts its facilities as providing the stage for shopping for education and business solutions across a wide range of products and services, as well as encouraging networking and eventually job placement. In Knowledge Village, academic programs, as well as professional and vocational programs, are provided. Two-year training programs in human resources, customer relations, accountancy, tourism, marketing, budgeting, cost control, information technology, biotechnology, and design arts are offered. The National Institute for Vocational Education, based in Knowledge Village, is one such recently established institution to meet demand for training in vocational skills (Dubai Education Council, 2007).

The goal of Knowledge Village is to consolidate programs that do not require specialized on-the-job training facilities and that entail duplicate efforts by multiple government or quasi-government organizations, such as those of the UAE's major oil companies. Abu Dhabi Oil Company, for example, continues to provide specialized training to its employees but will be able to recruit graduates of Knowledge Village, who will already have received preparation in English communication and "soft" skills. Programs at Knowledge Village are co-educational and are available for both nationals and non-nationals, the ultimate goal being to increase the share of nationals in the student body (Dubai Knowledge Village, 2004a). Eventually, the university-based and more-advanced degree programs in Knowledge Village will move to Academic City, a project costing 12 billion dirhams ($3.3 billion) that is set for completion in 2012 in Dubai. Knowledge Village will focus on job-training-based programs; Dubai Academic City will host four-year academic institutions of higher learning (Za'za', 2006; Dubai Knowledge Village, 2004a). As in Knowledge Village, foreign institutions in Academic City will operate on a private basis, responsible for covering their expenses through tuition and fees.

Major training and research initiatives are also being implemented in the emirate of Abu Dhabi. CERT, an offshoot of HCT, is a partnership of internationally renowned academic institutions and multinational organizations in the technology and business-solutions fields formed to carry out and promote research in the UAE.[21] This partnership is designed to provide human resource training and skills development for Emiratis through their participation in research and development activities (UAE federal e-government portal, 2006c; CERT, 2008a). Graduates of CERT receive two certificates, one from CERT University and one from the partnered international academic institution. This dual-degree approach caters to demand at the local UAE market and labor markets in other nations, which could encourage foreign residents to apply.

CERT's partnership with academic institutions and industry has culminated in Abu Dhabi's own "knowledge" city, named Education and Research City, which will be a nexus of learning consisting of a primary/secondary school, college or university, research center, and convention center with an attached five-star hotel. HCT, as well as other existing higher education institutions, will be a part of Education and Research City. The Education and Research City site will also house an early childhood center to aid in teacher training and will provide services to on-site staff. Education and Research City's goal is to develop first-rate research facilities as a way to attract top faculty. A computer and research center will provide opportunities for faculty to conduct research and teach at the university. Education and Research

---

[21] The CERT website (CERT, 2008b) lists the following (among others) as partners in the technology and business fields: Queen's School of Business (Canada), CERT Thales Institute (France and Abu Dhabi), MIT [Massachusetts Institute of Technology] Sloan School of Management (U.S.), Global Pacific Group (Australia), and IBM (U.S.).

City will be co-educational and available to both nationals and non-nationals (CERT, 2008a).

While efforts at training the national labor force remain the priority of the federal and local governments in the UAE, efforts have also gone into expanding education services for non-nationals from the region who wish to pursue post-secondary options close by. This stems from the recognition on the part of UAE officials that the size of the national population will not reach the levels required to sustain the labor force needs of the economy, even if goals for increasing the share of nationals in the workforce and in the private sector are achieved (as discussed below, in the context of Emiratisation). Nonetheless, as the government explores different ways of addressing its human resource needs, a dual purpose is served by expanding education opportunities for both nationals and non-nationals: economic diversification by providing education and training services in demand in the region, and the training of nationals and non-nationals alike to fill the labor demands of an expanding local and regional economy.

Emiratisation: Nationalizing the Workforce

A second focus of reforms in the UAE, specifically designed to reduce the reliance on expatriate workers, is Emiratisation, or the nationalization of the workforce. Emiratisation is the broad term used to describe a set of policies and laws that involve increasing the share of Emirati citizens employed in a particular sector. These policies are intended not just to reduce the overall reliance on foreign imported labor in absolute terms, but also to increase the share of jobs held by nationals in crucial and high-growth-potential sectors, such as oil and gas production, banking, insurance, trade, and, more recently, tourism. Banking, for example, is one sector that has been targeted because of its growth potential and because of the professional opportunities it offers could attract nationals. Other sectors that have been specifically targeted for Emiratisation include insurance and trade, with expectations that other sectors will be added in the future (CLMRI, 2005). Although our focus in this discussion is on efforts to increase the share of nationals in the private sector, a push to replace non-nationals with nationals in the government sector is also occurring (Hanka, 2006). The UAE

Ministry of Labour is generally responsible for overseeing the progress made in Emiratisation (UAE federal e-government portal, 2006c).

Boys' schools in the UAE continue to rely on expatriates to fill the ranks of classroom teachers. One report suggests that as of 2003–2004 (the academic year for which we could find information), only 6 percent of teachers in boys' schools were nationals, which means that 94 percent were expatriates. The same report indicates that nationality was more evenly split among female teachers: Emiratis made up approximately one-half of the female teaching force. Recently, the Ministry of Education took steps to increase the share of both male and female Emirati teachers, replacing over 500 expatriates in the subjects of mathematics, Arabic, and English (Hanka, 2006). The official website of the ruler of Dubai, His Highness Sheikh Mohammed Bin Rashin Al Maktoum, states that the plan is to move toward 90 percent Emiratisation of the teaching staff by 2020 and that an office in the Ministry of Education—the Planning, Development, and Evaluation Office—has been established to oversee this transition (His Highness Sheikh Mohammed Bin Rashid Al Maktoum, 2008). Numerous policies have been implemented as part of the nation's Emiratisation goals, all aimed at affecting the supply side of the labor market (e.g., the relative attractiveness of the public and private sectors in pay and benefits) and the demand side (e.g., employer incentives or mandates to employ nationals in a given sector of the economy). Another strategy targets both the demand and the supply side by facilitating the matching of workers to jobs.

Making the Private Sector More Attractive to Emiratis. The UAE government recognizes that enhancing the benefits associated with jobs outside the public sector is one way to lure Emiratis to work in the private sector. As noted earlier, the loss of employment-related benefits in going from a government job to the private sector has generally been one of the largest obstacles keeping nationals from joining the private sector.

One of the main benefits nationals did not want to lose is participation in the national pension plan. Historically, only Emirati nationals working in the government sector could participate in the national plan. But as of September 1999, a new social security and pension law stipulated that nationals could participate in a national pension plan while working in the private sector. Government employee retirement benefits, disability benefits, life insurance, and end-of-service bonuses would be transferred to the new national program. Thus, Emirati government employees leaving for the private sector would not lose benefits they had accrued. The government set up a new, autonomous authority, the General Authority for Pensions and Social Security, to manage the system; it began operating in 1998. Established with an initial grant from the government totaling 500 million UAE dirhams (approximately $135 million), the Authority's purpose is to manage and invest citizens' retirement benefits (UAE federal e-government portal, 2006c). Local affiliates of the General Authority for Pensions and Social Security, such as the Abu Dhabi Retirement and Pensions Fund, established in 2000, require contributions to the fund from all employers in Abu Dhabi with Emirati staff who wish to participate in the program (Abu Dhabi Retirement Pensions and Benefits Fund, 2008).[22]

Inducing Employers to Increase Their Employment of Emiratis. The sucesss of Emiratisation is also contingent on inducing employers in the private sector to hire more nationals. One strategy has been to impose specific targets for the share of nationals to be employed in a given sector. The earliest law explicitly setting employer quotas was issued in 1998. A Council of Ministers resolution promulgated that all banks must increase their share of local staff by 4 percent annually. This was followed by a recommendation in 2001 and a formal resolution in 2003 outlining a 5 percent annual increase in the share of Emirati staff in insurance-sector companies (CLMRI, 2005). A 2004 resolution by the Council of Ministers further extended quotas to the trade sector, stating that "all companies in the trade sector that include 50 employees or more shall employ citizens with a ratio of 2 percent yearly" (UAE Council of Ministers, 2004, p. 1). This law obliges the trade sector to increase the share of nationals in their workforce by 2

---

[22] According to information on the Abu Dhabi Retirement Pensions and Benefits Fund website, employees contribute 5 percent of their monthly salary and employers contribute 15 percent. The government of Abu Dhabi contributes an additional 6 percent (Abu Dhabi Retirement Pensions and Benefits Fund, 2008).

percent each year. An Emiratisation target of 2 percent as a starting point was set for 2005, with few companies in the trade sector able to comply (Golden, 2006).

The Ministry of Labour is authorized to categorize companies based on whether they have met their Emiratisation quotas. Companies failing to meet the Emiratisation requirements must pay a fee determined by their classification: The closer they are to meeting their quota, the lower the fee. Successive failure to reach quotas may lead to suspension of transactions being filed at the Ministry (UAE Tanmia, 2005).

In addition to the quotas and compliance mandates, the government has established a number of policies designed to restrict the flow of foreign workers into the country and to mitigate the reliance on foreign imported labor for the long term. Such policy levers as minimum wage requirements, taxes on businesses importing labor, taxes on salaries of imported labor, and higher visa and residency processing requirements have all been employed (Al-Fakhri, 2004). These policies are all intended to make the hiring of Emiratis rather than non-nationals more competitive on the basis of cost, but they do not address the need to train nationals so that they are more competitive on the basis of skills and workforce preparedness.

Matching Workers to Jobs. Another component of Emiratisation, also overseen by the Ministry of Labour, is the establishment of mechanisms to facilitate the transfer of Emiratis from the government to the private sector. This effort entails creating job banks to link private-sector employers with individuals who are searching for employment, whether they are preparing to enter the workforce for the first time or are re-entering the workforce. Another purpose of these job banks is to determine whether job seekers have further education and training needs. In some cases, the job bank provides the needed training with its own resources; in other cases, external service providers are identified.

A number of specific job-matching programs have been launched, the most significant of which was in 1999 when Tanmia was established as part of the Ministry of Labour. Tanmia's broad mission is to address the needs of job-seeking citizens by offering career counseling and training and identifying job market opportunities that best match the individual's skills. In addition, as part of a broader set of activities, Tanmia engages in formulating labor strategies for the UAE. Part of its long-term mission is to eliminate unemployment of nationals, reduce the reliance on foreign labor (especially in the high-skill fields), and train nationals in skills that are competitive both nationally and internationally. While the main Tanmia office is in Dubai, there is coordination across local offices in each of the emirates.[23]

Tanmia's role includes providing career counseling and guidance, both to adult nationals seeking jobs and to students in schools and universities, through its Center for Career Guidance and Planning. This Center interacts with public and private organizations in an effort to identify areas of need in the workforce and relays information back to education institutions to set up an appropriate training program. The Center also issues products covering a wide array of topics, ranging from information on colleges and universities to guides on successful business practices. It has been building relationships among education institutions in the UAE and businesses to enhance career guidance assistance for students. The Employment and Skills Development Center of Tanmia provides the skills training needed to prepare individuals for the workforce and tracks graduates of the program to assess their progress. This group directly connects with institutions that are required to or plan to increase the employment of nationals to help them determine the best way to achieve those goals. The training, much of which is in English, is outsourced to external contractors (UAE Tanmia, 2008).

Other entities affiliated with Tanmia include the Public Authority for National Development and Employment (PANDE), established in 1999, which maintains a database of individuals searching for jobs in order to link them to employers. A similar electronically maintained job bank in the planning stages, the Labor Market Information System (LMIS), will help forecast job opportunities for nationals so as to assist them in targeting particular sectors in their search for employment.

---

[23] A report released at the end of 2005 indicated that for that year up until November, Tanmia had successfully placed 1,845 nationals seeking employment into jobs and provided training for 1,220 job seekers (UAE Tanmia, 2006).

Once it is fully operational, this system will also facilitate labor market research that can be used in labor-related policymaking (UAE federal e-government portal, 2006b). Currently, the CLMRI is one such internal entity under Tanmia that will use these data and engage in labor market research. The *UAE Human Resources Report, 2005* is a product of CLMRI's efforts to disseminate information on human capital issues (CLMRI, 2005). The LMIS is intended to provide data and information that allow more in-depth and sophisticated labor market analyses to be conducted. To ensure that the LMIS is serving labor market planning and research needs, a mechanism to assess its effectiveness should be put into place.

In addition to the PANDE and LMIS job banks, the Ministry of Labour will be providing its own electronic job bank by allowing citizens to sign up on the Ministry's website and fill out a form that will help identify their areas of expertise and interest and link them to employers (UAE federal e-government portal, 2006b).

Progress to Date. Success with these various policy levers as part of Emiratisation has been mixed. While compliance laws, in the form of quotas and penalties for not meeting them, have achieved some breakthroughs in increasing the employment of nationals in the private sector, evidence suggests that competing national priorities, such as market liberalization, have undermined the sustained success of these policy levers. Indeed, despite policymakers' promising view that companies in the private sector will be able to increasingly employ nationals by providing "good working conditions and strong career prospects," progress has been slower than anticipated, and there have even been setbacks in achieving Emiratisation goals (CLMRI, 2005, p. 65).

Of the three sectors that have had Emiratisation laws in place, the banking sector has faced the requirements long enough that an assessment of progress to date can be made. In its examination of Emiratisation in the banking sector, CLMRI found that the sector increased its share of Emiratis from 14.1 percent to 26.4 percent of the workforce between 1999 and 2004 (CLMRI, 2005). This is still 10 percentage points below the quota set by the government for 2004, but it exceeds the percentage of nationals in other industries in the private sector. The factors mentioned earlier—a longer working day, a six-day workweek, and other job requirements—continue to make it difficult for the private sector, including banking, to meet its Emiratisation goals.

Each year the quota for Emiratisation increases by 4 percentage points for the banking sector, which despite making considerable gains, continues to struggle to meet the requirements. Recent data released for 2005 indicate that the banking sector was only able to achieve an increase of approximately two percentage points in the share of Emiratis in the workforce from 2004 to 2005, going from 28 percent to 30 percent. The total number of Emiratis reported as employed in the banking sector in 2005 was 6,975 out of a total of 23,219 employees (Emirates Institute for Banking and Financial Studies, 2006). The difficulty in keeping up with the quota may have something to do with the fact that the banking sector's fastest expansion is occurring in the free zones, which independently issue permits to foreign workers and thus are not directly subject to Ministry of Labour Emiratisation requirements (CLMRI, 2005).

The UAE is facing a formidable challenge in seeking to balance the goal of successfully channeling its citizens into productive work while fostering a business-friendly environment in an effort to diversify its economy (Sfakianakis, 2005). Moreover, the long-run effectiveness of these Emiratisation policies remains questionable as long as employers continue to find foreign workers who, compared with Emiratis, are significantly more prepared, more skilled, and cost less. Thus, the Emiratisation policy initiatives depend in part on the success of the education and training efforts discussed earlier.

Private-Sector Promotion and Economic Diversification
In addition to its efforts to advance the skills and training of the Emirati workforce and to reduce the reliance on foreign labor, the UAE has continued to pursue aggressive privatization and diversification strategies by providing incentives to international companies to establish regional headquarters and branch offices in the country. International companies with the potential for growth have been invited to open branches in free zones. This in turn has promoted economic diversification, which has become an important strategy for the UAE, particularly for emirates such as Dubai. The *UAE Yearbook 2006* cites avia-

tion, port facilities, tourism, finance, and telecommunications as the main areas of focus for expansion. Non-oil exports accounted for more than half (52.3 percent) of all exports during the 2000–2004 period, a growth of more than 20 percentage points since the 1980s, when non-oil exports accounted for only 29.5 percent of all exports (UAE Ministry of Information and Culture, 2006).

Several large-scale projects related to the UAE's oil and gas industries have been well under way since the 1990s to promote further growth in the country's industrial and manufacturing base. Abu Dhabi Oil Company, which oversees oil and gas production in Abu Dhabi, established venture companies in oil and gas transport, industrial refining, and petrochemicals. Both Abu Dhabi and Dubai participate in the Dolphin Project, a partnership with Qatar to channel natural gas into industrial growth and development ventures in the region in hopes of attracting further international investment in gas-related industries. The UAE has also experienced growth in the number of factories producing cement, building materials, aluminum, and chemical fertilizers. This growth has in large part resulted from the UAE seeking to expand its refinery capacity to process crude oil into value-added products and to create favorable business conditions in order to encourage growth in new industries. The government of the UAE reported that 1,695 factories employing 145,000 people were in operation in 1999 (UAE federal e-government portal, 2006a, 2006d).

Privatization in the UAE has been fostered by the establishment of free zones. The Jebel Ali Free Zone, which was purported to house 6,000 companies as of the end of 2006 and which represents a vast array of industries, has encouraged partnerships between local, regional, and international companies to take advantage of the infrastructure and basic services, along with the exemption from tax and labor laws (Sharma, 2007). This free zone is considered an important contributor to Dubai's local economy (Jebel Ali Free Zone, 2008). As more companies establish branch offices in Dubai and other emirates' free zones, the private sector will contribute an increasingly greater share to the UAE's overall economy (UAE federal e-government portal, 2006a).

However, while free zone projects encourage rapid diversification of the economy and are seen as vital to securing the nation's future, they also undermine efforts at Emiratisation. All establishments in free zones may not be automatically exempt from national labor requirements, but local governments can decide how best to set their own economic, and thus employment, priorities (Al Roken, 2005).[24] Evidence suggests that companies in free zones operate with little to no restriction on who they hire. This is a major challenge to UAE public officials, because they are tasked with reconciling competing national and local priorities, all of which threaten to undermine the effectiveness of the respective policies. Other GCC nations also face these competing priorities, trying to balance nationalization goals with those connected with reducing an almost exclusive dependence for revenue on oil and gas production. Unless the UAE government can facilitate the training of Emiratis in the skills needed in these emerging sectors, increasing the share of the professional and skilled national workforce in the growing private sector will continue to be difficult.

Broad-Level Policy Goals Remain Focused on Improving the Performance of the Federal Government

While the federal government wields considerable authority in setting economic priorities, the local governments, particularly those of Dubai and Abu Dhabi, have engaged in their own large-scale human capital reform initiatives. The federal government is overseeing its own broad initiatives, such as Quality Management—to improve its human resource capacity—and an e-government program—to enhance policymaking that promotes national development. For example, the vision statement outlined in the e-government program states its objective as "[e]nabling integrated policy formulation and facilitating a knowledge-based world class government" (UAE federal e-government portal, 2006b).

---

[24] According to Najjar (2005):

> [T]he law also exempts free zones from being subject to federal civil and commercial laws although other federal laws in areas such as penalty, civil and criminal procedures, employment, and laws related to entry into the country and residence therein by aliens still take precedence. (p. 30)

The federal government directly addresses the issue raised in the 2003 *Arab Human Development Report* (UNDP, 2003) by specifically stating that its intention is to build a knowledge-based society. The e-government program stresses the importance of the federal government keeping up with changes occurring in the economic sectors and playing the role of engaging in effective policymaking to promote the nation's development. There are statements in the strategy suggesting that the government intends to reduce inefficiencies and outsource services that could be provided more efficiently outside the government sector. Also included is a call for better data collection and information sharing in an effort to build a "world class" government that engages in data-driven decisionmaking (UAE federal e-government portal, 2006b).

As the federal government articulates goals related to improving its own functioning, much of its activities support local emirate-based initiatives designed to promote human capital development. As the UAE moves toward less dependence on oil as a base for its economy, it will have to coordinate the various economic diversification schemes that are fast becoming the lifelines of its future economic viability and well-being.

We have described the UAE's efforts to address the human resource challenges that the country is facing. In doing so, we focused on education and training initiatives, as well as employment policy levers to increase the share of nationals in the workforce. We found that the country is investing significant resources in reforming K–12 education, providing post-secondary education and training institutions, and establishing communities to promote research and creation of knowledge capital. These efforts are in their early stages, however, and it will take time before they produce tangible outcomes.

We also found that labor market initiatives such as Emiratisation have helped increase the share of nationals in the workforce, but that established goals have not been consistently met. This is partly because Emiratisation depends on the success of education and training initiatives, but it also a reflection of conflicting policies intended to encourage diversification and expansion of the private sector. Since much of the growth of the private sector has been occurring in the free zones, where labor requirements are not strictly enforced, progress toward Emiratisation goals has been counteracted.

We next describe the importance of establishing systems to evaluate progress toward the goals of these human capital reform initiatives.

Efforts at Data Collection and Dissemination to Improve Policymaking Are in the Early Stages

Given the important but competing priorities that UAE policymakers face, the capability needed to collect and analyze education and labor market data must be established so that appropriate policy decisions can be made and progress against goals can be continuously measured. We discuss the types of data available on the UAE and efforts taken to collect additional data to assist in long-term policymaking. We then discuss broad-level policy goals set forth by the UAE federal government to achieve human capital objectives and build the human resource base needed to fuel the rapidly expanding and diversifying economy.

Data Collection Efforts at the National Level

The UAE has undergone a number of major data collection efforts. The country has a history of conducting censuses—the first in 1968 (prior to the federation's establishment), followed by those in 1975, 1980, 1985, and 1995 (after its establishment). The most recent census was in 2005 (also transliterated from Arabic to "Tedad 2005"), and the next census is scheduled for 2010, in synchronization with censuses in the other GCC countries (UAE Ministry of Economy, undated). The federal organization of the UAE dictates that large-scale data collection efforts must be coordinated among the different emirates. The Dubai government oversaw its own data collection effort; the Abu Dhabi government census agencies managed data collection efforts for the remaining emirates.

Up until the 2005 census, the UAE did not publish detailed tabulations from prior censuses or specialized surveys on the numbers of Emiratis versus non-Emiratis. It is difficult to determine with exact precision the numbers of nationals and non-nationals and to calculate accurate population and labor force estimates by nationality. Population data are essential in assessing the demand for government services, such as education, health, and other infrastructure, and for determining economic priorities. It is possible that these data are available for government planning purposes but not to the broader research community.

Collecting information on the labor force is also crucial in policymaking, particularly in monitoring progress toward Emiratisation, one of the most important policy priorities for the UAE. With economic growth and diversification occurring, it is especially important for the nation to monitor Emiratisation's effects on developing Emirati human capital. Since certain sectors have been targeted as priorities for Emiratisation, collecting and disseminating information on the employment of nationals versus non-nationals by sector will also help facilitate studies and examinations of this issue. Notably, the UAE does not collect labor force data through a specialized labor force survey, so such information is only available at a national level from the periodic censuses.

The Ministry of Economy collects data and information on economic variables, including sector-reported performance and employment. While sector-reported employment is helpful in getting an indication of national versus non-national distribution, it does not provide a comprehensive view of total employment of nationals versus non-nationals by type of economic activity. The anticipation is that after the full set of results from the 2005 census is publicly disseminated, this information will become available.

CLMRI, the arm of Tanmia that conducts research on the labor market, is also responsible for collecting and disseminating labor information and is developing the LMIS mentioned previously. CLMRI is charged with collecting data and disseminating findings to the public, as well as conducting research and preparing reports intended to inform policymakers and assist in developing the nation's labor strategy. Further dissemination of CLMRI data is necessary to build research capital that can aid in policymaking. One of the areas closely monitored by CLMRI is the growth of the foreign workforce, including growth in the free-zone area, where Emiratisation policies are not strictly applied. Monitoring changes that occur in the labor force makeup as a result of the establishment of free zones provides critical information for policymaking.

Data on education are available through the Ministry of Economy. The data mostly cover student enrollment and characteristics, including breakdowns by nationality, as well as information on staffing. Until recently, the UAE did not administer a national assessment other than a final exit exam required for the secondary school certificate (high school diploma). The Ministry of Education made a decision to discontinue the final secondary school exit-exam system during academic year 2006–2007 in favor of a comprehensive formative, as well as summative, evaluation of student progress from the primary years, beginning in grade 4, to the secondary years, and ending in grade 12 (UAE Ministry of Education, 2006d). Data currently available on performance include the percentages of students that have passed or failed the secondary school certificate exam. Unlike some of the other Gulf nations (for example, Qatar and Kuwait), the UAE has not participated in international student assessments such as TIMSS, PISA, and PIRLS, which focus, respectively, on mathematics and science, life skills, and reading comprehension. The administration of internationally benchmarked independent assessments such as these can assist the UAE not only in understanding how well its education system is doing, but also in developing policies to improve and address shortcomings of this system.

Summary

Over a period of only 15 years, the UAE has witnessed tremendous growth—the nation's GDP and population have doubled. These developments have brought important opportunities but have also created significant challenges. Much of the population growth is from in-migration of non-nationals to meet labor market needs. As of 2005, Emiratis made up just 22 percent of the total population of the UAE; the remaining portion was made up of foreign residents of different nationalities. The distribution of nationals versus non-nationals is even starker in the labor force: Emiratis are just 8 percent of the total workforce. An important factor driving this disparity is the low labor force participation of Emiratis: just 19 percent of working-age females, and 69 percent of working-age males.

Another important issue is that although the share of Emirati females enrolled in UAE government secondary and post-secondary institutions is notably higher than the share of Emirati males, the labor force participation of Emirati females is low, suggesting that education outcomes are not appropriately aligned with workforce needs. A large segment of the more-educated working-age population of nationals is not participating in the workforce. Furthermore, findings from labor market studies suggest that nationals require additional training to be adequately prepared to meet the needs of the workforce, particularly in technical skills and the "soft skills," such as communication, customer service, and interpersonal relations. The emirates of Abu Dhabi and Dubai have been promoting economic diversification and privatization, which means that Emiratis must ultimately be prepared to meet the needs of newly emerging sectors. Emiratis have traditionally expected to be automatically eligible for employment in government jobs. These indicators are troubling and could undermine long-term sustainability of the growth and development achieved so far. Continued heavy reliance on a largely foreign labor force may hinder the development of a national human resource base with the skills needed in a rapidly globalizing economy.

In our analysis of secondary data sources and discussions with UAE policymakers, we found acknowledgment of the country's human resource challenges. To address these issues, the country has embarked on a number of initiatives, which we have summarized in Table 4.14.

The UAE has implemented a number of initiatives to enhance the human capital of its citizen population. Investments in education and training are examples of these initiatives; many of them have only recently been implemented, however, and will take time to produce tangible results. Labor market policies, such as Emiratisation, are strategies intended to increase the share of nationals in target sectors over a shorter time frame than can be achieved through education and training initiatives. However, Emiratisation goals have not been consistently met; and at the national level, the establishment of free zones, where

Table 4.14
Summary of Education and Labor Market Reforms Under Way in the UAE

Reform Categories and Subcategories

Education and training

   Primary and secondary education

      Formation of education councils to oversee education reform and align education outcomes with national workforce needs

      Implementation of new models of schooling emphasizing bilingual education (Arabic and English), greater support and training for principals and teachers, and a student-centered instructional approach in select government schools

      Promotion of private- and public-sector partnerships to manage K–12 schools

      Decentralization of decisionmaking authority and granting of more autonomy to K–12 schools

   Post-secondary and post-graduate education

      Requirement for academic accreditation of post-secondary education institutions

      Student internship programs to develop better links with local business community

      Establishment of theme cities to attract international post-secondary academic and training institutions' branch campuses

   Training system

      Establishment of institutions to provide retraining and match job-seeking nationals to vacancies

Labor market and economy

   Labor market reforms

      Establishment of goals for employment of nationals in private sector, residency restrictions, and penalties for hiring non-nationals to increase the share of Emiratis in the workforce

      Expansion of pension benefits for nationals beyond the government sector to encourage nationals to seek employment in the growing private sector

   Other economic reforms

      Allowance of foreign ownership of companies in selected sectors

      Establishment of free zones exempt from government requirements

companies are not subject to labor laws and requirements, may further slow down Emiratisation's progress.

Progress in achieving both the short- and the long-term goals through these initiatives is best assessed by putting into place mechanisms for the collection and analysis of education and labor market data that can be used for research by multiple stakeholders to produce findings that will inform decisionmaking. These mechanisms can also provide information that will assist policymakers in appropriately balancing priorities and modifying policies to successfully reach the multiple national goals.

CHAPTER FIVE
Sultanate of Oman

The Sultanate of Oman, situated at the entrance to the Arabian Gulf, is historically and economically unique compared with the other Gulf nations in this study. Its history is one of independence from foreign occupation since its leadership deposed Portuguese colonists in the mid-1700s, and one of alternating between trade and expansionism, and isolation (Cecil, 2006).

Oman is dealing with a less than certain economic future because its oil reserves—its major source of revenue since oil was discovered here in 1964—are quickly being depleted. This uncertainty about Oman's economic future has forced its leadership to take measures to promote the sustainability of the country's economy and the employability of its people through a number of education and labor market initiatives. Since the mid-1990s, the government has increased funding for sectors that can provide sustainable economic growth, such as agriculture and fishing. It has also encouraged tourism and constructed light industrial parks with the objective of exporting consumer goods. In addition, the government has embarked on a long-term strategy to enhance the skills and human resources of its citizenry through reforms to the education system and by encouraging the opening of private higher education institutions and training centers.

This chapter provides an overview of the measures Oman has recently taken to address the human resource needs of its population in the face of the dwindling supply of oil. We first provide important background information on Oman, including information on its political history, economy, population, education system, and labor force. We then use the analytic framework presented in Chapter One to discuss the human resource challenges that the country faces and to describe the national policy development and implementation process of major reforms under way in the country, focusing on those reforms that affect the education system and the labor market, as listed in Table 5.1.

Our analyses are informed by information gained in interviews with government officials and leaders in the private sector,[1] as well as in analyses of secondary data. We close our analyses with a discussion of the data resources that can be used to assess the effects of underway policy changes and conclude the chapter with a summary of our key findings.

Overview of Oman

The Sultanate of Oman is in the southeastern quarter of the Arabian Peninsula and covers approximately 309,000 square kilometers. According to Oman's 2003 census, 2,340,815 people inhabit Oman, of

Table 5.1
Human Capital Reforms Covered in Oman Case Study

Reform Categories and Subcategories
Education and training
Primary and secondary education
Post-secondary and post-graduate education
Training
Labor market and economy
Labor market reforms
Economic privatization
Economic diversification

---

[1] Appendix A lists the organizations and government ministries in which we held our interviews.

whom 559,257, or 24 percent, are expatriates. Figure 5.1 shows Oman's location on the Arabian Peninsula. The country is bordered to the west by the UAE and Saudi Arabia, including the Rub al Khali, or Empty Quarter (not pictured); it is bordered to the southwest by Yemen.[2]

**Figure 5.1
Map of Sultanate of Oman**

SOURCE: U.S. Department of State, 2007b.
RAND MG786-5.1

---

[2] The Rub al Khali historically formed a natural barrier between the Sultanate and the Arabian interior, contributing to Oman's isolation and reliance on the sea for its livelihood. The Al Hajar Mountains, which form a belt between the coast and the desert from the Musandam Peninsula to the city of Sur, at Oman's easternmost point, form another barrier (Metz, 1994).

Oman's territorial waters stretch into the Arabian Sea and Indian Ocean to the south and east, and to the north into the Gulf of Oman, which is shared by Iran. The Musandam Peninsula, located above the northernmost tip of the UAE, is also part of Oman; it is adjacent to the Strait of Hormuz, a vital transit point for world crude oil coming from the Gulf nations.

Oman has a heterogeneous population—vestiges of its long history of trade within the Arabian Gulf, with South Asia, and with Africa and Europe. Its population is composed of a number of ethnic groups that include Arab, Baluchi, South Asian (primarily Indian, Pakistani, Sri Lankan, and Bangladeshi), and African. Over 75 percent of its population is Muslim,[3] and approximately 25 percent is Hindu or Christian. Arabic is the official language, but English, Baluchi, Urdu, and other South Asian dialects are also common (U.S. Department of State, 2007b).

The Sultanate of Oman has two distinct geographic areas: the coast and the interior. It is divided into eight administrative divisions; three of them are called governorates (Muscat, Dhofar, Musandam), and the other five are called regions (Al Batinah, Ash Sharqiyah, Ad Dakhliyah, Adh Dhahirah, Al Wusta) (Oman Ministry of National Economy, 2005b). Muscat serves as the nation's capital and commercial hub.

Political History

In contrast to other countries in the region, Oman has enjoyed relative autonomy for most of its modern history. The most recent colonial presence was the Portuguese, from 1507 to 1650. They were finally expelled by Sultan Bin Saif Al Yarubi in 1650, the date which most consider to be the start of Oman's complete independence. In 1738,

---

[3] All Omanis are Muslims. The majority are Ibadi Muslims, followers of Abd Allah Bin Ibad. Approximately 25 percent are Sunni Muslims; they form the largest non-Ibadi minority and live primarily in Sur, its surrounding area, and Dhofar. The rest of the Omanis are Shiites, a minority that includes the Khojas, the Baharina (of Iraqi or Iranian descent), and the Ajam (of vague origin but generally considered to have originated in Iran). These Omanis live along the coast of Al Batinah, in the Muscat-Matrah region. (Metz, 1994)

Omani Arabs defeated Persian attempts to take over the country, ushering in an era of prosperity.

In 1804, Sayyid Said Bin Sultan acceded to the throne and nurtured his country's economy and commercial activities. He made Zanzibar Oman's second capital and established diplomatic relations with Europe and the United States. Oman prospered during this time and held colonies in East Africa and across the Gulf. During World War I, however, Oman's economy and trade links declined, and the country became relatively isolated, remaining that way until 1970, when Sultan Qaboos Bin Said came to power, and a rebellion in the southern region of Dhofar was quelled. Sultan Qaboos immediately began to reestablish links with the rest of the world. He remains Oman's head of state (Oman Ministry of Information, 2008b).

Although Oman does not have a constitution, Sultan Qaboos issued a royal decree in November 1996 that promulgated the "Basic Statute of the State," a constitution-like document defining the state's basic functions. Among other things, the Basic Statute defined the type of government as *sultani* and enshrined the sultanship as hereditary among the male descendants of Al Said (the male descendants of Sayyid Turki Bin Said Bin Sultan).[4] It also instituted a prime minister, barred government ministers from holding interests in companies doing business with the government, established a bicameral legislature, and guaranteed basic civil liberties for Omani citizens. An independent judiciary is also provided; however, the Sultan retained the right to overturn judicial decisions on appeal. Oman's legal system is broadly based on English common law but adheres to Islamic law, with the Sultan having the ultimate appeal (Rabi, 2002; U.S. Department of State, 2007b).

---

[4] Leadership in much of the Gulf comprises large ruling families with a great number of clans and family branches. This is not the case in Oman, however, because the Al Said family is relatively small, numbering fewer than 100 male members. Sultan Al Qaboos is childless and there is therefore no obvious heir apparent. The Basic Statute provides the Al Said family with a formula for selecting a new sultan: If the Royal Family Council fails to reach an agreement within three days of the throne falling vacant, it must turn to a letter left behind by Sultan Qaboos in which he designates the successor.

The Basic Statute created a new institution, the State Council (Majlis Al Dawla), whose 57 members are appointed by the Sultan and serve three-year terms. The State Council runs in parallel to the elected body, the Consultative Council (Majlis Al Shura), which debates matters referred to it by the Sultan. The State and Consultative Councils together form the bicameral body known as the Council of Oman (Majlis Oman) (U.S. Department of State, 2007b). The State Council is dominated by tribal leaders, former officials, and dignitaries. The Sultan appointed four women to this council when it was first established. The State Council is charged with reviewing all recommendations that emerge from the Consultative Council after that council reviews and studies the needs of the public. The State Council is also tasked with "serving the philosophy of the state as a whole" (Rabi, 2002, p. 46).

Inaugurated in 1991, the Consultative Council is a representative institution with 59 members representing the 59 *wilayats*, or districts, in Oman.[5] In 1994, the government expanded so that districts with more than 30,000 people would hold two seats, one of which would be appointed directly by Sultan Qaboos. As a result, the Consultative Council increased to 80 members in 1994, 82 members in 1997, and had 83 members in 2006 (Cecil, 2006). Its role is to relay the interests of the local communities to the central government and to inform its constituents of the government's plans and policies. Members are elected directly by voters. In the most recent elections, held in October 2005, approximately 74 percent of registered voters (194,000 persons) voted to elect the 83 seats (U.S. Department of State, 2007b).

The Consultative Council has no formal legislative powers—all such powers remain with the Sultan. However, this council serves as a conduit of information between citizens and government ministries. The elected assembly is therefore relatively restrained. The Consultative Council may question government ministers in public or private, review all draft laws on social and economic policy, and recommend

---

[5] The Sultanate of Oman is divided into eight administrative regions further subdivided into 59 districts. Each district is governed by a wali, who is responsible to the Ministry of Interior.

legislative changes to the Sultan, who makes the final decisions. The Consultative Council can recommend new laws or changes to existing ones and has the authority to study the five-year development plan current at the time (these plans are discussed in the next section) and monitor its implementation. Much of the council work is done in committees, of which seven are permanent: Legal, Economic, Health and Social Affairs, Education and Culture, Services and Development of Local Communities, Environment and Human Resources, and Follow-up and Implementation (Rabi, 2002). Neither of these two councils is given the authority to discuss or question the government on matters related to foreign policy or defense, issues that are of personal interest to the Sultan.

Economic Development
Oman's economic development has gone through three phases since Sultan Qaboos came to power: (1) rapid expansion, between 1970 and 1986, in which growing oil wealth made funds available for improvements in Oman's agriculture and fisheries industries, for the beginnings of industrialization, and for provision of a wide range of social services (Rabi, 2002); (2) economic retrenchment and rationalization, between 1986 and 1989, as a result of the 1985–1986 oil price collapse; and (3) stabilized growth, since 1990 (Metz, 1994; Fasano and Iqbal, 2003).

After assuming power in 1970, Sultan Qaboos soon enhanced the country's infrastructure and oversaw the establishment of modern government and administrative institutions with the proceeds from the production and sale of oil. By the mid-1980s, virtually all regions of the country were linked by a transportation system and a telecommunications network. In addition, a new deepwater port, an international airport, electricity-generating plants, desalination plants, schools, hospitals, and low-cost housing were established. Ministerial government and the civil service were expanded, and limited participation in the political process was created in 1981, with the establishment of the State Consultative Council (Al Majlis Al-Istishari Lil-Dawla); in 1991, with the formation of the Consultative Council, which superseded the State Consultative Council; and in 1997, with the establishment of the State Council (discussed above) (Metz 1994; Rabi, 2002; Cecil, 2006).

Increased wealth from oil revenues also brought an improvement in the standard of living for Omani citizens. As noted in Chapter One, the World Bank presently classifies Oman as upper middle income. Figure 5.2 shows that per capita GDP, measured in constant U.S. dollars, more than doubled between 1970 and 2004 (the most recent year of available figures), rising from about $4,000 to $9,000. GDP growth was more volatile in the 1970s and early 1980s but has ranged between –2 percent and 6 percent since 1990.

Although economic growth and structural change have occurred rapidly in Oman over the past three decades, Oman still lags some of its Gulf neighbors in these areas (see, for example, Chapters Two and Three, which discuss Qatar and the UAE, respectively). This lag is partly the result of Oman's relatively late discovery of oil, in 1964, with production not starting until 1967. Oil was discovered in neighboring

Figure 5.2
Trends in GDP per Capita and GDP per Capita Growth in Oman, 1970 to 2004

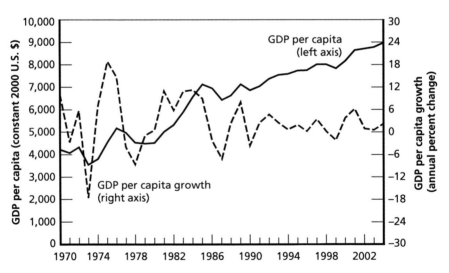

SOURCE: World Bank, 2007.
RAND MG786-5.2

Arab countries in the late 1930s, and its exploitation occurred in the late 1940s, directly after World War II (Metz, 1994).

Not only has Oman had to play catch-up with its Gulf neighbors; it also has smaller resources. Its proven reserves in oil were estimated in 1992 at 4.6 billion barrels—small in comparison to the reserves of other Gulf states. It was estimated that at the mid-1992 production rate of 725,000 bbl/day, Oman's crude reserves would permit 17 years of output; Saudi Arabia's output, in contrast, was estimated at nearly 350 years (Metz, 1994). Estimates of Oman's oil production as of 2005 were 769,000 bbl/day and reserves of 6.1 billion barrels, whereas Qatar's estimated oil production was about the same, 765,000 bbl/day, and oil reserves of 15 billion barrels. The UAE's oil production is much higher than that of both Oman and Qatar: 2.378 million bbl/day and reserves of 97.8 billion barrels (OPEC, 2006).

Population Composition and Change

Oman's economic progress and structural improvements have brought about a rapid growth in population. According to 2005 figures, Oman has a population growth rate of 3.5 percent per year, one of the highest in the world (Oman Ministry of National Economy, 2005d). In turn, the government faces the challenge of meeting the education and employment needs of its growing population. Using data from the World Bank, Figure 5.3 shows the rapid growth of Oman's population from 1960 to 2006.

Much of the increase in population is the result of natural population growth of Omanis, rather than the rapid immigration of expatriates that has caused population growth in the two other Gulf countries in our study. Table 5.2 uses data from the Oman national population censuses administered in 1993 and 2003 to show the distribution of nationals and non-nationals, by age group, in the country in those years. As is evident from the table, a large portion (40.6 percent) of Omanis were under age 15 as of 2003. In 1993, the bulk (51.6 percent) of Omanis fell in the group age 0 to 14, and in 2003, more than half of Omanis were age 15 to 64 (working age). Of the non-nationals, individuals age 15 to 64 made up the majority (around 88 percent) of the population in both 1993 and 2003.

Figure 5.3
Trends in Population Total and Growth Rate in Oman, 1960 to 2006

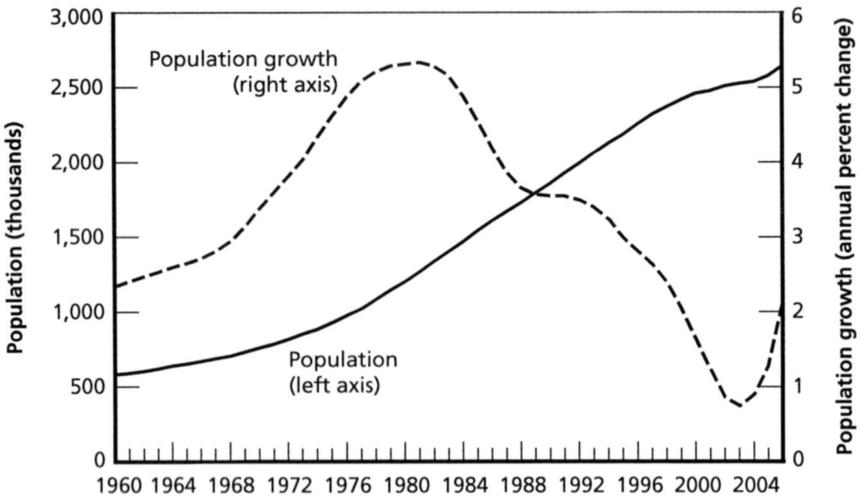

SOURCE: World Bank, 2007.
RAND MG786-5.3

Advances in Education

Oman's publicly funded education system (grades 1 through 12) has gone through a number of changes with the ascension of Sultan Qaboos.[6] Prior to 1970, there were 909 male students being educated in three schools and there was one technical/vocational school (the Industrial School, established by Petroleum Development Oman Company in 1967). Sultan Qaboos expanded education to all parts of the country on the premise that all citizens have the right to education and that education is a vehicle for social advancement and progress (Oman Ministry of Information, 2008b).[7] By academic year 1989–1990, almost 100

---

[6] The Oman government provides free education to children starting in grade 1. Kindergarten, which is not part of the government education system in Oman, is provided by the private sector and requires payment of tuition.

[7] Until 2004, the education system was guided by the policymaking body of the Council for Education, chaired by the Sultan and operated by the Oman Ministry of Education and Youth (Metz, 1994; Oman Ministry of National Economy, 2004). The Council for Educa-

Table 5.2
Population in Oman, by Nationality and Age Group, 1993 and 2003

Nationality and Age Group	Population					
	1993			2003		
	Number (1,000s)	Percent Distribution		Number (1,000s)	Percent Distribution	
		By Nationality	By Age Group		By Nationality	By Age Group
National	1,483	73.5	100.0	1,782	76.1	100.0
Age 0–14	765		51.6	723		40.6
Age 15–64	673		45.4	1,001		56.2
Age 65 and up	44		3.0	57		3.2
Non-national	535	26.5	100.0	559	23.9	100.0
Age 0–14	62		11.6	69		12.3
Age 15–64	471		88.1	487		87.0
Age 65 and up	2		0.3	4		0.7
Total	2,018	100.0	100.0	2,341	100.0	100.0
Age 0–14	827		41.0	791		33.8
Age 15–64	1,144		56.7	1,489		63.6
Age 65 and up	46		2.3	61		2.6

SOURCES: Oman Ministry of National Economy, 2005b, Table E; and authors' calculations.

NOTES: The Oman census tables provide only percentages of population by age groups and nationality, as well as total population for Omanis and non-Omanis. Figures given here for age groups are estimates computed from the percentages.

percent of Omanis in the related age group were enrolled in primary schools, up from 53 percent in 1977–1978. The percentage of females

---

tion has since been replaced by the Council of Higher Education, chaired by the Minister of Diwan of Royal Court and operated by the Oman Ministry of Higher Education.

attending primary schools also rose rapidly during this period, going from 37 percent in 1977–1978 to 97 percent in 1989–1990. Secondary school enrollment lagged that of primary school; it rose from 8 percent of the related age group in 1977–1978 to 48 percent in 1989–1990 (Metz, 1994). Official figures for 2005–2006 record 568,074 students in government schools (275,597 males and 292,477 females). In 2006, 1,046 schools existed across the country: 357 boys' schools, 317 girls' schools, and 372 mixed-gender schools. In addition, 28,183 students attend the Sultanate's 132 private schools—15,735 males and 12,448 females. There are also three schools for those with special needs and a number of private schools for children of non-nationals working in the Sultanate (Oman Ministry of Education, 2006).

Table 5.3 shows that males and females attend primary school at similar rates but that enrollment is not yet universal. The net enrollment ratios indicate that children may be delayed in entering school at the normal age or may repeat one or more grades, circumstances that would cause them to be older than expected for their grade.[8] Enrollment ratios are similar for males and females at the preprimary level as well, although the 8 percent rate is the lowest of the four countries in our study. There is some decline in the enrollment ratio for females at the secondary level, and yet females are overrepresented at the post-secondary level. These two conditions signal that more female than male graduates of secondary school choose to continue their education at the post-secondary level.

Labor Force Trends: The Labor Force Is Growing and the Share of Females Is Rising

In the last several decades, as shown in Figure 5.4, labor force growth in Oman has been slower than overall growth in the working-age population.[9] The labor force participation rate was over 60 percent in the mid-to-late 1990s but dropped to 58 percent from 2003 to 2006.

---

[8] Interestingly, the UNESCO estimate of the rate of primary grade repetition in Oman is just 1 percent as of 2004 (UNESCO, 2006).

[9] The World Bank defines the labor force as persons age 15 to 64 who are economically active, meaning they are employed or they are unemployed and actively looking for work.

Table 5.3
Gross and Net Enrollment Ratios in Oman, by Education Level and Gender, 2006

Education Level	Gross Enrollment Ratio		Net Enrollment Ratio	
	Males	Females	Males	Females
Preprimary	8.3	7.8	n.a.	n.a.
Primary	81.4	81.9	72.6	74.1
Secondary	89.7	86.3	76.9	76.6
Post-secondary	17.6	19.2	n.a.	n.a.

SOURCE: World Bank, 2007.
NOTE: n.a. = not available.

Figure 5.4
Trends in Working-Age Population, Labor Force, and Labor Force Participation Rate in Oman, 1980 to 2006

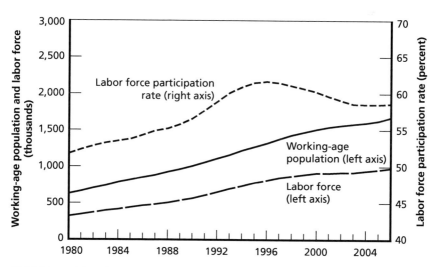

SOURCE: World Bank, 2007.
NOTE: Population and labor force take into account persons age 15–64.
RAND MG786-5.4

The next three tables examine the labor force in Oman in more depth using data from Oman's 1993 and 2003 national censuses.[10] Table 5.4 shows the distribution of Omanis and non-Omanis in the labor force. In general, we see a noticeable increase in the Omani share in the labor force between census years. In 1993, only 38.6 percent of the labor force was Omani, whereas by 2003, Omanis made up 50.7 percent of the labor force.

Table 5.5 illustrates the labor force participation rate (also known as the rate of economic activity), which Oman's Ministry of Economy defines as the percentage of the population age 15 and over that is in the labor force. Here, the increase in Omani females age 15 and over in the labor force from 1993 to 2003 is particularly apparent: 6.7 percent to 18.7 percent. At the same time, the percentages for their male counterparts decreased slightly: 68.1 percent to 64.7 per-

Table 5.4
Distribution of Labor Force in Oman, by Nationality, 1993 and 2003

Nationality	Labor Force			
	1993		2003	
	Number	Percent	Number	Percent
National	272,397	38.6	442,517	50.7
Non-national	432,401	61.4	430,949	49.3
Total	704,798	100.0	873,466	100.0

SOURCE: Oman Ministry of National Economy, 2005b, Table L.

---

[10] The Oman national census defines the labor force as those who are employed or unemployed, as follows. To be employed is to be an individual age 10 or above who practiced work of economic value for at least one hour during the week preceding the night of the reference time, regardless of whether the work was performed inside or outside the housing units. An individual is also considered employed if he/she did not engage in productive work during the week of reference time but satisfies one of two conditions: (1) works for others but did not practice that work because of a holiday, ailment, or difficult circumstances; (2) originally self-employed (i.e., working for himself/herself) but did not practice the work because of difficult circumstances or because of the nature of the work itself. To be unemployed is to be an individual age 10 or above who is capable of performing work and did not perform any kind of work during the week preceding the census reference night even though he/she was seriously looking for work (from Oman Ministry of National Economy, 2005b).

Table 5.5
Labor Force Participation Rates in Oman, by Nationality and Gender, 1993 and 2003

Nationality	Labor Force Participation Rate (percent)			
	1993		2003	
	Males	Females	Males	Females
National	68.1	6.7	64.7	18.7
Non-national	99.0	55.2	97.7	55.0

SOURCE: Oman Ministry of National Economy, 2005b, Table N.

cent in 2003. The reason for this decrease could be that Omani males delayed their entrance into the labor market with schooling or that they had difficulty finding work. It is also clear from this table that non-nationals, especially the males, were very active participants in the labor force in 1993 and 2003: About half of the non-national females in the working-age population were economically active in both years, and nearly 100 percent of their male counterparts were.

Table 5.6 highlights the gender distribution of the economically active population in Oman. For the past 10 years, the increase in the labor force participation rate among Omani females has led to an increase in their share in the labor force. In 1993, only 8.6 percent of working Omanis were females; in 2003, that percentage had risen to 22.2 percent.

Table 5.6
Gender Distribution in Oman Labor Force, by Nationality, 1993 and 2003

Nationality	Labor Force (percent distribution)			
	1993		2003	
	Males	Females	Males	Females
National	91.4	8.6	77.8	22.2
Non-national	89.6	10.4	85.5	14.5
Total	90.3	9.7	81.6	18.4

SOURCE: Oman Ministry of National Economy, 2005b, Table L.

Human Resource Challenges Faced by Oman

Wealth from oil and gas revenue distributed by Sultan Qaboos has brought about enhanced infrastructure development and significant education and health benefits for the Omani people. However, similar to the situation in the two other Gulf countries in our study, these benefits are overshadowed by a number of human resource challenges. In this section, we highlight the most-salient issues noted by our interviewees: the concentration of Omanis in public-sector employment, high unemployment rates among young Omanis, an education system that is not producing workers with the skills required by employers, a training system that lacks coordination, and underlying concerns about disparities in living standards. We discuss each of these challenges in turn, describing problems using the most-recent population, education, employment, and labor market data available within the country.

Omani Employees Are Concentrated in the Public Sector

Using data from the 2003 Oman national population census, Tables 5.7 and 5.8 provide a snapshot of worker's distribution across different sectors and occupations as of 2003. It is evident from these tables that Omanis are well represented in the public sector and underrepresented in the private sector. However, nationals in Oman are more evenly distributed across the private and public sectors than are nationals in our two other Gulf countries, the UAE and Qatar.

Table 5.7
Distribution of Persons Employed in Public and Private Sectors in Oman, by Nationality, 2003

	Public Sector		Private Sector	
Nationality	Persons Employed	Percent Distribution	Persons Employed	Percent Distribution
Total	123,045	100.0	482,632	100.0
National	99,076	80.5	74,816	15.5
Non-national	23,969	19.5	407,816	84.5

SOURCES: Oman Ministry of National Economy, 2005d; and authors' calculations.

Table 5.8
Percent Distribution of Persons Employed in Oman, by Economic Activity and Nationality, 2003

Economic Activity	Nationals	Non-Nationals
Public administration and defense; compulsory social security	46.3	4.2
Education	12.5	3.2
Wholesale and retail trade; repair of motor vehicles, motorcycles, and personal and household goods	6.9	15.4
Transport, storage, and communications	5.5	2.5
Manufacturing	4.4	10.8
Health and social work	4.2	2.4
Mining and quarrying	3.8	1.9
Construction	3.2	25.5
Fishing	2.4	0.4
Financial intermediation	2.3	0.4
Agriculture, hunting, and forestry	2.1	10.0
Real estate, renting, and business activities	1.8	2.5
Hotels and restaurants	1.1	4.5
Other community, social, and personal service activities	0.6	1.8
Electricity, gas, and water supply	0.6	0.5
Activities of private households as employers and undifferentiated production activities of private households	0.2	12.1
Extra-territorial organizations and bodies	0.1	0.1
Not stated	2.0	1.8
Total	100.0	100.0

SOURCE: Oman Ministry of National Economy, 2005b, Table P.

Table 5.7 shows that 80.5 percent of government employees are nationals and that only 15.5 percent of those employed in the private sector are nationals. Table 5.8 shows that the largest occupational category for nationals is public administration and defense: 46.3 percent of working nationals are in these fields. The second largest occupational category is education: 12.5 percent of working nationals are teachers and administrators.

Oman Has Relatively High Unemployment Rates, Particularly for Its Youth

Oman's leadership is deeply concerned with promoting the employability of its citizens because the number of job seekers entering the labor market is projected to increase by 212 percent in the next two decades as its youth population (age 0 to 14) continues its sustained growth beyond 2020 (Rabi, 2002; Lussier, 2007). Oman is experiencing the second-highest rate of growth of young people between age 15 and 24 in the MENA region (Hutton, 2003); about 43 percent of Omanis are under age 15 (Oman Ministry of National Economy, 2008b), and an estimated 30,000 young Omanis enter the job market each year (McInerney, 2005). The 2004 unemployment rate in Oman has been estimated at around 15 percent (U.S. State Department, 2007b).[11]

According to the *Oman Human Development Report, 2003* (Oman Ministry of National Economy, 2004), the majority of job seekers are dropouts from general education or recent graduates from secondary school. They do not have post-secondary educations or professional and technical skills that allow them to find work in a labor market that rewards higher education and professional skills. The report (p. 135) states the following:

> [I]f this basic mismatch between the outputs of the existing educational system, which is built upon academic education, and the requirements of the labor market for more professionals and technicians continues, Omanis will be faced with a hideous rise in unemployment. This will have enormous negative impacts on human resources development and on sustainable human development universally.

---

[11] The unemployment rate is defined as the percentage of the population that is available for and looking for work that pays the wage prevalent in the market.

Omanis Are Not Obtaining the Types of Education Needed to Compete in Oman's Economy

Given the challenges in the school-to-work transition and the relatively low representation of Omanis in private-sector employment, it is relevant to ask whether Omanis are well prepared by the country's education system to enter the 21st century workplace. The *Oman Human Development Report, 2003* asserts that the high rates of unemployment exist among graduates of secondary school because they lack the skills and competencies necessary for productive work (Oman Ministry of National Economy, 2004). It points to faults in Oman's education system that perpetuate the unemployment problem:

- Lessons are restricted to theoretical knowledge and not closely linked to the concept of work.
- There is a negative attitude toward technical and vocational education, and it is reinforced by certain policies, such as elite students being selected for academic higher education while those who perform less well go into vocational specialization.
- Available resources, such as schools, books, and teachers, are not sufficient.
- School is non-obligatory.
- The absorptive capacity of higher education institutions is limited. In 2000, 42 percent of secondary school graduates entered institutions of higher education, which means 58 percent turned to the labor market.
- Studying abroad is costly and thus unaffordable for most Omani secondary school graduates.

One consequence of this poor schooling is that children experience high rates of grade failure, dropping out, and grade repetition (see Table 5.9).

Furthermore, officials in the Ministry of Education and Ministry of Higher Education report that students who do go on to higher education are not graduating in the high-demand fields of science and technology. Although the enrollment rate in higher education institutions for those age 18 to 24 increased from 5 percent in 1993 to 12.6

Table 5.9
Gross Rates of Student Dropout, Grade Failure, and Grade Repetition in Oman, by Education Level and Gender, 1999–2000

Outcome and Education Level	Gross Rate (percent)	
	Males	Females
Dropout		
Primary	1.2	1.4
Preparatory	6.0	3.2
Secondary	4.4	7.4
Grade failure		
Primary	9.1	6.0
Preparatory	16.6	6.6
Secondary	10.6	5.0
Grade repetition		
Primary	9.1	6.0
Preparatory	17.2	6.7
Secondary	11.6	5.5

SOURCE: Oman Ministry of National Economy, 2004, Table 5-6.

percent in 2000 (Oman Ministry of National Economy, 2004), the general perception of our respondents was that there are not enough graduates in the science and engineering fields to fill the needs of Oman's labor market. There is, however, an abundance of graduates in the humanities and in teaching. For example, at Sultan Qaboos University, Oman's national university, 61 percent of first-year students were enrolled in the education, arts and social sciences, and commerce and economics fields as of 2000–2001, and 39 percent were enrolled in the engineering, science, medicine, and agriculture fields.

More-recent figures draw further attention to this issue, although the numbers are improving. Table 5.10 is based on data collected on first university degrees by the U.S. NSF. According to these data, in 2000, only about 10 percent of Omani students graduating with a first degree were in the science and engineering fields (217 students out of a total

Table 5.10
Breakdown of First University Degrees Granted in Oman, 2000

	Degrees Granted (number)		
	Males	Females	Total
All fields	1,353	991	2,334
Science and engineering fields	146	71	217
Physical/biological sciences	36	15	51
Computer sciences	7	0	7
Agricultural sciences	5	40	45
Engineering	105	9	114
Social/behavioral sciences	0	0	0
Non-science and non-engineering fields	1,207	920	2,127
No. of persons in 24-year-old population	21,000	20,000	41,000
	Ratio of Persons Getting Degree to Population of 24-year-olds (percent)		
	Males	Females	Total
First university degree	6.4	5.0	5.7
Natural sciences or engineering degree	0.7	0.4	0.5
Social/behavioral sciences degree	0.0	0.0	0.0

SOURCE: NSF, 2006, Tables 2-37 and 2-39.

of 2,127). As Table 5.11 indicates, 56 percent of students registered in Sultan Qaboos University in 2004–2005 were majoring in the fields of education, arts, social sciences, and commerce; 44 percent were majoring in the fields of engineering, science, medicine, and agriculture.

Officials from the Oman Ministry of National Economy attested to the improvements in post-secondary education outcomes over the previous four years. They noted that private-sector leaders with whom they communicated had expressed more satisfaction with the quality of recent graduates from post-secondary institutions in Oman than they had in years past. According to our respondents, private-sector leaders also seemed pleased that the government was making a genuine effort to improve the skills of the country's graduates.

Table 5.11
Number of Students Registered for Bachelor's Degree in Oman, by College, Field of Study, and Gender, 2004–2005

	Students Registered for Bachelor's Degree		
College and Field of Study	Females	Males	Total
Sultan Qaboos University	5,975	5,957	11,932
Humanities and social sciences			
College of Education	1,697	1,090	2,787
College of Arts and Social Sciences	1,452	763	2,215
College of Commerce and Economics	726	977	1,703
Sciences and engineering			
College of Engineering	332	1,380	1,712
College of Science	850	716	1,566
College of Medicine and Health Sciences	495	480	975
College of Agriculture and Marine Science	423	551	974
Private colleges	11,850	9,828	21,678
Humanities and social sciences			
Shari'a and Law	162	552	714
Education[a]	5,192	3,462	8,654
Literature	859	330	1,189
Languages	15	1	16
Sciences and engineering			
Medicine and Pharmacy	415	111	526
Engineering	351	1,457	1,808
Computers	1,447	1,196	2,643
Commerce and Administrative Sciences	2,484	1,936	4,420
Sciences	118	26	144
Other[b]	969	1,309	2,278
Total	17,825	15,779	33,610

SOURCE: Oman Ministry of Higher Education, 2005a.

[a] Enrollment figures are combined for Colleges of Education in Oman and other private colleges that offer education as a field of study.

[b] Examples are information technology, hospitality, and tourism.

Income Inequality Is Another Area of Concern for Human Capital Development

As discussed in Chapter Two, Oman's 2004 GNI per capita of just over $9,000 places it among the countries defined by the World Bank as upper middle income. This level of per capita income is less than one-half that of Qatar and the UAE, both of which are defined as high-income countries. The UNDP HDI also places Oman at "medium" human development, below Qatar and the UAE, which are each at the "high" level of human development. Likewise, the Human Poverty Index that the UNDP computes based on various indicators (such as survival and literacy rates, nutrition and income levels, and basic infrastructure) places Oman at a lower standard of living than all three of the other countries in our study (UNDP, 2005).

Even though Oman has not yet developed an official poverty line, concerns about living standards have received attention in Oman's overall focus on human capital development (Oman Ministry of National Economy, 2004). The level of living standards and disparities across the Oman population have both been documented in a series of household income and expenditure surveys. The latest available published data are for 1999–2000. In the absence of a poverty measure, the 1999–2000 living standards survey data have been used to assess satisfaction among the Omani population on such outcomes as food, health, education, residence and environment, time use, social security, personal safety, and economic opportunities (Oman Ministry of National Economy, 2004). These data indicate that there are considerable disparities in the levels of satisfaction with living standards, particularly by geographic area (satisfaction is lowest in rural areas) and by education level of family head and family consumption (satisfaction decreases with the head of family's education level and family consumption). Family income and consumption also vary considerably by geographic area (again, satisfaction is lowest in rural areas) and are positively correlated with education level of family head. When poverty is gauged by the fraction of households whose food expenditures exceed 60 percent of total consumption, the poverty rate ranges from 2 percent, in the capitol region of Muscat, to 41 percent, in the most impoverished but sparsely populated region of Al Wusta.

While we did not identify data showing a link between low living standards and investments by families in their children's human capital, the 1999–2000 household income and expenditure data show that satisfaction with education outcomes is lower for families whose head has a low level of education (58 percent for families whose head has no formal education versus 70 percent for those whose head has a post-secondary education) (Oman Ministry of National Economy, 2004). In the poorer, rural regions outside the major metropolitan areas or further into the country's interior, access to primary and secondary schools is lower in terms of distance, and enrollment ratios lag those of wealthier urban areas. Thus, addressing disparities in family economic well-being is one potential approach for improving human capital attainment for more-disadvantaged persons.

The income data for Oman also reveal that family income is higher, for both Omani and non-Omani families, when the family head is employed in the public sector rather than the private sector. This may explain at least part of the nationals' attraction to public-sector employment; it also signals one of the challenges of moving more Omanis into the private sector (Oman Ministry of National Economy, 2004).

Approaches to Reform in Oman

Oman is facing a two-fold challenge to its stability and future growth (see Figure 5.5). First, Oman's dwindling oil resources have lowered the capacity of the public sector to employ Omani nationals and have necessitated changes in the country's economic structure. Second, the skills demanded by the labor market are not being met by the growing youth population that is entering the labor force. According to discussions with officials at the Oman Ministry of Civil Service, the growing youth population is placing a large demand for employment on the public sector, a sector that is saturated. In addition, the population needs more skills to compete in the new, knowledge economy.

These two issues are creating concerns about employing recent secondary and post-secondary school graduates. To address these con-

Figure 5.5
Schematic of Challenges Faced by Oman: Need to Meet the Challenges of a Changing Economy

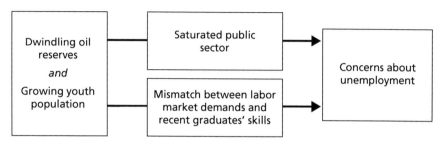

RAND MG786-5.5

cerns, Oman has implemented policies to diversify its economy and promote the growth of the private sector. Likewise, steps are being taken to develop the human capital of Omani nationals so that they are employable in major industries. In 1995, a conference was held to consider the future direction of the country's economic and social development. Out of this conference came what is known as Oman's Vision 2020, which states that the "acquisition of global knowledge, information and technology, and the development of advanced human skills are becoming essential prerequisites for progress" (as quoted in Oman Ministry of Education, 2004, p. 8). The Vision lists the following goals for Oman to achieve by the year 2020:

- An efficient and competitive private sector
- A diversified, dynamic globalized economy
- Well-developed human resources
- Sustainable development within a stable macroeconomic framework.

To reach these goals, the leadership in Oman has instituted a number of formal five-year development plans to promote diversification of the economy and the economic well-being of its citizens. Each plan focuses on macroeconomic balance and sustainable growth, economic diversification, private-sector development, and human resources development (Oman Ministry of National Economy, 2005a).

At the time of our study, Oman was at the end of the sixth plan (for 2001–2005) and at the beginning of the seventh (2006–2010), which are the second and third phases of Vision 2020's long-term strategy (1996–2020).

Two main goals of the sixth five-year development plan are (1) to raise citizens' rates of economic participation in the labor market and to harmonize labor market needs and education system outputs; and (2) to increase the contribution of the diversification sectors and improve the performance and productivity of the private sector. To achieve these goals, Oman's leadership is pursuing five interrelated approaches for developing the country's human resources and its economy:

1. Changing education curriculum and structure
2. Promoting the establishment of private universities and colleges
3. Increasing the number of vocational training opportunities and linking vocational training to private-sector needs
4. Diversifying the economy away from reliance on oil
5. Promoting privatization measures in the labor market.

The first three of these approaches pertain to the education system and the development of human resources. The last two address issues in the labor market and broader economy. We focus on the education reforms first.

Efforts to Reform the Education System and Develop Human Resources Are Under Way

Oman's Ministry of National Economy states that the "Development of Human Resources and upgrading the skills of Omani nationals—to keep abreast of technological changes, to meet the demands of a knowledge-based economy and of increasing globalization—[have] been and [continue] to be a policy area of highest importance in Oman's developmental planning" (Oman Ministry of National Economy, 2005c, p. 19). Oman's leadership has devoted substantial funds to promoting the development of human resources. The sixth five-year development plan allocated 473.3 million Omani rials (O.R.) by mid-

May 2005 to the "social structure" sector, which includes education, vocational training, health, information and culture, religious affairs, and social and youth centers. Total investment on education in the 2001–2004 period was about O.R. 234 million. Of this, O.R. 120 million was spent on general education, and O.R. 114 million was spent on higher education (Oman Ministry of National Economy, 2005a).[12]

The sixth five-year plan had a number of objectives for developing Oman's human resources:

- Increasing the percentage of intake in higher education institutions of graduates with general certificates, as well as upgrading and spreading basic education. The goal is to enable Omani youth to fill new employment opportunities and substitute for non-nationals, specifically to "increase the productivity of Oman's youths and prepare them to participate in establishing the pillars of [the] Knowledge Economy and improve the quality of their lives" (Oman Ministry of National Economy, 2005a, p. 29).
- Encouraging the expansion of private education
- Developing programs for the abolishment of illiteracy
- Expanding special-education facilities
- Developing education through:
  – Abolishing the double-shift system in schools
  – Developing research in education
  – Developing the assessment and evaluation system
  – Expanding the use of technology in schools
  – Developing the curriculum.

Since the mid-1990s, Oman has made steady progress in developing the human resources of its citizens by instituting changes to the structure and curriculum of the primary and secondary education system, post-secondary education reforms, and vocational training initiatives.

---

[12] In February 2008, 1 Omani rial was equivalent to U.S. $2.60.

Changes in Primary and Secondary Government-Funded Education
Having achieved the initial goal of providing education for all children in Oman, the government has recently changed priorities to focus on enhancing the quality of that education so that it is in line with the technological needs of the new, knowledge economy. The 1996 *Basic Statute of State* set general objectives for the education system: "to raise and develop the general cultural standard, promote scientific thought, kindle the spirit of research, respond to the requirements of economic and social plans, build a generation that is physically and morally strong and takes pride in its nation and heritage and preserves its achievements" (Oman Ministry of Education, 2004, p. 9).

To achieve these goals and to address the high repetition and dropout rates noted in Table 5.9, above, the structure and curriculum of the education system in Oman has changed in recent years. Most schools follow a "General" education system of 12 years: primary for six years, preparatory for three years, and secondary for three years. "Basic" education, which is 10 years in length, started replacing the General education system in academic year 1998–1999 for grade 1 and 2 students in 17 primary schools. By 2006–2007, 589 out of 1,642 schools were following the Basic education system, teaching over 250,000 students out of a total of over 813,000 (Oman Ministry of National Economy, 2008c). This Basic education reform is an attempt to improve critical thinking, problem solving, English knowledge, self-dependence, and the entrepreneurial spirit of youth. The first group of students to go through Basic education will be completing grade 12 in 2009.

The Basic education system comprises two cycles: The first cycle is from grade 1 to grade 4; the second cycle is from grade 5 to grade 10. Those who complete and pass the second cycle are promoted to two years of study, grades 11 and 12, of "post-Basic" education (Oman Ministry of Education, 2004). Students have the option of leaving school after grade 10 but must go to school for all 12 years if they want to enter higher education. The school year has been expanded from 160 days to 180 days, classroom periods from 35 minutes to 40 minutes, and the school day from 4 hours to 5 hours (Rassekh, 2004).[13]

In addition to establishing a structure for the progression across grades and extending the hours of study, the Basic education reform brings a number of curricular changes. The General education syllabus emphasizes Arabic language and Islamic studies, whereas the Basic education curriculum provides these subjects along with more teaching time for scientific, technical, vocational, and mathematical subjects (Oman Ministry of National Economy, 2004; Oman Ministry of Education, 2004). Compared with students in General education, Basic education students in grades 1 through 10 spend 44 percent more time on Arabic language, 89 percent more time on science, 90 percent more time on mathematics, and 122 percent more time on English language (Oman Ministry of Education, 1998).

Correspondence with officials at Oman's Ministry of Education pointed to other changes accompanying the Basic education reform:

- English is introduced in grade 1, rather than grade 4, as it had been in the earlier, General education system. According to our respondents in the Ministry of Education, English previously was not taught for functional use, and students outside of Oman's capital, Muscat, had very few opportunities to use the language. Since most higher education programs are now taught in English, youth need to learn how to *use* English. Presently, other subjects are not being taught in English, but policymakers are weighing the advantages and disadvantages of teaching other subjects, such as mathematics and science, in English.
- Information technology and environmental life skills are in the curriculum.
- Science laboratories and learning resource centers are provided.
- Curricular materials emphasize the acquisition of transferable skills rather than theory or abstract concepts alone. Materials

---

[13] Five hours is comparable to the length of a school day in Qatar's and the UAE's Ministry of Education schools.

provide students with opportunities for experiential learning and offer real-life contexts for application.
- Learning is student centered. According to our respondents in the Ministry of Education, the General education system was more teacher centered, which encouraged students to learn passively. One goal of the student-centered approach is to encourage students to be more self-reliant, since this is a skill they will need in higher education.
- Schools are encouraged to devise individual learning programs to meet the needs of both low- and high-achieving students.
- Cycle 2 schools (grades 5 to 10) are required to have at least one career guidance counselor per 500 students in anticipation of students' entering the labor market or post-Basic education grade 11. The Oman National Career Guidance Center provides trained counselors to work in schools.
- Assessments have shifted from testing memorization of information to testing higher thinking skills. A wide range of testing instruments has been introduced, including the replacement of an all-inclusive final exam with more-frequent formative classroom assessments to inform teachers of students' continuous progress.
- Classroom organization has changed. Schools are encouraged to rearrange classrooms so that they are more student centered.
- The qualifications of teachers with only two-year degrees were upgraded through in-place bachelor's degree programs in conjunction with University of Leeds for English language teachers and with Sultan Qaboos University for teachers of other subjects.
- Teachers are encouraged to use learning resources, various instruction methods and technologies, and materials—books, compact discs, and computers—in the classroom.

Officials at Oman's Ministry of Education explained that the post-Basic education in grades 11 and 12 aims to prepare students for life after school, whether for higher education or entry into the labor market. The post-Basic education offers a core curriculum plus a number of electives from which students can choose. The first set of students was set to enter the post-Basic education grade 11 in 2007–2008.

Courses being developed included computer programming, communications, computer engineering, graphic arts, geography, photography, fashion studies, entrepreneurship and accounting for small businesses, introduction to marketing, and hospitality and tourism, to name a few. To graduate, students would have to pass the exam for a General education certificate and complete a graduation project.

Although these changes were set to occur while most schools continued under the General education system, a number of improvements were also made to the General education system so that students in that system could reap similar benefits. These included

- The development of textbooks and teacher guides aligned with the Basic education system goals and phased into the General education schools
- As of September 2004, the commencement of General education school students' use of the Basic education books in grade 1; after that, introduction of new books annually in each successive grade
- The introduction of assessment reforms in the General education system schools so that assessments would rely less on rote memorization (Oman Ministry of Education, 2004)
- To make the curriculum relevant to the needs of students, the curtailment of the practice of tracking students into an arts or science stream in grades 11 and 12; secondary school students are instead offered a core curriculum with optional courses to choose from (e.g., pure mathematics or applied mathematics, which includes economics)
- As of 2006–2007, the requirement that secondary schools have one career guidance counselor per 500 students.

The Basic education reform seems to be taking hold, but it is still too early to tell with any confidence. According to data provided by officials from the Oman Ministry of Education, rates of school dropout and grade repetition have declined from previously levels. Comparison of the numbers in Table 5.9 and those in Table 5.12 shows that school performance has improved for both males and females at all educa-

Table 5.12
Gross Rates of Student Dropout and Grade Repetition in Oman, by Education Level and Gender, 2005

Outcome and Education Level	Gross Rate (percent)	
	Males	Females
Dropout[a]		
Primary	0.2	0.2
Preparatory	2.3	1.1
Secondary	4.2	2.0
Grade repetition[b]		
Primary	0.6	0.9
Preparatory	0.7	0.7
Secondary	1.4	0.5

SOURCE: Oman Ministry of National Economy, 2005d.
[a] Government and private schools.
[b] Government schools only.

tion levels: Dropout and grade repetition rates went down in all school levels from 2000 to 2005.

Post-Secondary Education Reform Efforts

Commensurate with its efforts to enhance the learning experience of its children, Oman has made great strides in expanding its post-secondary education choices. Sultan Al Qaboos University was established in 1986, and a number of other private colleges and universities have subsequently opened. In 1994, the Oman Ministry of Higher Education was established by Royal Decree 2/94 to implement education and research plans and supervise programs offered by institutes of higher education.

In 1996, Royal Decree 41/96 invited the private sector to open institutes of higher education (Oman Ministry of Information, 2008b). A large and diversified system of private higher education has been built in a little over a decade. According to officials from the Oman Ministry of Higher Education, the system of private higher education grew rapidly from one college in 1995 to the present complement of 22, including three private universities, with close to 17,000 new entrants each year (16,842 in semester one of 2005–2006). Private colleges and universities as of academic year 2004–2005 are listed in Appendix D.

To encourage private higher education institutions, the Oman Ministry of Higher Education is authorized to give a package of incentives to private universities that includes free land, exemption from taxes and duties, and an O.R. 3,000,000 matching grant from public funds. Total government expenditure increased from about O.R. 362 million in 2000 to O.R. 514 million in 2004—an average annual growth of about 9.2 percent (Oman Ministry of National Economy, 2005a). The government encourages investment in private higher education in the hopes of encouraging students to pursue such new fields of study as engineering, information technology, and business. Although the increased presence of institutes of higher education has expanded local options for Omanis, the number of slots appears to be below what is needed to fill the demand for higher education from Omani secondary school graduates. A considerable number of Omanis go abroad for their post-secondary education (Oman Cultural Office, 2008).

While increasing the opportunities for post-secondary education has been an important accomplishment, giving thousands of students access to higher education in Oman, the Ministry of Higher Education is also focusing on quality improvement. In September 1998, Oman issued a decree establishing a Council for Higher Education. One function of this council is to accredit institutions of higher education. Whether state or privately owned, all institutions of higher education must conform to the requirements of Oman's System of Quality Assurance in Higher Education and be accredited by the Accreditation Board of the Council for Higher Education. The Oman Ministry of Higher Education oversees and manages this process. In addition, all higher education programs must be accredited and fully recognized under the National Qualifications Framework for Higher Education in Oman, which was approved by the Council for Higher Education for adoption by the Accreditation Board. According to officials at the Ministry of Higher Education, a number of initiatives are under way within the Ministry to further improve the quality of institutions of higher education, including the development of a network among Oman's higher education institutions for the purpose of improving quality assurance practices and sharing best practices. Training of Accreditation Board Secretariat staff and Oman Ministry of Higher Education staff in world standard quality assurance practices has already begun.

In addition, the Oman Ministry of Higher Education has embarked on a plan to develop a system of higher education that is both comprehensive and diverse, covering the full range of programs available in modern countries. To that end, the Ministry has been working with the Oman Ministry of Education to formulate a comprehensive strategic plan for education at all levels—primary, secondary, and post-secondary. The major objective of the proposed strategic plan is to align Oman's systems of education with labor market needs to help Oman gain a competitive advantage in the global economy. The plan emphasizes "learning that is fit for purpose" in helping students acquire the skills needed for the job market and for higher education, and it places a high priority on both the quantity and quality of education—i.e., on expanding the provision of education while improving the quality of education to reach international standards at all levels from early childhood education and Basic education to post-graduate studies. The proposed strategic plan includes five integrated strategies: management of Oman's system of education, student participation and progression through that system, building of quality at all levels, research and development, and funding to support the reformed education system.

The Oman Ministry of Higher Education has also instituted a number of structural changes to the higher education system to accommodate the growing needs of Oman's labor market. Following Oman's success over the past decade in training a sufficient supply of teachers to meet internal needs, five of the six government Colleges of Education were converted to Colleges of Applied Science offering information technology, communications, design, and international business administration. According to Ministry of Education officials, the new colleges aim to assist in human resource development to meet the needs of Oman's increasingly diversified economy.[14]

Oman is also committed to educating all segments of the Omani population. The Oman Ministry of Higher Education provides scholarships for students from low-income Omani families to enter post-secondary education. The goal is to have one or two children in each family educated beyond secondary school. Educating females has also become a priority. The first colleges for females in Oman, the Mazoon College for Management and Applied Sciences and Al-Zahra College for Girls, opened in 1999 (Oman Ministry of Higher Education, 2005b).

Vocational Training Programs

To respond to the increased need to train Omanis so that they will be prepared for jobs in the private sector and to increase the quality and number of Omanis in the labor market in general, Oman's leadership established the Ministry of Manpower in 2002.[15] This Ministry provides vocational training and technical education for secondary school graduates who do not go on to college; it also compiles data on non-nationals, jobs, and levels of Omanization, or the extent to which Omanis are represented in the economy. The Oman Ministry of Manpower operates four vocational training centers and five technical colleges open only to nationals.[16] The centers deliver vocational programs

---

[14] A number of private colleges offer specialized programs in business, information technology, tourism and hospitality, medicine, marine science, and port management. The six government Colleges of Technology offer a full range of vocational and technical programs. Furthermore, Sultan Qaboos University has seven different colleges offering all the major higher education programs: engineering, information technology, medicine, science, agriculture, business, education, humanities, and law. The new private universities at Sohar, Nizwa, and Salalah also offer a diverse range of programs. Appendix D lists the programs of the colleges and universities.

[15] In 2002, the Ministry of Manpower and Social Development divided into the Ministry of Manpower and the Ministry of Social Development.

[16] The five technical colleges are the Higher College of Technology in Muscat, Al Musanna College of Technology, Ibra College of Technology, Nizwa College of Technology, and Salalah College of Technology.

on both semi-skilled and skilled levels; the colleges target the highly skilled technician level, running post-secondary programs only.

The Ministry of Manpower also partners with private-sector employers to train prospective employees for entry-level placements. Training usually lasts from 6 to 24 months. The Ministry introduced the partnerships to better serve the needs of private-sector employers. The hope was that councils would be established in each occupational sector. To date, only one business society, the Oman Society for Petroleum Services (known as OPAL), has been established to bring together companies in the oil and gas sector to support Omanization, workforce training and development, and use of best practices in employment and business (Oman Society for Petroleum Services, 2008). Other occupation sectors do not have official entities; instead, leading business people and members of the Ministry meet on an unofficial basis to determine training needs. According to officials from the Oman Ministry of Manpower, the Ministry spent O.R. 26 million in 2004 to solidify these partnerships and the trainings offered, by mutual choice of the employers and the Ministry.

Before the Oman Ministry of Manpower existed, training programs were imported from abroad. However, according to our interviewees in the Ministry of Manpower, most of these programs encountered challenges in the Omani context, attributed primarily to lack of coordination with the needs of the private sector. In response to the lessons learned from failed initiatives, the Oman Ministry of Manpower now develops its own curriculum and certification for public technical colleges and institutes. Students receive the Oman Vocational Qualification (OVQ). The Ministry uses recommendations from private-sector companies and receives informal feedback from them on how the programs are going.

Oman's Ministry of Civil Service offers training for Omanis employed by the government, tailored to each government agency's needs. Since the 1970s, training planning has been a major requirement of the Oman Ministry of Civil Service. It accomplishes this goal through a number of initiatives. First, it established the General Administration Institute in 1977, an institute that administers training and professional development of government employees. The training provided depends on the skills needed and the government organization—for example, some government institutions are looking for administrative assistance, others for finance, others for computer knowledge. Second, the Ministry created specialized training centers that are linked to specific government bodies: the Diplomatic Institute for the Oman Ministry of Foreign Affairs; the Agricultural and Fishing Training Center for the Oman Ministry of Agriculture and Fishing; and the Training Center for the Ministry of Municipalities, Environment, and Water Resources.

Third, the Ministry of Civil Service prepares and implements annual training programs for all government employees through a newly created Training and Preparations Department, which monitors and oversees the training of government employees in collaboration with the General Administration Institute and the specialized training centers. Article 56 of the Civil Services Law issued by Sultan Decree 120 in 2004 stipulates that the Ministry of Civil Service establish standards and criteria for annual training programs of all government ministries. These standards and criteria are developed as part of the Unified Training Strategy Project. Each September, as part of this project, the Training and Preparation Department distributes a training plan and provides standards that government ministries employ to design their training programs. The ministries then determine the training needs of their employees and submit a proposal to the Department, which discusses the proposals and submits a report to the Oman Ministry of Civil Service Council for endorsement. Once training proposals have been approved, government ministries can proceed with the needed training.

The fourth initiative is the Workforce Investment Program, which is internal to the Oman Ministry of Civil Service. This program seeks to change the work processes and operations within the Ministry of Civil Service as a way to improve productivity and increase efficiency. It does this by diagnosing Ministry employee training needs, distributing training opportunities among employees efficiently, assigning positions to employees in accordance with their qualifications, and improving the image of the Ministry by enhancing the work satisfaction and motivation of Ministry employees.

A law in place on January 1, 2006, sets new policies governing the Oman Ministry of Civil Service so that the Ministry is further involved in manpower planning in the government sector. New initiatives included are

- Determining the needs of the government sector.
- Working with the World Bank to develop a comprehensive framework for employment in the government sector.
- Simplifying procedures and processes of the kinds of services used by nationals so that nationals can look up jobs and information on the Internet.
- Building a database so that the procedures required by other ministries can be performed electronically (although other ministries may be averse to change and will need training on how to perform requests over the Internet).
- Classifying and defining government jobs and developing job descriptions that the Council of Civil Service and Council of Ministers will agree on.
- Commissioning a study to examine the government organizational chart to determine what the role of the civil services should be. Officials in the Ministry of Civil Service envision that the Ministry will move toward more of a consultancy role (e.g., providing assistance on classification and advising other ministries on legal status and other civil service laws).
- Centralizing the government job registration process. Some government jobs are not registered, and civil service laws apply only to those that are. For example, government bodies inform the civil service about jobs that are open. The civil service in turn advertises for those jobs and then organizes the evaluation and screening of applicants.

Training also exists within government ministries (e.g., to improve English or computer skills). Some current training initiatives are

- On-the-job performance-based standards.
- Skills identification and recruitment system in the government sector.
- Evaluation, support, and strengthening of existing government programs that provide training (e.g., Oman Ministry of Health professional training programs).
- Cooperation with Rotterdam Port to provide training on all levels of technical skills.
- Cooperation among Oman Ministry of Oil and Gas, the quasi-private and private oil sector, and education institutions such as the Maritime College, under the guidance and monitoring of the Training and Development Unit of the Oman Ministry of Civil Service. The oil and gas companies in Oman provide funds to support the training of prospective Omani employees.

In addition to these government-funding training initiatives, there are 150 private training centers in Oman. The Training and Development Unit of the Oman Ministry of Civil Service publishes a guide on private training centers that government bodies can turn to for training needs. This is seen as a way to increase collaboration between the public and private sectors and to better serve the human resource development needs of the government.

The challenge for many vocational training providers is to have nationals remain with a profession after they complete training. Similar to what happens in Qatar and the UAE, job-hopping of nationals is apparently common. Although no statistics are available to ascertain the numbers of Omanis that move from one job to another after completing a training program, leaders in the private sector and officials in the government ministries with whom we spoke expressed concern that this practice was rampant. Another challenge noted by many government officials with whom we spoke was that private-sector employers often lose nationals to the public sector. Generally, the private sector has not provided the same level of job security as the government sector, which affects their ability to retain Omanis. To address this issue, the government has recently provided comparable job protections for private-sector jobs held by nationals.

Labor Market Initiatives: Economy Diversification and Privatization Efforts

In addition to improving the quality of the Omani education system to enhance Oman's human resources, the government has taken steps to diversify its economy to improve economic stability and sustainability. It has also introduced measures to promote the employment of Omanis through Omanization policies.

As a way to reduce Oman's dependence on oil and expatriate labor, the government wants to increase its spending on industrial and tourism-related projects in the hopes that this will foster income diversification, job creation for Omanis in the private sector, and development of Oman's less developed interior region. Government programs offer soft loans and propose the building of new industrial estates in regions outside the capital area. The government is giving greater emphasis to Omanization, particularly in banking, hotels, and municipally sponsored shops benefiting from government subsidies. In addition, efforts are under way to liberalize investment opportunities in order to attract foreign capital (U.S. Department of State, 2007b).

The seventh five-year plan, already under way, has several key goals:

- To achieve growth rates, at constant prices, with annual averages of not less than 3 percent
- To upgrade citizens' standard of living and maintain the currently low levels of inflation
- To improve the general education output and expand higher education opportunities
- To prioritize the employment of nationals and formulate a clear and specific program for Omanization (Oman Ministry of National Economy, 2005a).

A number of initiatives to achieve the goals outlined in this five-year plan have taken effect. They are summarized here in terms of economic diversification, promotion of the private sector, and Omanization. Detailed descriptions are provided in Appendix E.

Economic Diversification. To stem the reliance on oil for its national wealth, Oman has pursued a number of economic initiatives over the past decade. In 2000, Oman opened a liquefied natural gas plant that has proven quite productive: Natural gas production was estimated in 2003 at 16.5 billion cubic meters, and natural gas reserves are at 829.1 billion cubic meters. Furthermore, the Omani Center for Investment Promotion and Export Development was established in 1996 to boost local and international private-sector investment in key economic sectors. A key function is to provide assistance to foreign investors. (Oman Ministry of National Economy, 2005c).

Oman is also actively developing its manufacturing and industrial sectors. It has opened two new ports, one in Salalah (1997) and one in Sohar (2002), in tandem with an industrial zone, and a new port was expected to be in operation in 2007 in the Duqum area. Manufacturing and industrial zones dot the country—in Rusayl, Sohar, Raysut, Sur, Nizwa, Buraimi, and the Al Mazunah Free Trade Zone. Efforts to develop the industrial sector reach back to the establishment in 1993 of the Public Establishment for Industrial Estates (PEIE), a government organization responsible for developing industrial land and acting as a liaison for manufacturing businesses and the Oman government. The PEIE assists companies in assembling sites, developing buildings, assessing infrastructure needs, reviewing incentives available for projects, and helping firms market and promote their products. It works closely with the Oman Ministry of Commerce and Industry; the Oman Chamber of Commerce; the Oman Center for Investment, Promotion, and Export Development; permit-issuing and regulatory organizations; and utility providers.

Each of these initiatives has bolstered Oman's economic sustainability through the years, lessening the country's reliance on dwindling oil revenues. Estimates for 2005 of GDP contribution by sector indicate that the industrial sector is at 40 percent, the services sector at 57 percent, and the agriculture sector at 3 percent.

Promotion of the Private Sector. To generate jobs for its citizenry and strengthen the industrial, trade, and commercial sectors, Oman's government has looked to ways to promote the private sector. From divestment strategies in public utilities and petroleum companies, to privatization laws that allow for 100 percent foreign ownership of companies in selected fields accompanied by lower tax rates, Oman is working actively to build a strong private sector. In doing so, Omani leadership has paved the way for lower reliance on the public sector as a primary form of employment for nationals and has looked for ways in which nationals can invest in, and therefore sustain, their own country.

Oman has established a number of tax free zones and technology parks in recent years to attract international investment and Omani business development. The most comprehensive technology park in Oman, Knowledge Oasis Muscat (KOM), is located outside of Muscat; it is dedicated to supporting technology-oriented businesses. KOM provides necessary infrastructure for businesses. Targeted tenants are entrepreneurs, researchers, and small- and medium-sized enterprises, or more established multinationals. KOM incentives include 100 percent foreign ownership, no personal income tax and no foreign exchange controls, tax and import-duty exemptions for eligible companies for five years (with option to renew for another five years), and duty-free access to products from Oman and GCC countries. KOM houses two private technical colleges, Waljat College of Applied Sciences and the Middle East College of Information Technology, to promote practical experience for students and research connections across faculty and businesses (Knowledge Oasis Muscat, 2008).

As a way to attract investment in Oman, the government has opened a number of free trade zones. Al Mazunah Free Zone, which has been operating since 1999, is located in Oman's southern region of Dhofar, close to the border with Yemen. It lies outside Oman's tax boundaries, and business personnel can enter Al Mazunah without a visa. Other developments on this front are a free trade agreement with the United States (the U.S.-Oman Free Trade Agreement) that was signed into U.S. law on September 26, 2006 (Bolle, 2006). Oman has also taken part in free trade agreement discussions among the GCC, of which it is a member, and the European Union and Turkey. An Arab Free Trade Area (which would include India, Pakistan, and Singapore) is a separate initiative (outside the GCC agreement) that is also in the planning stage.

Oman also promulgated the Foreign Capital Investment Law in 1994 to attract non-Omani investors. This law was amended in 2003 to allow non-Omanis to conduct a business in Oman with a license from the Oman Ministry of Commerce and Industry. Although foreigners are not allowed to own more than 49 percent of a company, exceptions of up to 65 percent and even 100 percent ownership can be made for "projects which contribute to the development of the national economy" upon the approval of the Council of Ministers (Oman Ministry of National Economy, 2005a, p. 47). In addition, companies in specific sectors, such as industry, tourism, and farming, can be exempt from taxes for up to 10 years.

The development of local markets to create jobs across the country, rather than just in Muscat, and to provide fiscal incentives for people to start their own businesses is a recent initiative. Oman offers soft loans and grants for young people to start businesses through the Sanad program (Oman Chamber of Commerce and Industry, 2008), which is managed by the Oman Ministry of Manpower. It operates a revolving fund of O.R. 2 million that offers small, subsidized loans of up to O.R. 5,000 to young people who leave school and unemployed Omanis, the goal being to foster self-employment. This program has contributed to the Omanization of trade and small businesses. Funds are dispersed by the Oman Development Bank, and the targeted sectors include grocery shops (sale of foodstuffs), vegetable and fruit shops, sale of ready-made garments, car washes, Internet cafés, butchery shops, and carpentry shops. A smaller program, Intelaca, trains Omanis to start businesses.

Other initiatives include a labor law adopted in May 2003 that gives employees more rights and sets a uniform minimum wage for nationals to replace the previous two-tiered (skilled and unskilled) minimum wage (Fasano and Iqbal, 2003).

Omanization. For much of Oman's modern history, a foreign workforce shaped the physical and administrative infrastructure of the country, with a large disparity between oil-producing and non-oil-producing companies. In 1990, nationals in the oil-sector workforce made up 61 percent. Among the major companies in the oil sector, nationals made up 61 percent of the workforce for Petroleum Development Oman, 53 percent for Elf Aquitaine Total Oman, 20 percent for Occidental Oman, and 21 percent for Japex Oman. In non-oil-producing companies, nationals on average made up 32 percent of the workforce as of 1990. In the banking sector, 70 percent of the work force was nationals; in the insurance sector, nationals were 24 percent; in the hotel sector, 19 percent (Metz, 1994). To ensure the employment of Omani people, the Omani government has developed a number of Omanization policies.

According to discussion with officials in the Oman Ministry of National Economy, Oman's goals have been to increase the proportion of nationals in the banking sector to 90 percent (which the country has done in recent years), in the industrial areas to 50 percent, and in construction to 35 percent. The sixth five-year plan outlines the following goals (Oman Ministry of National Economy, 2005a):

- Raising the Omanization ratios in private-sector establishments and increasing productivity in government bodies
- Increasing the Omani labor force from 17 percent to 50 percent of the total workforce population.
- Increasing the Omanization percentage in the government sector to 95 percent. (The Omanization percentage in the government sector was 75 percent in 1990 and decreased to 65 percent in 2000.)
- Increasing the Omanization percentage in the private sector to 75 percent. (This share increased from 25 percent in 1990 to 31 percent in 2000.)

Oman has taken steps to promote the employability of Omanis. More than 17 joint sectoral committees—with members from the private sector, public sector, and Oman Chamber of Commerce and Industry—have been formed to enhance and expand private-sector and government roles in the field of training and employment. These committees address the structure of labor and formulate training and Omanization plans, identifying such requirements as time schedules, employment relations, and wage policies (Oman Ministry of National Economy, 2005a). Based on the recommendations of these committees, the Ministry of National Economy has fixed Omanization targets in six areas of the private sector and offers certain benefits to businesses that meet Omanization targets. These rewards include a certificate for meeting Omanization targets, having the company name published in the local press, and preferential treatment in dealings with the Ministry (Oman Ministry of Information, 2008a).

The field of education has made great Omanization success. Historically, teachers in Oman have been predominantly non-nationals. This dependency on foreign staff often brought about high turnover rates and a lack of continuity. In academic year 1980–1981, only 618 of a total of 5,663 teachers, or 11 percent of the teaching staff, were nationals. By 1985–1986, the proportion had increased to 18 percent. The majority of Ministry of Education employees (55 percent in 1990) were also non-nationals: more than 70 percent Egyptians, and 30 percent Jordanians, Pakistanis, Sudanese, Indians, Filipinos, and others (Metz, 1994). The government has responded by emphasizing teacher training for nationals in order to create an indigenous teaching force. Furthermore, the government has made Omanization in the educational colleges a high priority. As of 2003, the total number of staff working in the educational colleges was 1,051; of these people, 633 were faculty, 94 of them nationals (approximately 15 percent of the total). Academic support staff numbered 213, of whom 205 were nationals (97 percent of the total) and 8 (4 percent) were non-nationals. Administrative staff were 100 percent nationals. Oman Ministry of Higher Education staff on scholarships for higher degrees (master's degrees and doctorates) numbered approximately 37, with a further 12 expected to go abroad for the same purpose in 2004 and 2005 (Oman Ministry of Information, 2008a).

Omanization efforts have also met success in the banking industry. According to discussions with officials from the Oman Ministry of National Economy, the largest area of Omanization has been the banking industry, with current estimates indicating that 91 percent of banking employees are nationals, which means the sector has reached its Omanization goals. Other successes include the hotel and hospitality sector, whose key to success has been funding for training and cooperation with private-sector employees. Transportation is also seen as a success for Omanization, because non-nationals are not permitted to drive cabs. Figure 5.6 gives the Omanization percentages by private-sector area for 2005.

Foundation for Data Collection in Support of Decisionmaking Is in Place

To be able to adequately determine the country's economic and labor market needs, Oman established, in 1997, the Oman Ministry of National Economy, which is responsible for nationwide planning and development, national expenditures, general workforce development, and nationwide statistical and survey development and administration (including the census). The primary mission of the Ministry of National Economy is to formulate economic policies and programs to

Figure 5.6
Omanization Rates, by Area of Private Sector, 2005

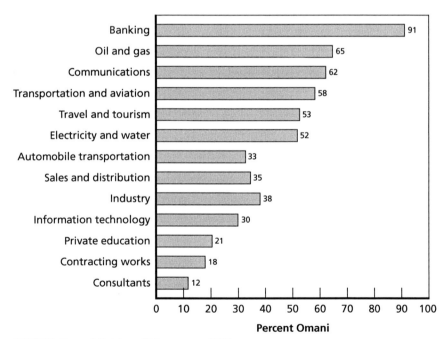

SOURCE: Oman Ministry of Manpower, 2006.
RAND MG786-5.6

achieve development objectives stipulated in Oman's Vision 2020 (Oman Ministry of Education, 2004). In addition to its own data collection efforts, the Ministry draws on data from other ministries to shape the five-year plans; it also monitors and evaluates implementation of programs under those plans. Additionally, it publishes a monthly statistical bulletin to disseminate economic, demographic, and social indicators (Oman Ministry of National Economy, 2008a).

The Information and Publication Center is one of the Oman Ministry of National Economy's offices and the main center for database processing and storage. It is also the main center for dissemination of economic and social statistics in Oman in order to ensure timely and efficient flow of information for the purposes of project formulation, monitoring and evaluation, and general research and public awareness (Oman Ministry of National Economy, 2008a). It develops two main databases, the Social Economic Database, which contains statistical data from 1970 on a number of major social and economic sectors, and the National Geographic Database, which contains data on all geographic levels (regions, districts, towns, and villages). The center also designs Oman's major surveys, such as the national census, household surveys, and establishment surveys (Oman Ministry of National Economy, 2008a). Royal Decree 29/2001, enacted April 7, 2001, entrusts the Directorate General of Economic Statistics and the Directorate General of Social Statistics of the Ministry of National Economy with the responsibility for collecting and disseminating statistics and for carrying out surveys and population censuses for Oman (Oman Ministry of National Economy, 2008b).

Oman's population and labor force data collection efforts include (IMF, 2005; Oman Ministry of National Economy, 2008b)

- *A decennial census.* The first population census, conducted in 1993, was expanded in 2003 to cover population, housing, and establishments. The census data include information on the labor force. Oman plans to participate in the 2010 census coordinated with the GCC.
- *A household expenditure and income survey.* An initial survey was fielded from 1991 to 1992; a second one spanned three years,

from 1999 to 2002. A third survey began in May 2006 and was to take place over 12 months. Ultimately, the Ministry of National Economy plans to conduct an ongoing survey over five consecutive years to allow sufficient sample sizes for estimation of small geographic areas.
- *A periodic labor force survey.* The first survey was conducted in 1996, and another followed in 2000. The most recent survey was fielded in 2006. Plans call for a survey every five years.

Other data collection efforts include an annual survey of business establishments and several specialized surveys of individual establishments.

The Ministry of National Economy established the Statistics Advisory Committee to organize the various surveys and data collection efforts of government entities in Oman. The first meeting was held in 2004. The Committee is working toward establishing a central database that will organize information about the surveys and statistical research under way in Oman. Other goals of the Committee are to coordinate and prioritize statistics plans of government units, unify statistical terminology, encourage research based on statistics, and approve any publications of official statistics results (Oman Ministry of National Economy, 2008a, 2008b). In an effort to organize and develop its economic, population, and manpower indicators, Oman joined the IMF's GDDS (IMF, undated; 2005).

In June 2005, a royal decree established Oman's National Science Research Council, which is mandated to

- Formulate a strategy with a nationally integrated plan for research and monitor its development
- Identify national research priorities and develop one or more programs to implement them
- Publicize the national research plan and its priorities with the objective of supporting research activities
- Support individual innovation and research programs in accordance with the set national research priorities
- Support scientific publications.

As part of its investment program, the National Science Research Council proposed the establishment of a Science and Technology Valley as a first step toward building a state-of-the-art science and technology center. The Science and Technology Valley is to bring together the future Sultan Qaboos University cultural center, the KOM, an industrial estate, the national Armed Forces Hospital, and the Sultan Qaboos University hospital. The Valley will include clusters for innovation and strategic studies, as well as a medical cluster, a cluster for oil and gas, and a cluster for water, environment, and biotechnology.

Summary

Given its large youth population, relatively wide disparities in income and quality of living standards within its citizenry population, and dwindling revenues from natural resources, Oman faces hurdles that the other two Gulf nations in our study, Qatar and the UAE, do not currently face. In 1995, Oman's leadership developed its Vision 2020, which laid out a set of five-year plans for enhancing Oman's economy that covered the education and labor market sectors (Ministry of Education, 2004). Compared to Qatar and the UAE, Oman has had the longest time to develop and implement a vision for its education and labor market.

Since 1995, Oman has been initiating reforms to its elementary, secondary, and post-secondary education systems, and it more recently began making improvements to its post-secondary education sector by bringing in foreign universities and vocational institutions. The government has also developed partnerships with private-sector employers to train nationals for the job market. A number of labor market reforms have also been initiated, such as an Omanization policy to encourage employment of qualified nationals in the private sector and to support entrepreneurial nationals who start their own businesses. Table 5.13 lists the gamut of reforms under way.

Oman's primary and secondary education reforms are intended to meet the needs of the globalized, knowledge economy. Seeking to gradually implement education changes in the country, members of

Table 5.13
Summary of Education and Labor Market Reforms Under Way in Oman

Reform Categories and Subcategories
Education and training
Primary and secondary education
School organizational change
Restructured curriculum
Training for teachers and administrators
Integration of information technology
Post-secondary and post-graduate education
Requirement for academic accreditation of post-secondary education institutions
Scholarship programs (for low-income students/in targeted fields and institutions)
Establishment of private higher education institutions
Training system
Establishment of technical/vocational colleges
Public-private partnerships to train nationals
Labor market and economy
Labor market reforms
Establishment of goals for employment of nationals in private sector, residency restrictions, and penalties for hiring non-nationals to increase the share of Omanis in the workforce
Equalization of worker rights or access to benefits in public and private sectors
Training and financial support for nationals to start new businesses
Other economic reforms
Allowance of foreign ownership of companies in selected sectors
Incentives to expand peripheral industries
Establishment of free zones exempt from government requirements
Implementation of free trade agreements and free trade zones
Divestment of government-owned companies

the Ministry of Education deliberately decided to transition the education system from the established General system to the new Basic system in only a few grades and schools each year. Therefore, the small proportion of students in the Basic program (rather than the General program) has not changed much since the reform's inception. In consequence, the portion of students graduating from the Basic system is small, making it difficult to tell whether the reform's goals are taking hold.

It is also difficult to determine whether the training initiatives under way in the country are meeting their intended goals. Numerous programs are available for nationals, but it is not clear whether there is an overall strategy or unifying force organizing these programs. When asked how the success of training programs is measured, our interviewees stated that the feedback received is informal in nature; there is no formalized feedback system that would enable officials to determine success.

While Omanization policies seem to be assisting nationals in finding jobs in the private sector, particularly in the banking sector, Oman is facing a contradiction similar to one being faced by the UAE: The existence of free trade zones, in which labor laws are not enforced, may significantly deter employers from hiring nationals. Furthermore, no link has yet been established between the education and manpower sectors to coordinate education, training, and employment initiatives. Perhaps Oman's strategic plan (still in draft form at the time of our study) will offset the lack of coordination among the sectors.

CHAPTER SIX
Lebanon

Lebanon, the one Arab country in our study that is not a Gulf state, borders disputed land and is caught in the heart of the Arab-Israeli conflict. Despite being geographically small, Lebanon has a heterogeneous population that represents diverse ethnic and religious groups and is thus particularly susceptible to the region's extended political turmoil. The 15-year civil war that began in 1975 demarcates a devastating period in the history of modern Lebanon. During the war, most of the country's infrastructure was damaged, hundreds of thousands of Lebanese were killed or injured, and around one-quarter of the population was displaced. The ramifications of the immense economic, social, and political destruction caused by this conflict continue to surface and obstruct full recovery 16 years after the war's end.

Lebanon faces a different mix of challenges than the three Gulf countries in our study face. In contrast to the countries that rely predominantly on natural resources and have large public sectors, Lebanon enjoys a strong and talented local workforce and a robust private sector. It has always compensated for its lack of natural resources by capitalizing on the wealth of its skilled local human resources. Yet the continued political instability has brought about a brain drain: Large numbers of skilled and qualified Lebanese citizens continue to leave Lebanon for countries all over the world in pursuit of a more prosperous and stable future. Lebanon also must contend with disparities in living conditions that generate differences in access to and quality of education opportunities. This chapter provides an overview of recent measures Lebanon has taken to develop, retain, and use the human resources of its population through economic reforms designed to promote economic growth and raise living standards and through efforts to create a more efficient and effective public sector.

We begin the chapter by providing background on Lebanon's political history, economy, population, education system, and labor force. We then highlight the key human resource challenges faced by the country using analyses of secondary data and information from interviews conducted with government officials and private-sector leaders from January to June of 2006, which was prior to the onset of the 2006 conflict between Hezbollah and Israel.[1,2] Third, we describe the policy approaches to addressing the human resource problems, listed in Table 6.1. In contrast to the other countries in this study, Lebanon has

Table 6.1
Human Capital Reforms Covered in Lebanon Case Study

Reform Categories and Subcategories
Education and training
Primary and secondary education
Post-secondary and post-graduate education
Training
Labor market and economy
Labor market reforms
Economic privatization
Economic diversification

---

[1] Our period of data collection, including in-country interviews, occurred for the most part prior to the armed conflict that erupted between Israel and Lebanon on July 12, 2006. Thus, much of the information we present reflects the situation in Lebanon and the focus of public-sector reform efforts prior to these hostilities. While many of the challenges we identified continue to be valid, in some cases they have intensified or become more complex as a result of the recent conflict and efforts to address the need the country's economic, political, and social recovery. The process of recovery may change Lebanon's priorities and reform efforts in directions neither addressed nor anticipated in our study.

[2] Appendix A lists the organizations and government ministries in which we held our interviews.

engaged in broader-based economic reforms, given its need to restore the health of its economy following the civil war and presumably the July 2006 altercations between Hezbollah and Israel that occurred within its borders. In consequence, Lebanon has not yet had the resources or attention to devote to more-focused education and training system reforms.

In the remainder of the chapter, we discuss the data resources available to assess Lebanon's progress in human capital development and other economic outcomes, concluding with a summary of our analyses.

Overview of Lebanon

A relatively small country, Lebanon covers 10,452 square kilometers in southwest Asia on the eastern coast of the Mediterranean Sea. Figure 6.1 is a map of Lebanon; as it shows, Lebanon is surrounded by Syria to the north and east and shares, on the south, a border with Israel, including the Israeli-occupied Golan Heights. Lebanon has a narrow coastal plain and two parallel mountain ranges separated by the fertile Bekaa Valley.

The country is divided into six administrative regions that are each headed by a governor: Beirut, North Lebanon, South Lebanon, Mount Lebanon, Nabatiyah, and Bekaa. Bekaa is the largest administrative region, followed by North Lebanon and Mount Lebanon (Lebanon Ministry of Environment, 2001). Beirut, the most populous city in Lebanon, serves as the capital and the center of commerce and trade.

One of the most distinctive features of Lebanon is its heterogeneous society characterized by varied ethnic and religious subgroups. The country is home to a number of religions, including several distinct Christian and Muslim sects. In particular, the present Lebanese Constitution officially acknowledges the following 18 religious groups: Maronite (Catholic), Greek Orthodox, Greek Catholics, Armenian Orthodox (Gregorian), Armenian Catholic, Syriac Orthodox (Jacobite), Syriac Catholic, Roman Catholic (Latins), Copts, Evangelical

**Figure 6.1
Map of Lebanon**

SOURCE: U.S. Department of State, 2007a.
RAND MG786-6.1

Christian (including Protestant groups such as Baptists and Seventh-Day Adventists), Chaldean Catholics, Nestorian Assyrian, Twelver Shiite, Sunni, Isma'ili, Druze, Alawite, and Jewish. Arabic, French, Armenian, and English are the primary languages spoken in Lebanon, with Arabic being the official language. The use of English in the business community is gaining ground, and English is increasingly spoken among Lebanese youth (U.S. Department of State, 2007a). In addition, the country encompasses a mosaic of cultures and ethnic groups that have assimilated to some extent over the centuries but still maintain some distinct divisions.

The delicacy of the subject of religious diversity and sectarian balance—and of the political and social implications of data related to that subject—has caused a reluctancy on the part of consecutive Lebanese governments to conduct a national census that would highlight the different religions' and groups' relative percentages of the population. The last national census, which was conducted in 1932, before the modern state was founded, demonstrated that Christians made up 55 percent of the population. The 1932 census stated that Maronites, the largest group among the Christian sects and at that time largely in control of the state apparatus, accounted for 29 percent of the total population (Maktabi, 1999). But since the 1800s, Muslim birth rates have been consistently higher than Christian birth rates, with the fastest population increase among Shiites. Today, there is general consensus in Lebanon that Muslims (Sunni, Shiite, and Druze) constitute a solid majority of the population. However, there are no figures to back this up, and estimates of the population shares of the three Muslim sects vary widely from one source to another. Nevertheless, it is still believed that no single sect, by itself, constitutes a majority of the population. The Shiites are believed to be the largest sect, estimated to be about 30 percent of the population (El Khazen, 2001; Panizza and El Khoury, 2001).

The rest of this section describes Lebanon's political history, economic development, population trends, education system, and labor market patterns.

Political History

Lebanon's political history[3] is rife with conflict and political change— it has endured centuries of different rulers and colonists from other regions—and the conflict and political change have carried over into its modern political scene. The Phoenicians lived along the Lebanese coast for more than 2,000 years (circa 2700–450 B.C.). The region came under the control of the Persian Empire and then Alexander the Great. Circa 64 B.C., the Romans conquered the Phoenician cities and

---

[3] Information in this section is drawn from Khouairy, 1976, Krayem, 1997, and U.S. Department of State, 2007a.

declared Beirut the capital of the entire Roman coastal region. Most of the Phoenician cities were Christianized during the 1st century and then followed the Arab conquest during the 7th century. Since the 7th century, the mountains of Lebanon have served as a sanctuary for persecuted and marginalized Christians and for Muslim sects. In the early 16th century, Lebanon became part of the Ottoman Empire, a status that continued until the end of World War I and the empire's collapse.

After World War I, the League of Nations gave France mandate over the five provinces that make up present-day Lebanon. Modern Lebanon's constitution, drawn up in 1926, specified a balance of political power among the various religious groups. The unwritten "National Pact" of 1943 ensured the representation of different religious communities in the government by stipulating a Maronite Christian president, a Sunni Muslim prime minister, and a Shiite speaker of the parliament. Independence in 1943 was followed by the withdrawal of French troops in 1946. Since independence, Lebanon has experienced periods of growth resulting from its favorable position as a regional center for finance, education, culture, and tourism, as well as periods of political turmoil and civil strife.

An incident that took place on April 13, 1975, paved the way for a devastating 15-year civil war. Unidentified gunmen opened fire at a congregation outside a church and killed four Phalangists. In apparent retaliation and believing the assassins to have been Palestinians, the Phalangists ambushed a bus passing through a Christian neighborhood, killing more than 24 Palestinian and Lebanese passengers. These events were followed by an escalation of violence as more incidents of revenge and religious-affiliation-based killing took place. A destructive civil war started soon after; by the end of its first year alone, there were 29 official militias in the country with a total membership of 200,000 citizens. During that first year, more than 10,000 people were killed and about 40,000 were injured. Approximately 100,000 Lebanese citizens immigrated to the Americas, Europe, Africa, and Australia; another 60,000 left for different Arab countries.

In 1989, a negotiated end to the war was reached in Ta'if, Saudi Arabia, when a committee of the Arab League succeeded in bringing

Lebanese parliamentarians together to agree on a national reconciliation accord. The Ta'if agreement constituted a compromise among the Lebanese deputies, political groups and parties, and militias and leaders, and was the right formula to end the war internally. Many political and administrative reforms were deemed crucial by the Ta'if agreement for the sustainability of peace in Lebanon, a number of which were incorporated in constitutional amendments adopted in 1990. These included an expansion of the Chamber of Deputies to 128 seats to be divided equally between Christians and Muslims.

Estimates of the damage resulting from the Lebanese civil war speak to the magnitude of conflict's costs: More than 100,000 people were killed, and 200,000 were left injured or disabled. Up to one-fifth of the pre-war resident population, or about 900,000 people, were displaced from their homes. One in every five Lebanese citizens—mostly professionals and skilled workers—left the country, and about 250,000 emigrated permanently.

Today, Lebanon is a parliamentarian republic with a sectarian-based electoral system of proportional representation; the Lebanese people have the right to change their government using democratic practices. The constitution gives the people the right to select their representatives at the parliament every four years through direct elections, and the parliament is responsible for electing a new president every six years. Together, the president and parliament choose the prime minister. The parliament enjoys robust political power over the cabinet of ministers through its constitutional right to question ministers about their decisions on policy issues. The parliament also plays a critical role in the country's financial affairs through its authority to pass the budget.

Economic Development

Since its independence in 1943, Lebanon has benefited from its multilingual talent pool, its favorable geographic location, and its modern financial sector, compensating for its lack of natural resources. Following the civil war, the Lebanese government faced the challenging tasks of addressing post-war reconstruction and development and rebuilding public confidence. The government then faced this task again, in 2006, following the conflict between Hezbollah and Israel that took place within Lebanon's borders.

The 15-year civil war destroyed or severely damaged most of Lebanon's infrastructure; the UN estimated the damage to physical assets at $25 billion (Eken et al., 1995). Public institutions were severely weakened, and the quality of services provided to citizens deteriorated throughout the war. Real GDP growth was 6 percent per annum from 1965 to 1975, and GDP per capita reached $2,250 in 1975. In 1980, five years into the civil war, GDP was estimated to have declined 40 percent compared with the 1974 GDP.[4]

Figure 6.2 shows the trajectory of GDP per capita (measured in constant 2000 U.S. dollars) since 1989, one year before the end of the civil war, using data from the World Bank. The first signs of economic recovery can be seen in 1989 and 1990, when the growth in GDP per

Figure 6.2
Trends in GDP per Capita and GDP per Capita Growth in Lebanon, 1989 to 2006

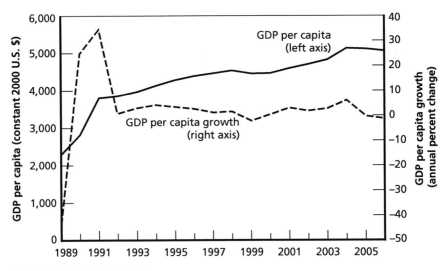

SOURCE: World Bank, 2007.
RAND MG786-6.2

---

[4] The historical GDP figures in this paragraph were provided to us by the Lebanese Ministry of Economy.

capita soared at an annual rate of 25 percent and 35 percent, respectively. Since 1992, the rate of GDP per capita growth has been fairly stable, in the range of 1 percent to 5 percent per year (with the exception of 1999). GDP growth was somewhat higher through 1995 (a range of 5 percent to 8 percent between 1992 and 1995) than the growth in GDP per capita shown in Figure 6.2. The latter grew more slowly as a result of the more rapid growth in the population that was caused by the return of individuals who had left the country during the civil war. However, as of 2005, 15 years after the civil war ended, Lebanon's per capita income was still one-third below its 1975 level (World Bank, 2007).

After years of internal fighting and civil chaos, the rebuilding of Lebanon came with a high price tag. In the period immediately following the civil war, the Lebanese government aspired to attain high economic growth as a way to improve living standards (Lebanon Ministry of Social Affairs, 2004). The national strategy had two main goals: (1) rebuild and modernize the infrastructure and institutional capacity of the country's different sectors, and (2) achieve financial and monetary stability by decreasing inflation, stabilizing the national currency, and controlling the budget deficit. The underlying assumption was that achieving these dual goals would create the right set of circumstances to successfully attract investment to the private sector. However, the needed level and timing of external investment did not materialize. Thus, the government relied heavily on domestic currency financing to cover the expenditures for rebuilding in order to secure the newly established civil peace and regain public confidence.

By the end of 1992, the net public debt (i.e., gross public debt minus public-sector depositions with the banking system) had already reached the equivalent of 46 percent of GDP.[5] Despite early warning messages from international organizations, public-sector debt continued to accumulate. The net public debt reached 92 percent of GDP by 1997 and jumped to 141 percent by 2000. The problem continued to grow; net public debt reached 158 percent of GDP by 2005. Public debt

---

[5] The public debt figures cited in this paragraph, provided to us by the Lebanese Ministry of the Economy, are based on annual reports produced by the Lebanese Ministry of Finance and the Banque du Liban.

servicing, which includes only interest payments on domestic and foreign loans, represented close to 49 percent of revenues in 1992, almost 85 percent in 1997, and 92 percent in 2000.

At the same time, and as a result of focused efforts, the country witnessed a strong recovery in the years following the civil war, as much of the country's infrastructure was rehabilitated and most of the basic public services were restored. As seen in Figure 6.2, per capita real GDP had nearly doubled from its level in 1989, just prior to the end of the civil war. With the establishment of civil peace and the initiation of major reconstruction projects, Lebanon began to regain its role as a tourist and commercial center in the region. Lebanon posted a 5 percent real GDP growth in 2004, with inflation running at 3 percent (Lebanon Ministry of Economy and Trade, 2007).

Lebanon's economic recovery benefited from its free market economy and long history of liberal commercial practices. The Lebanese economy is service oriented, with the service sector representing 33 percent of GDP as of 2002 (Lebanon Ministry of Economy and Trade, 2005). The service sector includes business services, services of maintenance, services of hotels and restaurants, various personal services, health services, education services, and financial services. Banking has traditionally played a major role in Lebanon's economy. Lebanon effectively places no restrictions on capital movement or foreign exchange and strictly enforces bank secrecy. Also as of 2002, the industry sector—ranging from food and beverage industries, to metals, machinery, and equipment, and including jewelry making and printing works—represented 12 percent of GDP. In 1999, an estimated 24 percent of the Lebanese territory was cultivated, the main crop categories being wheat, vegetables, fruit, tobacco, and olives (Lebanon Ministry of Environment, 2001). There is considerable livestock farming in the country, as well.

Population Composition and Change

Lebanon's population has fluctuated in recent decades in response to periods of conflict and recovery. As Figure 6.3 shows, Lebanon's population was nearly 1.9 million people as of 1960, and there was steady growth in the range of 2 to 3 percent per year until the civil war

Figure 6.3
Trends in Population Total and Growth Rate in Lebanon, 1960 to 2006

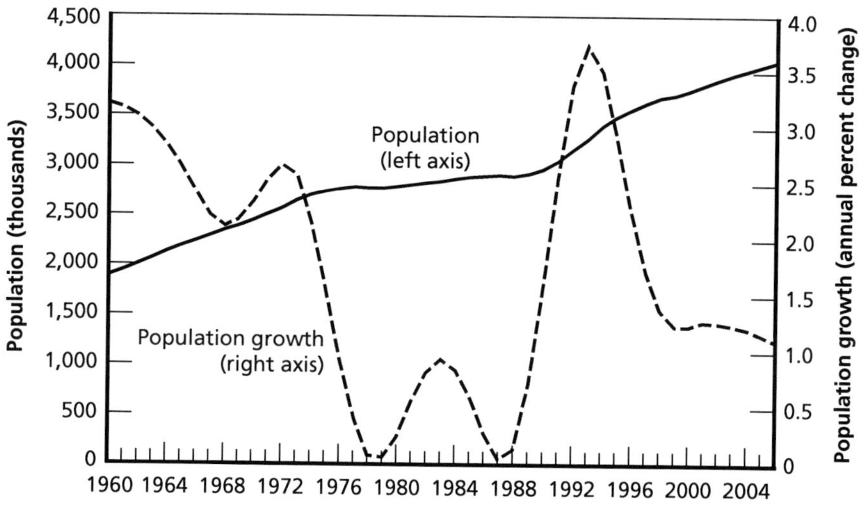

SOURCE: World Bank, 2007.
RAND MG786-6.3

began, in 1975. The population leveled off at approximately 2.7 million through the 1980s and declined further before the war ended, in 1990. In the immediate aftermath of the war, the population grew as those who had left the country because of the conflict returned. Over the more recent years shown, population growth has been a steady 1 percent per year, with an estimated population of 4.0 million persons in 2006.

As noted earlier, Lebanon has not had a complete population enumeration since 1932, and there are no routine population-based surveys on topics such as the labor force, education, or health.[6] The documentation of the national survey of living conditions that was done in 2004 provides tabulations of population distribution by various characteristics (Lebanon Central Administration for Statistics, 2005,

---

[6] A population and housing survey was conducted in 1994 to 1996, and we provide some results on living conditions from that survey below. We also discuss, in a later section covering data resources for the country, a few other periodic surveys that have been conducted.

2006).[7] Table 6.2 provides data from this source on the population distribution by age and gender.[8] The 2004 total population figure of 3.7 million is about 200,000 persons higher than the World Bank number reported in Figure 6.3, above. These figures indicate that 27 percent of the population is under age 15 and that nearly 8 percent is age 65 and above. Females outnumber males by a small margin only in the group of persons age 15 to 64.

Table 6.3 reports results for the distribution of the population by age and nationality. Figures from the 2004 national survey of living conditions indicate that Lebanon's population is heavily made up of citizens: Lebanese make up 93 percent, and non-Lebanese make up the other 7 percent. Non-citizens have a somewhat greater share in the working-age group, those age 15 to 64: Non-citizens constitute 71 percent of this age group, compared with 65 percent for citizens. This is consistent with the expectation that a primary reason for non-citizens to be in the country is to work. However, as we discuss below, there is a large contingent of foreign workers that is not counted in official population figures because these workers reside in housing not included in the sampling frame (e.g., the Palestinian refugee camps, work places, and construction sites) (UNDP, 1997). Including the expatriate workforce would increase the share of the non-Lebanese population beyond what is shown in Table 6.3.

---

[7] Tables 6.2 and 6.3 are based on data from the preliminary release of the 2004 survey results (Lebanon Central Administration for Statistics, 2005). While the population counts reported in Table 6.2 change by a small amount based on the final results, released in 2006 (Lebanon Central Administration for Statistics, 2006), the percent distributions are unchanged. Population figures by nationality, shown in Table 6.3, were only reported in the preliminary release. Thus, we also rely on the same source for Table 6.2 so that the population totals will be consistent. In other tables based on the 2004 survey, we rely on the results reported in 2006.

[8] The sampling frame for the 2004 survey excluded the Palestinian camps (Lebanon Central Administration for Statistics, 2006).

Table 6.2
Population in Lebanon, by Age Group and Gender, 2004

Age Group	Males Number	Males Percent	Females Number	Females Percent	Total Number	Total Percent
0–14	536,313	28.7	486,565	25.8	1,022,878	27.2
15–64	1,189,163	63.7	1,259,446	66.8	2,448,609	65.2
65 and up	142,746	7.6	139,552	7.4	282,298	7.5
Total	1,868,222	100.0	1,885,563	100.0	3,753,785	100.0

SOURCE: Lebanon Central Administration for Statistics, 2005, Table 4.

Table 6.3
Population in Lebanon, by Nationality and Age Group, 2004

Nationality and Age Group	Population Number	Percent Distribution By Nationality	Percent Distribution By Age Group
Lebanese	3,505,950	93.4	100.0
Age 0–14	961,013		27.4
Age 15–64	2,271,854		64.8
Age 65 and up	273,083		7.8
Non-Lebanese	247,835	6.6	100.0
Age 0–14	61,865		25.0
Age 15–64	176,754		71.3
Age 65 and up	9,216		3.7
Total	3,753,785	100.0	100.0
Age 0–14	1,022,878		29.2
Age 15–64	2,448,608		69.8
Age 65 and up	282,299		8.1

SOURCE: Lebanon Central Administration for Statistics, 2005, Tables 6 and 7.

Advances in Education

The Lebanese education system reflects the influence of the French during its mandate, as well as the dominant Arab culture. Following independence in 1946, the government established the Ministry of Education and Higher Education and the Ministry of Vocational and Technical Training (the latter is now a directorate under the former following a reorganization in 2000) (Haddad, 2004; European Training Foundation, 2006). Arabic was specified as the primary language of instruction, although Lebanon remains the only Arab country that has consistently taught a foreign language starting in grade 1 (French and, more recently, English are the prominent secondary languages taught in school) (UNDP, 2003). Free primary education was introduced in 1960, yet as described in more detail below, private schooling remains an important element of education for a large segment of Lebanese children. Today, compulsory education begins at age 6 and continues through the six years of elementary education and three years of junior secondary education (UNESCO, 2006). The non-compulsory secondary level includes three more years and offers both an academic and a vocational track. In addition, preschool was introduced in the middle 1990s as part of public education offerings, but it is also available in private schools.

Table 6.4 shows gross and net enrollment ratios for Lebanese students by education level. These ratios are based on data from 2007 World Bank development indicators and Lebanon's 2004 national survey of living conditions. World Bank figures indicate that nearly three of every four preschool-aged children are enrolled in preprimary education (this is the highest enrollment ratio at this level of the four countries in our study). Primary enrollment is essentially universal for males and females (note that gross and enrollment rates are higher in the Lebanese survey data than in the World Bank data). The net enrollment ratios for both sources indicate that fewer children are progressing through school in step with their age, either because of delayed entry or grade repetition. Indeed, UNESCO figures indicate that the grade repetition rate at the primary level in Lebanon was 11 percent in 2004, which is the highest grade-repetition rate among the four countries in our study (UNESCO, 2006). Data from the 2004 Lebanese

Table 6.4
Gross and Net Enrollment Ratios in Lebanon, by Education Level and Gender, 2004

Education Level	Gross Enrollment Ratio		Net Enrollment Ratio	
	Males	Females	Males	Females
World Bank				
Preprimary	75.2	73.7	n.a.	n.a.
Primary	108.7	104.8	93.6	92.7
Secondary	84.9	92.6	n.a.	n.a.
Post-secondary	44.9	50.4	n.a.	n.a.
Lebanon's 2004 National Survey of Living Conditions				
Primary	111.7	109.0	92.7	92.7
Junior secondary	92.0	104.0	65.0	72.5
Secondary	58.8	65.7	39.2	45.6

SOURCES: World Bank data are from World Bank, 2007; Lebanon's 2004 national survey data are from Lebanon Central Administration for Statistics, 2006, Tables 2-3, 2-4, and 2-5.
NOTE: n.a. = not available.

survey further show that 10 percent of females and 12 percent of males are older than would be expected if they were progressing on time through the primary level. Within each primary grade, the age-grade delay reaches 29 percent for females and 33 percent for males (Lebanon Central Administration for Statistics, 2006).

Enrollment ratios at the junior secondary level (grades 7 through 9) are reported only in the 2004 Lebanese survey and thus appear only in that panel of Table 6.4. Together with the secondary enrollment figures reported by both sources, it is evident that enrollment ratios decline for both males and females in moving to higher levels of education, although the drop is larger for males than for females. Again, the gap in gross and net enrollment rates indicates significant delays in grade progression. The age-grade delay at the senior secondary level, considered within each class, reaches 51 percent for males and 48 percent for females (Lebanon Central Administration for Statistics, 2006). Starting at the junior secondary level, females are more likely than males to be enrolled in school. The overrepresentation of females also holds at the post-secondary level (figures only available from the World Bank in this case).[9]

The Lebanese education system has long been characterized by a high rate of private-school enrollment. Lebanese schools are divided into three major categories in terms of their auspices and fee structure: public schools, tuition-free private schools supported by government funds (for preschool and elementary levels only), and fee-based private schools. While public schools follow similar organizational and administrative patterns and are more or less similar in their curriculum offerings, private schools are distinctly different in their educational approaches, curriculum content, and overall management methods. Private schools can either belong to individuals, associations, or sectarian and religious groups. The Lebanese law guarantees the freedom of these schools by exempting them from falling under the jurisdiction of the Ministry of Education or any other governmental entity.

Table 6.5 shows that 63 percent of all school students in Lebanon were enrolled in private schools—either free or fee-based—in academic year 2004–2005. The share in public schools rose with each successive education level, increasing from 23 percent at the preschool level to 53 percent at the secondary level. There is only limited information about the differences in education outcomes among the different types of schools. What little evidence there is suggests that the public and tuition-free private schools, which are where more disadvantaged children are concentrated, are of lower quality. At the same time, the supply of public schools is not sufficient to serve all children in some poor regions, so families there turn to subsidized private schools,

---

[9] Although females are overrepresented in higher education, the reverse is true for vocational education. For example, during academic year 2000–2001, males represented 55 percent of students enrolled in vocational institutions (Lebanon Ministry of Social Affairs, 2004).

Table 6.5
Student Enrollment in Lebanon, by Education Level and Type of School, 2004–2005

Education Level	Public		Tuition-Free Private		Fee-Based Private	
	Number	Percent	Number	Percent	Number	Percent
Preschool	34,248	22.7	23,155	15.4	93,207	61.9
Elementary	154,907	34.2	91,039	20.1	206,661	45.7
Junior secondary	86,803	43.8	0	0.0	111,256	56.2
Secondary	61,664	53.3	0	0.0	54,006	46.7
Total	337,622	36.8	114,194	12.5	465,130	50.7

SOURCE: Lebanon Ministry of Education and Higher Education, 2006.
NOTE: The secondary school enrollment figures include only those students on the academic track.

which can be of mixed quality (UNDP, 1997). Education outcomes are better in the fee-based private schools, which attract more economically advantaged students (Lebanon Ministry of Social Affairs, 2001).

As noted above, Lebanon places a priority on foreign language instruction. In 1995, public schools were allowed to teach mathematics and science in French or English (UNDP, 2003). As of 2004–2005, only 32 percent of public schools used English as the primary foreign language; the rest mainly used French (Lebanon Ministry of Education and Higher Education, 2006). In contrast, English is the dominant foreign language in private schools: As of 2004-2005, private schools that used English as the primary language of instruction made up 68 percent of all schools. In both public and private schools, the use of French has been declining in favor of English.[10]

Since the early 1950s, Lebanon has experienced steady growth in the number of its higher education institutions, fostering the country's reputation as the educational and cultural center in the region.

---

[10] Statistics from academic year 2000–2001 show that there was a notable increase in the number of public and private schools that used both languages at the same time (Lebanon Ministry of Education and Higher Education, 2003).

In 1973–1974 (prior to the civil war), 50,403 students were enrolled in higher education institutions. By 1997–1998, that number had increased to 87,330, and by 2004–2005, it had increased to 141,479 (Lebanon Ministry of Social Affairs, 2004).[11] This was accompanied by a steady increase in the number of higher education institutions: from 10 in 1973, to 24 in 1997, to 33 in 2001, to 38 in 2004. The sole public university in the country, Lebanese University, attracted close to 60 percent of all higher education students in Lebanon in 2000–2001. However, this university faces formidable competition from private institutions and suffers from poor equipment and lack of modern scientific course offerings (Lebanon Ministry of Social Affairs, 2004). Private institutions of long standing and worldwide renown include the American University in Beirut (founded in 1866) and St. Joseph's University (founded in 1875). English and French, respectively, are the primary languages of instruction for these two institutions, along with Arabic.

Technical/vocational education and training are also delivered through a mix of public and private institutions. During academic year 2002–2003, enrollment in technical and vocational education programs comprised nearly 67,000 students, 54 percent of whom were in private programs (European Training Foundation, 2006). Private providers include for-profit schools and schools operated by not-for-profit NGOs, the latter with subsidies from the Lebanese government or local or international donors. These institutes offer training in such areas as accounting, social work, and physical therapy. Public technical programs include those at the Technical Institute of Tourism, Technical Teachers Institute, Industrial Technical Institute, and Higher Institute for Marine Science.

These investments in education have produced what is a highly literate population in comparison with the populations of other countries in the Middle East, and Lebanon's illiteracy rate has continued to decline despite the civil war (UNDP, 2002). In 1970, the share of the

---

[11] In academic year 2004–2005, females represented 54 percent of enrolled students (Lebanon Ministry of Education and Higher Education, 2006). In addition, Lebanese citizens accounted for 91 percent of all students enrolled in higher education institutions.

population age 10 and above that was illiterate stood at 22 percent. This share declined to 12 percent in 1997 and was at 8 percent in 2001 (Lebanon Ministry of Social Affairs, 2004). However, illiteracy rates for females have been about twice as high as those for males throughout these years. The level of illiteracy overall and the male-female gap reflect, in part, educational differentials for older age groups that were educated in prior decades, when human capital investments were not as large. More relevant is the illiteracy rate for the younger population, those persons educated in more recent years—a rate that has also been declining over time. Indeed, the estimated illiteracy rates for males and females age 15 to 24 were 3 and 7 percent, respectively, as of the 2000–2004 period (Population Reference Bureau, 2005).

Labor Force Trends

Data from the World Bank since 1980, plotted in Figure 6.4, provide perspective on the trends for the population of working age, those in the labor force, and the labor force participation rate.[12] As the figure indicates, the trend in the size of the labor force showed little or no change during the civil war period, followed by a period of increase; the labor force participation rate, however, initially declined in the immediate post-civil-war period. These data indicate that the labor force participation rate reached about 55 percent in 2004, which is about the same rate attained in 1989, the last year of the civil war.

In addition to demographic information, Lebanon's 2004 national survey on living conditions collected information about employment and unemployment. However, the published tabulations indicate that the proportion of the population age 15 to 64 that was in the labor force was 47 percent, a lower share than Figure 6.4 reports (Lebanon Central Administration for Statistics, 2006).[13] The survey report indicates that 76 percent of employed persons age 15 to 64 were

---

[12] The World Bank defines the labor force as those persons age 15 to 64 who are economically active, meaning they are employed or they are unemployed and actively looking for work. Lebanon's Central Administration for Statistics uses the same age range in its definition of the labor force.

[13] There is no clear explanation for the discrepancy. If the labor force participation rate is measured for the population age 15 and above (rather than age 15 to 64), the result is 44

Figure 6.4
Trends in Working-Age Population, Labor Force, and Labor Force Participation Rate in Lebanon, 1980 to 2006

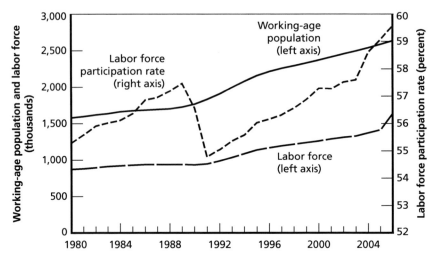

SOURCE: World Bank, 2007.
NOTE: Population and labor force take into account persons age 15–64.
RAND MG786-6.4

male, leaving females with a 24 percent share of those employed (Lebanon Central Administration for Statistics, 2006). The gap in the labor force participation rate between males and females reported in Table 6.6—73 percent versus 22 percent as of 2004—is somewhat larger than that seen for male and female nationals in Qatar (see Table 3.7) but similar to the gap for Oman's nationals (see Table 5.5). As seen in the table, females' labor force participation has been rising in Lebanon over time, and their share of the workforce has likewise been increasing. Nevertheless, their rates of labor force participation remain low, especially considering the relatively high rate of female participation in post-secondary education.

---

percent, which is even lower. The Lebanese Central Administration for Statistics uses the International Labour Organization's international standards for defining employment and unemployment (Lebanese Central Administration for Statistics, 2006).

Table 6.6
Labor Force Participation Rates in Lebanon, by Gender, 1970 to 2004

	Labor Force Participation Rate (percent)	
Year	Males	Females
1970	84.0	16.0
1997	77.3	21.7
2001	75.7	25.0
2004	73.4	22.3

SOURCES: Figures for 1970, 1997, and 2001 are from Lebanon Ministry of Social Affairs, 2004, Table 4.1; figures for 2004 are from Lebanon Central Administration for Statistics, 2006, Table 3-1.

The distribution of male and female workers across sectors has also shifted over time.[14] Table 6.7 indicates that most working females in 2001 were in the education and business sectors. It also indicates that between 1975 and 2001, female participation declined considerably (from 23 percent to 4 percent) in the agriculture and fishery sector while increasing considerably in the business sector (from 6 percent to 21 percent). At the same time, Lebanese females represented only 6 percent of executives and high-ranking managers in small companies as of 2001 (Lebanon Ministry of Social Affairs, 2004).

Chapter Two noted the difference in the size of the private sector between the three Gulf nations in our study and Lebanon. In 2004, 86 percent of those employed in Lebanon were working in the private sector, and just 13 percent were working in the public sector (Lebanon Central Administration for Statistics, 2006).[15] Lebanon's private-sector share has increased gradually over time: It was 80 percent in 1997 and 82 percent in 2001 (Lebanon Ministry of Social Affairs, 2004). Lebanon

---

[14] The distribution of employment by sector and gender is not tabulated in the report on the 2004 national survey (Lebanon Central Administration for Statistics, 2006).

[15] The residual 1 percent worked for international organizations, civil or partisan organizations, or organizations from other sectors not classified as private or public.

Table 6.7
Distribution of Workforce in Lebanon, by Sector and Gender, 1970 and 2001

	Percent Distribution			
	1970		2001	
Sector	Males	Females	Males	Females
Agriculture and fishery	18.1	22.5	7.7	3.5
Manufacturing (including electricity, gas, and water)	18.6	20.4	14.8	11.5
Construction and building	7.8	0.3	11.9	0.5
Business (including restaurants and hotels)	19.3	6.1	29.4	21.0
Transportation and communication	8.2	2.3	8.3	2.2
Financial brokerage and companies' servicing	3.5	3.0	6.7	11.0
General management	7.9	10.3	10.0	2.7
Education	3.2	16.5	4.5	29.4
Health and social work	0.7	3.1	2.1	10.7
Other	12.7	16.1	4.6	7.5
Total	100.0	100.0	100.0	100.0

SOURCE: Lebanon Ministry of Social Affairs, 2004, Table 4.6.

is also distinguished for its tradition of entrepreneurship, particularly in contrast to the Gulf countries in our study. Data indicate that 29 percent of those employed reported that they were self-employed, working alone or with family members, and another 5 percent were classified as employers (Lebanon Central Administration for Statistics, 2006).

Human Resource Challenges Faced by Lebanon

Lebanon differs in several important ways from the three other countries in our study, so it is not surprising that the human resource challenges reflect a different mix of issues. Even so, some of the themes in our discussions of the three Gulf countries are echoed in Lebanon. Issues that are more salient in Lebanon include brain drain and the prevalence of poverty. Concerns shared by the other countries in this study include the quality of the primary and secondary education systems, high rates of unemployment (especially among youth), and the preparation of secondary and post-secondary graduates for the world of work.

Outcomes of Primary and Secondary Education System Are Not Up to International Standards

Although Lebanon has made tremendous progress in raising education enrollment rates and narrowing the gender gap, the system of primary and secondary education is widely perceived as failing to produce sufficient numbers of graduates with the skills required for direct entry into the labor market or continued study at the post-secondary level (UNDP, 1997, 2002). The proliferation of education reform initiatives and laws has focused on upgrading and improving equipment and other material supplies, rather than promoting institutional development and student performance (Lebanon Ministry of Social Affairs, 2004). Basic education for the first nine years was guaranteed via a 1998 law that introduced mandatory and free education for all Lebanese children in the elementary and junior secondary levels. However, full enforcement of this law has yet to take place, as indicated by the enrollment ratios at the junior secondary level reported in Table 6.4.

One of the challenges in any attempt to assess the quality of the primary and secondary education systems in the region (as noted in earlier chapters, for the three other study countries) is the lack of student assessments, whether aligned to country education standards or international standards, at various grade levels. This is slowly changing. Qatar and Oman participated in international assessments for the first time in 2006 and 2007, respectively; Lebanon participated in the 2003 and 2007 TIMSS (Gonzales et al., 2004; Mullis et al., 2004).[16] Table 6.8 shows the average scale scores in mathematics and science for Lebanon's grade 8 students on the 2003 TIMSS assessment (the most

---

[16] Students were tested in either English or French.

Table 6.8
Average Scale Scores on the 2003 TIMSS Assessment for Lebanon and Comparison Countries

Country	Grade 8 Mathematics	Grade 8 Science
Lebanon	433	393
Jordan	424	475
Iran	411	453
Tunisia	410	404
Egypt	406	421
Bahrain	401	438
Palestinian National Authority	390	435
Morocco	387	396
Saudi Arabia	332	398
United States	504	527
International average	466	473

SOURCE: Gonzales et al., 2004, Tables 3 and 9.

recent administration with publicly available reports at the time of this monograph's publication). For comparison purposes, it also shows the scores for the other Middle East countries that participated, as well as the international average and U.S. scores. In mathematics, Lebanon's score places it 31st of the 45 countries taking the test and 30 points below the international average. However, the same score places it above all eight of the other countries in the region that took the test. Notably, Lebanese males scored significantly higher than Lebanese females on the mathematics test (Mullis et al., 2004). The science score for Lebanon is even more problematic: It is 80 points below the international average, places Lebanon 41st of the 45 countries, and puts Lebanon last among the eight countries in the region. Note that the U.S. benchmark, while well above the scores for Lebanon (about 70 and 135 points higher in mathematics and science, respectively), is far from the top of the international standing: The United States ranks 15th in mathematics and 9th in science among the 45 countries participating in the assessment.

The TIMSS includes an assessment of the mathematics and science curricula of the participating countries; this assessment revealed that Lebanon's mathematics curriculum was not consistent with international standards. Lebanon was one of the six (of 45 total) countries whose curriculum, through grade 8, covered less than half of the topics on the TIMSS assessment (Mullis et al., 2004). Notably, Lebanon was one of the 14 countries whose grade 8 mathematics teachers were not required to have a university degree.

Coupled with Lebanon's high rates of grade repetition and declining enrollment rates as students age (discussed above), these test results signal that there are issues with the efficiency and quality of the primary and secondary education system. In terms of student achievement, considerable progress is needed for Lebanese students to perform at the level of their peers in developed and newly developing countries.

The Higher Education System Is Strong and Depends on the Private Sector

As mentioned earlier, Lebanon has long been considered a regional center for higher education, possessing an array of high-quality private universities and colleges that attract students from throughout the Middle East and beyond.[17] While considered one of the best in the Arab world, the Lebanese education system faces challenges in generating sufficient numbers of graduates in fields required for the 21st century workplace, especially the high-technology-reliant workplace that Lebanon aspires to achieve.

In some respects, Lebanon is a success story in terms of higher education in the region. Table 6.9 shows data assembled by the NSF indicating that there were about 15,000 first university degree graduates in Lebanon in 2001. As the table shows (bottom panel), when the numbers of graduates (by gender and in total) granted a first univer-

---

[17] Lebanon also has relatively more students at the post-secondary level studying abroad, an estimated 7 percent, with most enrolled in institutions in France, followed by the United States (Bhandari and Chow, 2007).

Table 6.9
Breakdown of First University Degrees Granted in Lebanon, 2001

	Degrees Granted (number)		
	Males[a]	Females[a]	Total
All fields	4,778	6,616	11,394
Science and engineering fields	1,309	1,650	2,959
Physical/biological sciences	348	326	674
Computer sciences	254	164	418
Agricultural sciences	10	18	28
Engineering	371	106	477
Social/behavioral sciences	326	1,036	1,362
Non-science and non-engineering fields	3,469	4,966	8,435
No. of persons in 24-year-old population	31,800	31,400	63,200
	Ratio of Persons Getting Degree to Population of 24-year-olds (percent)		
	Males	Females	Total
First university degree	15.0	21.1	19.7
Natural sciences or engineering degree	3.1	2.0	4.3
Social/behavioral sciences degree	1.0	3.3	2.7

SOURCES: NSF, 2006, Table 2-37; NSF, 2004, Table 2-35.

[a] Data are for 2000.

sity degree for the year are expressed as a fraction of the 24-year-old population, the results are all close to 20 percent. This is one of the highest rates of graduates with a first university degree in the Middle East—and higher than the rates in Qatar and Oman, for which the NSF also reports similar figures (see Tables 3.13 and 5.10), and than the Middle East average of 8 percent (NSF, 2006). Table 6.9 also shows these degrees by major field of study. Degrees in fields outside science and engineering dominate: They number approximately 8,400, compared with approximately 3,000 in the science and engineering fields. And in the science and engineering degrees category, the share for the physical, biological, computer, and agricultural sciences and engineering is even smaller—about 1,600 degrees for the year. When expressed in terms of the share of the 24-year-old population that is obtaining these degrees, this equals just 4 percent. The separate results shown for males and females in Table 6.9 reveal that females are overrepresented among graduates receiving a first university degree (21 percent, versus 15 percent for males) but are underrepresented among those receiving degrees in the critical fields of the natural sciences and engineering (2 percent, versus 3 percent for males).

As noted above, all universities in Lebanon except for the Lebanese University are private entities with tuition and fees. Although the majority of post-secondary students in Lebanon are enrolled in the tuition-free public university, the relatively high cost of attending some of the private higher education institutions might be preventing more secondary graduates from pursuing advanced studies. For example, the average undergraduate tuition at the Lebanese American University, as of 2006–2007, is $11,200 per year (Lebanese American University, 2008). The issue of cost is particularly relevant given the high levels of poverty that have prevailed in Lebanon, an issue we discuss further below.

There appears to be little relationship between major studied and future career; college graduates and new entrants to the workforce seem to accept any job that becomes available to them (Lebanon Ministry of Social Affairs, 2004). The vocational training system also generates supplies of graduates that are not well matched to the needs of employers (European Training Foundation, 2006). On-the-job training and professional development opportunities are not widespread.[18]

---

[18] A study conducted by the National Employment Agency in 1999 showed that organizations in Lebanon spend an average of 2 percent of their salaries' bill on training (Lebanon Ministry of Social Affairs, 2004).

Brain Drain Has Diminished the Benefit of a Strong Higher Education Sector

One of the most significant effects of Lebanon's political and economic instability in the past several decades has been the departure of its educated elites to other parts of the Middle East and to Europe, North America, and Australia. This departure was facilitated by long-standing migration patterns—Lebanese have migrated to major economic centers in Africa, Asia, Europe, and the Americas since the late 19th century. But the civil war spurred a dramatic increase in the number of emigrants. A recent survey indicated, for example, that 46 percent of Lebanese families reported having at least one family member who lives in a foreign country and who emigrated from Lebanon sometime between 1975 and 2001. These emigrants were drawn from the younger members of society: Nearly 37 percent were age 30 to 39. Most of these people were males (64 percent), and the main reason given for deciding to leave the country was to look for a job elsewhere. Results also reveal that 58 percent of unemployed youth were considering emigration as a response to their poor economic conditions, and that 1.5 to 2 percent of the economically active population had been emigrating every year between 1996 and 2001 (Kasparian, 2003).

A recent UNDP analysis by Ozden (2006) sets the magnitude of the brain drain in Lebanon in recent decades in the context of other countries in the Middle East. Based on census data from 1990 and 2000 for OECD countries (the destinations), Ozden traces migration patterns for nearly 200 source countries, including Lebanon, capturing over 90 percent of the global brain drain.[19] These data reveal that approximately 250,000 immigrants in OECD countries were of Lebanese origin as of 1990, and the number was somewhat higher in 2000. When viewed as a share of the labor force, immigrants in OECD countries who were Lebanese made up almost one-sixth of the labor force in 1990 and about one-seventh as of 2000—both underestimates because the analysis did not account for Lebanese that migrated to other Middle Eastern countries. This ratio is about two times as large as Morocco's,

---

[19] The data do not capture migration to non-OECD countries, such as the Arabian Gulf countries and higher-income areas of Asia and Africa (e.g., Singapore and South Africa).

the country that ranked second on this indicator among Middle East countries in both 1990 and 2000. Even more relevant is the number of emigrants with a post-secondary education as a share of the home country population with a post-secondary education. Lebanon had the highest ratio in the Middle East in 1990 and in 2000: College-educated emigrants equaled nearly 40 percent of the college-educated population in Lebanon as of 2000—twice the rate of Morocco and Iran, which ranked second and third on this measure of brain drain. Educated Lebanese were more likely to leave the country during the years of turmoil than afterwards, because they had the resources to do so and better economic prospects in the destination countries (Ozden, 2006).

Ozden's (2006) analysis shows some lessening of the brain drain between 1990 and 2000, when resolution of the civil war provided an impetus for some Lebanese emigrants to return. Even so, the implication is that Lebanon must contend with a labor force that does not fully reflect the past history of human capital investment in the population. Moreover, the educated population in Lebanon remains highly mobile and may not be ready to make a full commitment to the country's labor market in the face of continued political instability and civil unrest. As seen in Table 6.10, which is based on data from Lebanon's 2004 national survey of living conditions, the educational attainment of the labor force in Lebanon is heavily weighted toward persons with less than a secondary education. The fraction with a university degree is just 21 percent, and nearly 60 percent achieved no more than the junior secondary level.[20]

Unemployment Is High Among Youth in Particular and Foreign Workers Compete with Lower-Skilled Lebanese

Despite the recent success of the post-war economic recovery in Lebanon, unemployment remains significant, especially for the younger

---

[20] The share with a college degree has changed little from its 2001 level of 21.1 percent, although it did increase substantially from 1970 to 1977, going from 4.3 percent to 16.7 percent (Lebanon Ministry of Social Affairs, 2004). At the same time, the percentage of the labor force that was illiterate or semi-illiterate decreased from 64.7 percent in 1970 to 15.3 percent in 1997 and then 11.5 percent in 2001.

Table 6.10
Educational Attainment of Labor Force in Lebanon, 2004

Educational Attainment	Labor Force	
	Number	Percent
Illiterate	40,269	3.5
Reads and writes	42,729	3.7
Preschool	10,226	0.9
Elementary	324,555	28.1
Junior secondary	264,333	22.9
Secondary	191,761	16.6
University	239,133	20.7
Unknown	2,207	0.2
N/A	38,980	3.4
Total	1,062,096	100.0

SOURCES: Lebanon Central Administration for Statistics, 2006, Tables 82 and 100; and authors' calculations.

NOTES: N/A = not applicable. Numbers may not add to total because of rounding.

population. As seen in Table 6.11, the labor force, or economically active population, was 1.06 million, and about 92,000 were unemployed, for an unemployment rate of 8 percent. The numbers for population subgroups indicate that females were more likely than males to be unemployed (10 percent versus 7 percent). Even more striking is the high rate of unemployment among the youngest age groups: 27 percent for those age 15 to 19, 17 percent for those age 20 to 24, and 9 percent for those age 25 to 29.[21] It is also interesting to note that the unemployment rate is higher for those with a junior

---

[21] Unemployment data show that females were less likely than males to be unemployed in 1970 and 1977 but that this trend had reversed by 2001 (Lebanon Ministry of Social Affairs, 2004). The pattern of unemployment rates by age evident in Table 6.11 was similar in 1970, 1997, and 2001.

Table 6.11
Unemployed and Unemployment Rates in Lebanon for Economically Active Population, by Gender, Age Group, and Educational Attainment, 2004

	Unemployed (number)	Labor Force (number)	Unemployment Rate (percent)
Gender			
Male	64,975	872,578	7.4
Female	27,118	281,611	9.6
Age group			
15–19	16,603	61,564	27.0
20–24	29,075	168,221	17.3
25–29	15,948	183,178	8.7
30–34	9,348	166,069	5.6
35–39	6,082	143,985	4.2
40–44	5,755	135,540	4.2
45–49	3,339	106,388	3.1
50–54	2,701	85,457	3.2
55–59	1,423	59,354	2.4
60–64	1,819	44,435	4.1
Educational attainment			
Illiterate	2,281	40,269	5.7
Reads and writes	2,651	42,729	6.2
Preschool	557	10,226	5.4
Elementary	25,627	324,555	7.9
Junior secondary	24,018	264,333	9.1
Secondary	16,829	191,761	8.8
University	19,913	239,133	8.3
Unknown	219	2,207	9.9
Total	92,093	1,062,096	8.0

SOURCES: Lebanon Central Administration for Statistics, 2006, Tables 69a, 80a, 82, 98, and 100; and authors' calculations.

NOTE: Numbers may not add to total because of rounding.

secondary degree or higher level of education (8 to 9 percent) compared with those with the lowest levels of education (5 to 6 percent).

Note that while these figures are high enough to be of concern, estimates made by international organizations such as the European Training Foundation and World Bank place the incidence of unemployment 8 to 10 percentage points higher than the 8 percent average rate shown (European Training Foundation, 2006).

The employment situation in Lebanon is also affected by the large number of non-Lebanese working in the country, either formally or informally, mainly as unskilled and semi-skilled workers in such jobs as construction, seasonal agriculture, and municipal and sanitation work (UNDP, 1997; European Training Foundation, 2006). There is a general belief that lower-skilled Lebanese workers must compete with mainly Syrian and Egyptian counterparts who are willing to accept jobs for lower wages. Given the high unemployment rates in the country, this situation has created tension and stirred much debate. However, there are no data available to shed light on the exact size of the non-Lebanese workforce. One estimate places the foreign worker population at 1.4 million (80 percent from Syria), a figure that would exceed the size of the official workforce shown in Table 6.11 (European Training Foundation, 2006). Other estimates place the number of foreign workers at several hundred thousand (UNDP, 1997).

Material Deprivation Is High and Disparities in the Standard of Living Are Large

Lebanon is classified as an upper-middle-income country by the World Bank, and had a GNI per capita of $6,040 in 2004. To date, Lebanon does not have an official poverty line that could be used to assess the fraction of the population below a given absolute or relative standard of living. Yet the extent of material hardship and the disparities in living conditions across population groups and geographic areas have long been areas of concern and the focus of social policy (Lebanon Ministry of Social Affairs, 2001). Studies conducted before and after the civil war indicate that income equality improved prior to the onset of the war and then deteriorated as a result of the conflict. Poverty, or material deprivation, has been consistently associated with agricultural households, households living on the outskirts of the major cities, and households with low levels of education (UNDP, 1997).

Income and expenditure data from the 1994–1996 population and housing survey reveal substantial regional disparities in average household incomes and expenditures (UNDP, undated). In the absence of an official poverty line, this survey has been used to assess the extent of material deprivation in the population based on various measures of living conditions, such as housing (number of rooms, area, heating source), water and sewage, education (enrollment and attainment), and economic status (number of cars, dependency rate, occupation, and unemployment) (Lebanon Ministry of Social Affairs, 2001). Based on an index of unsatisfied basic needs, 32 percent of households and 35 percent of individuals were classified as living below the satisfaction threshold, with 7 percent of households and individuals having a "very low" degree of satisfied needs. At the other end of the scale, 26 percent of households and 23 percent of individuals were classified as having a high or very high level of basic needs satisfaction. Households were also asked in the survey to estimate the income necessary to meet their basic needs. By that measure, 37 percent of households had inadequate income.

There is a strong association between educational attainment and living conditions: 70 percent of those who were illiterate fell below the satisfaction threshold, compared with just 2 percent of those with a university education (Lebanon Ministry of Social Affairs, 2001). Moreover, children from households with low levels of well-being were found to be more likely to attend public schools or tuition-free private schools and thus more likely to receive a lower-quality education. As a result, they were more likely to experience such problems as delayed school entry, grade repetition, and school dropout, all of which reduce their chances for post-secondary education and eventual labor market success.

Approaches to Reform in Lebanon

As discussed in the prior sections, Lebanon faces a set of highly challenging domestic and external circumstances that affect the course of reform efforts aimed at addressing its human resource issues (see Figure 6.5). In the aftermath of the civil war, national consensus about the state's political, economic, and social direction has yet to be achieved by the various groups in Lebanon's diverse society. Thus, government policies, initiatives, and programs are often stalled or even abandoned from lack of internal agreement. On the regional level, the absence of an Arab-Israeli peace settlement and the resulting ongoing political instability create uncertainty and exacerbate tensions between different Lebanese groups with varying political orientations. While good progress has been made toward economic recovery and future growth prospects are promising, the large debt burden limits the resources available for public-sector investments in human capital development initiatives.

Yet Lebanon enjoys several advantages in comparison to the other three countries in our study. It has, for example, a capable and multilingual workforce, an unrestricted economy, an advantageous geographical position on the Mediterranean Sea, a moderate climate, and an advanced financial and banking sector. Moreover, in the past few years, Lebanon has benefited from a number of international and regional changes that led to considerable improvement of its tourism

Figure 6.5
Schematic of Challenges Faced by Lebanon: Need to Achieve Political Stability While Addressing Human Resource Issues

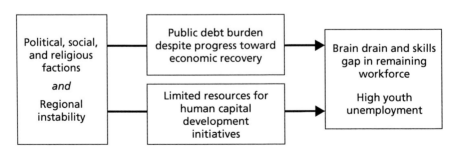

RAND MG786-6.5

sector. Increasing numbers of Arabs are opting to spend their vacations, and retain their funds, in Lebanon rather than in Western countries in the aftermath of September 11, 2001. This, coupled with rising oil prices, has positively affected capital flows in the country.

In a presentation made by the Lebanese government to donors in New York on September 19, 2005, the priorities of the planned economic and social programs focused on (World Bank, 2005)

- Modernizing the economy
- Addressing fiscal and debt sustainability challenges
- Improving governance and reforming the public sector
- Improving social conditions and strengthening social safety nets.

To address fiscal and debt sustainability challenges, the plan aimed to rationalize public expenditures, embrace viable public reform programs, introduce a global income tax, and reform tax and debt management administration. A central piece of the plan called for the use of proceeds from privatization for debt reduction. To modernize the economy, the plan called for trade liberalization, development of capital markets, and improvement of the investment climate.

The plan also called for a comprehensive strategy to restructure public institutions and overhaul the civil service through a human resource plan designed to improve governance capacities and reform the public sector. Public finance transparency, civil service reform, procurement reform, reducing red tape, and improving and enforcing anti-corruption measures were all expected to be major components of the strategy. Finally, reinforcing social safety nets and developing targeted programs to reach poverty clusters through NGOs and municipalities were viewed as ways to improve social conditions. The plan included reform of social security, institutionalization of current social fund projects, and rationalization of public social expenditures.

In terms of the types of reforms examined in our study, Lebanon has not incorporated reforms in the primary and secondary education, higher education, or training domains comparable to those described for the three Gulf countries. Rather, Lebanon's efforts have largely focused on broader reforms to the economy and to the labor market, with the latter reforms being specific to the civil service sector. Thus, in the discussion that follows, we focus on the recent reform efforts in the two relevant areas.

Economic Reforms Are Under Way

In recent years, the Lebanese government has undertaken major steps to advance economic growth and modernize the public sector.[22] To address the alarming accumulation of public debt, major debt restructuring in 2003 (following a meeting of major international donors known as the Paris II Conference) incorporated longer maturities and lower interest rates. The debt service was lowered to about 11 to 12 percent of GDP in 2005, down from 16 to 17 percent in the 2000–2003 period. The primary deficit dropped significantly, eventually (since 2002) turning into a surplus.

More efforts have been made to address the public debt by improving public-sector revenues. The Lebanese government introduced tax reform measures to improve tax collection, started auditing larger taxpayers in a systematic manner, and introduced a tax regularization law in 2001. It also introduced a 10 percent value-added tax (VAT) that became applicable in February 2002, and a 5 percent income tax that became applicable in February 2003. In addition, many institutional and administrative reform projects were developed and implemented to arrive at a lean and more efficient public sector. Examples include modernizing management practices and automation at a number of public entities, streamlining procedures and automating deed registration at the Land Registry, and establishing streamlined and standardized operating procedures at Customs in conformity with international standards. As part of efforts to reduce public expenditures, the government undertook a number of structural measures to rationalize public-sector employment and redefine the role of the state (these are discussed below, with other efforts to reform public institutions). It is worth noting that previous restructuring efforts, of the national airline company (Middle East Airline) and the public television station (Tele-Liban), resulted in discharging over 2,000 public employees.

---

[22] This section draws on World Bank, 2005.

As part of its ongoing economic reforms, the Lebanese government paid special attention to international competitiveness and trade. A solid commitment to the Lebanese pound, which has been pegged to the U.S. dollar since September 1999, resulted in better levels of confidence in the country's national currency. An earlier membership in the Greater Arab Free Trade Area in 1997 was followed by signing the Euro-Med Partnership Agreement with the European Union (EU) in 2003. As part of a broader partnership with EU countries and a robust program of cooperation, the agreement provides for free access of Lebanon's industrial exports, most agro-industrial exports, and a large number of agriculture exports. The EU decided to grant Lebanon a five-year grace period on the dismantling of tariffs. Lebanon has also been making solid steps toward membership in the WTO. In 2000, a number of measures were introduced in this regard, including an open sky policy and a WTO-compatible customs law. More efforts toward WTO accession are under way.

On the privatization front, the Lebanese government announced plans to privatize some major economic sectors, including telecommunications, electricity, water, gas exploration, and the ports. To facilitate these goals of privatization, the Higher Council for Privatization (HCP) was established as an authority in charge of planning and implementing the privatization program and its relevant operations. Discretionary power over the broad parameters of the privatization program is allocated between the Council of Ministers and the HCP in a way that allows the Council of Ministers to approve all matters before their implementation by the HCP. It is worth noting that the estimated total valuation of enterprises with the potential for privatization is quite small in relation to the total debt (10 to 15 percent). However, the announced overarching rationale for privatization focuses on reducing public cost, enhancing quality of provided services in a number of key sectors, and stimulating overall economic growth.

On the investment promotion front, the Lebanese Council of Ministers issued a Directive in 1994 to establish the Investment Development Authority of Lebanon (IDAL) and spearhead Lebanon's investment promotion efforts. The Authority was restructured and supported by the enactment of Investment Development Law 360 in 2001. IDAL's mission includes promoting domestic and foreign business entities and stimulating Lebanon's economic and social development. It also focuses on promoting Lebanon as a viable investment destination and seeks to foster, facilitate, and retain investments in the country. Over the past few years, IDAL has benefited from the regional economic boom and succeeded in attracting a sizable number of investments, especially in sectors such as tourism (business, medical, and environmental tourism), industry (particularly for sectors with high export rates, such as jewelry, equipment, food, chemicals, cement, and printing products), agriculture, information technology, and communications.

However, and despite all efforts, the economic and political reform objectives are far from being accomplished. Lebanon still faces severe macroeconomic imbalances, with debt reaching 175 percent of GDP and limited employment-generating growth, resulting in higher levels of poverty and emigration.[23] According to the World Bank (2005), 46 days are needed to register a business, compared with the best practice of one day. Contract enforcement takes 721 days, three times as long as the OECD average (World Bank, 2005). Even with the establishment of IDAL, the investment climate continues to suffer from high taxes, tariffs, and fees; corruption in government and in the courts; and inadequate protection of intellectual property. The announced privatization program has not progressed as a result of deep in-country division over its approach and underlying philosophy.

Efforts to Reform Public Institutions Are Concurrent with Economic Reform

The 15-year civil war prevented the advancement and modernization of the Lebanese public sector during those 15 years and damaged much of its physical and administrative infrastructure. Attention to human capital development and the introduction of technological and communication advancement tools was lacking during that time, putting the Lebanese public sector at a great disadvantage compared with the public sectors of countries around the globe.

---

[23] The debt-to-GDP ratio, which is based on data provided to us by the Lebanese Ministry of the Economy, is consistent with figures reported in a World Bank (2005) study.

The post-war Lebanese government recognized the importance of creating a lean and efficient public administration capable of providing quality and timely services to its citizens. The Office of the Minister of State for Administrative Reform (OMSAR) was established in 1993 as the main body concerned with developing and implementing short- and long-term plans for reforming public institutions and processes. OMSAR's mission is to bring the Lebanese public administration system into the 21st century through best practices that raise productivity and deliver efficient and transparent services to the public and private sectors (Lebanon OMSAR, 2001). The major donors for OMSAR's projects are the Word Bank, Arab Fund for Economic and Social Development, EU, and UNDP.

Major national policy priorities in the area of administrative reform can be grouped under four objectives (Lebanon OMSAR, 2001):

1. Promotion of citizen-oriented public administration
2. Reduction of the size and cost of public administration
3. Development and establishment of modern management capacities in key sectors/agencies
4. Development and reform of laws and regulations to accompany other areas of reform.

These objectives were arrived at through a cross-government, consultative process that led to the formulation of a national administrative reform strategy for Lebanon. In turn, OMSAR developed an array of donor-funded projects that address these objectives and seek to attain the stated goals.

In connection with the first objective, information gathered from OMSAR officials and public documents indicates that a number of initiatives are under way that seek to create a citizen-oriented public-sector administration—i.e., one that is responsive to the needs of the people it is designed to serve. These initiatives include simplifications of procedures; establishment of reception offices in public buildings to assist citizens; development of a national e-strategy to incorporate information technology in business, government, and society; approval of an "Ombudsman" law by Parliament in 2005; a proposal to pass a

"Child Ombudsman" law; and the establishment of a series of documents on citizens' rights in the fields of health, environment, public safety, culture and heritage, democracy, and others.

For the second objective, which is to reduce the size and cost of public administration, the Lebanese government identified and released a large number of public employees that were deemed "surplus." The government also initiated a project to examine the status of the surplus workforce from contractual, legal, and social perspectives in order to arrive at viable solutions that satisfy cost reduction goals while addressing the circumstances of this group of workers. Current estimates indicate that there are approximately 5,000 surplus employees and that the majority of them have been reassigned to different administrations that had vacant positions (Lebanon OMSAR, 2006).

The third objective, that of establishing modern management practices and capacities, was tackled by developing and implementing a number of reform projects that strive to implement best practices identified in the field of public management. Principles of organizational performance management and measurement were introduced and institutionalized in a number of public entities to improve efficiency and effectiveness; a human resources strategy, as well as a communication strategy, was developed for the Ministry of Finance; and capacities were built within local municipalities to enable them to build local development plans and implement projects related to hard waste management.

In support of the fourth objective, basic laws are being updated to modernize standards and improve public-sector efficiency and transparency. As of March 2007, a new public accounting law that streamlines budgetary procedures and strengthens treasury controls was before parliament, and a new procurement law that would establish a public procurement regime based on international standards was under review by an inter-ministerial committee.

One of the challenges that reform programs face in the Lebanese public sector relates to human resources. Although there are many vacant positions in several public agencies, especially in the areas of management and information and communication technology, the Lebanese government is unable to hire new staff to fill these vacancies.

This is mainly because of the surplus, or excess, of unskilled staff who were hired into the public sector during the civil war years and who continue to consume a large portion of the personnel budget.

Over the past few years, the government embraced a number of initiatives and reforms to address these human resource needs: introduction of a new recruitment system for the enrollment of governmental senior positions that follows a transparent, well-founded criteria-based selection process; creation of the Ecole Nationale d'Administration (National School of Administration), which is in charge of providing pre- and in-service training to public-sector employees; and establishment of human resource management units in each government ministry to better address and respond to human resource needs in each agency.

In addition, OMSAR initiated a number of major human capital reform projects during the past five years (Lebanon OMSAR, 2001, 2006), including

- Development of a modern job classification system with job descriptions and evaluation procedures
- Development and adoption of human resource practices, such as a testing and recruitment system, performance evaluation system, and promotion system
- Capacity building and training, especially in areas of management, human resources, and information and communication technology.

Assessments of multiple training needs for all grade-level civil servants have been taking place since 1995. Project implementation work also revealed the need for specialized human resources for effective and sustainable operations.

The Office of the Prime Minister is the ultimate entity in charge of evaluating and measuring progress in the achievement of reform goals. The Office requires monthly progress reports to monitor achievements in all projects undertaken by OMSAR. This reporting mechanism is also applicable to all public entities and follows a standardized reporting template.

Only Limited Demographic, Economic, and Labor Market Data Are Available to Monitor and Evaluate Progress

The collection of demographic, economic, and labor market data in Lebanon has fluctuated over time, commensurate with economic and political situations and the underlying tensions among the different population factions. As noted earlier, Lebanon has not implemented a nationwide census since 1932, and no data collection efforts since that time have incorporated questions that would allow estimates of the size of its ethnic and religious subgroups. Efforts to collect data also stalled during the civil war, making it difficult to measure the demographic and economic impact of the conflict, as well as the progress of recovery since its end. More recently, as the economy has recovered and tensions subsided, several nationwide surveys have been implemented that capture aspects of the population distribution, labor market situation, and living standards:

- The 1994–1996 population and housing survey collected by the Ministry of Social Affairs in collaboration with the United Nations Population Fund (UNFPA)
- The 1997 labor force survey undertaken by the National Employment Office in cooperation with UNDP (this survey updates the 1970 labor force survey conducted by the Directorate of Statistics, then part of the Ministry of Planning)
- The 2004 national survey of living conditions conducted by the Central Administration for Statistics.

Other surveys have been collected by NGOs—for example, the 2002 youth entrance to the workforce and immigration study that was fielded by researchers at the University of Saint Joseph.

Central authority for the collection and dissemination of the full range of economic, demographic, and social data for Lebanon rests with the Central Administration for Statistics, an independent agency established in 1979. The Administration is charged, on its own or in collaboration with other ministries, with coordinating the production and maintenance of statistical data for Lebanon, including national accounts, balance of payments, and other economic data, as well as executing required sample surveys to collect needed social, demographic, and economic data. Like Qatar and Oman, Lebanon has joined the IMF's GDDS, thereby signaling its commitment to further develop a comprehensive data collection strategy consistent with international standards. The Central Administration for Statistics has responsibility for implementing the standards under the GDDS.

Summary

Lebanon is striving to rebuild the country's infrastructure and reform its economy in the aftermath of civil war. In doing so, it faces a challenging set of human resource hurdles. Similar to the other countries in this study, Lebanon has made tremendous progress in raising primary and secondary school enrollment rates and narrowing the gender gap. Yet a widely held view, confirmed by international assessments of student performance, is that the country's primary and secondary education system is not adequately preparing Lebanese students to succeed in today's knowledge economy. The picture is also mixed at the postsecondary level of the education system. Lebanon's rate of granting university degrees is one of the highest in the Middle East. However, similar to what is happening in the other countries in our study, relatively few students graduate in the science, mathematics, or engineering fields, which are high-demand fields for workers in sectors of the economy such as banking and information technology, where growth is targeted. This mismatch in skills among both the non-college-bound and the college-graduate population has resulted in high unemployment rates among the country's youth. Furthermore, the political and economic instability of the recent past has caused Lebanon to lose many of its best and brightest, thereby diminishing the value of one of the region's best systems of higher education. Like Oman, Lebanon must also contend with the need to raise living standards among a substantial share of the population: upwards of one-third of Lebanon's people according to some estimates of material deprivation.

Our analyses of available secondary data sources and interviews with government officials in the country show a widespread understanding of the challenges that the country faces. To address these human resource challenges, Lebanon has focused its most recent efforts on broad-based reforms of its economy and public sector. This strategy recognizes the need to put the country on a path toward sustained economic growth and higher living standards. Unlike the Gulf countries in this study, Lebanon has not undertaken major reforms of its education and training systems or the labor market more generally. Instead, it has focused on economic recovery, part of which has entailed improving the efficiency of government. Table 6.12 summarizes the reform efforts under way in Lebanon.

Lebanon has made important gains since the end of the civil war, but a number of challenges continue to jeopardize the sustainability of reforms put in place to date and the commitment to implement future reform programs: the ongoing instability in the internal political situation, as well as the spillover effects of conflict in the region; the fragile state of the economic recovery, including the impact of public debt accumulation; and the shortage of qualified senior staff in the

Table 6.12
Summary of Education and Economic Reforms Under Way in Lebanon

Reform Categories and Subcategories
Education and training
Primary and secondary education
Participation in international assessments
Labor market and economy
Other economic reforms
Divestment of government-owned companies
Implementation of free trade agreements and free trade zones
Training and other supports for more-efficient public administration

government ministries capable of undertaking the reform activities. Of particular concern to the Lebanese government is the fact that ongoing reforms do not entail enforceable transparency and accountability components. A shared view expressed during our interviews was that in order to successfully push the administrative reform agenda forward, concepts of transparency and accountability, as well as structured reporting, need to be fully integrated into all ongoing and future reform programs. Recent efforts to collect data on housing, the labor market, and living conditions are certainly a step in the right direction. However, we found that in Lebanon, just as in the other study countries, the use of collected data to inform future policy initiatives is limited.

CHAPTER SEVEN
Conclusions

The countries examined in this study are facing a number of human resource challenges, to a large extent reflecting the range of issues affecting countries throughout the Arab region. Our four study countries are at various stages of implementing reforms and policy initiatives to address these challenges. We found that while the motivations for these reforms and other initiatives are oftentimes similar, the countries' specific approaches can be distinctly different. More common across the study countries is a gap between implementation of reforms and evaluation of whether they are having the intended effect. In many cases, the reforms have only recently gotten under way, so it may be too early to measure their impact. In other cases, the lack of systematic assessment stems from gaps in the data available for tracking the effects of policy changes.

In this chapter, we synthesize what we learned from our four study countries about the human resource challenges they face, the range of reforms and other initiatives that have been implemented or are under way, and the extent to which these changes are being or can be evaluated with existing data. We conclude by highlighting a benefit of making policy evaluation an integral part of the reform process, in order for all countries in the region to benefit from lessons learned and knowledge gained from the extensive changes that are under way.

Significant Human Resource Challenges

Table 7.1 summarizes the array of significant human resource challenges that our four study countries face. Each row in the table delineates a challenge affecting at least one of the countries; one check mark indicates that the particular challenge affects the country in that column. Two check marks side by side in a column indicate that the issue is having an even greater effect on that particular country.

The first challenge, relevant for the three Gulf countries, and most prominently the labor-importing resource-rich countries of Qatar and the UAE, is the heavy reliance on non-nationals to meet labor force needs for both skilled and unskilled workers. The dominance of non-nationals in the workforce stems both from the relatively small population base from which rapid economic growth took place following the discovery of oil and gas, and from the relatively low labor force participation rate of nationals, particularly in the private quasi-government sectors where few nationals are employed.

Table 7.1
Human Resource Challenges Affecting Study Countries

Challenge	Lebanon	Oman	Qatar	UAE
Labor force made up mostly of non-nationals; low labor force participation among nationals		√	√√	√√
Employment of nationals focused in government sector; private-sector employment less attractive to nationals		√	√√	√√
Unemployment rates high among young first-time workers	√	√	√	√
Education and training system not preparing students well for the workforce	√	√	√	√
Brain drain diminishes benefit of a strong higher education sector	√			
Disparities in living standards affect access to and quality of education opportunities	√	√		

NOTES: √ = issue affects country; √√ = issue is relatively more prominent in this country than in the others.

Having a large expatriate population in the labor force poses a political and economic conundrum for rulers in the Gulf countries. On one hand, few if any nationals are willing to take jobs performed by expatriates because they perceive these jobs as being of lower prestige (such as low-skilled jobs) or offering arduous working conditions (such as positions outside the government sector). Moreover, research conducted in Qatar found that potential employers believe that nationals lack the skills necessary to compete in higher-skilled jobs, such as English language skills and information and communication technology skills (Stasz et al., 2007). On the other hand, this system is not self-sustaining. Expatriate workers have terminal residency permits that allow them to be in the country for a limited time, and they must be "sponsored" by a national employer. Further, children born to an expatriate in a Gulf country are not citizens of that country; the child is a citizen of the parents' country of origin. Officials we spoke with in Qatar, the UAE, and even Oman considered expatriate workers to be, at minimum, not vested in the country's development because of their status as temporary residents and, at most, potential security threats or even criminal threats because of their lack of allegiance to the country.

Linked to the issue of high proportions of non-national workers in our three Gulf countries is the issue of relatively low labor force participation rates for nationals. In Oman, Qatar, and the UAE, the labor force participation rates for male and female nationals are 15 to 40 percentage points lower than those for non-nationals. And for cultural and religious reasons, the rate for female nationals is considerably lower than that for male nationals, despite the tendency for females to have higher educational attainment. Thus, the labor capacity of the citizen population—both male and female—is underutilized.

A second issue faced by the Gulf countries in our study—again, most importantly for Qatar and the UAE—is the concentration of national workers in the public sector. This reflects the historically preferential treatment nationals have received in the public sector, where compensation, working conditions, job security, and prestige are higher than is found in the private sector. Government jobs in Qatar, the UAE, and, for a limited time, Oman have been a way to transfer the wealth derived from oil and gas exploitation to the country's citizen population. In effect, employment in the public sector has become a form of welfare granted by the ruling elite in the resource-rich Gulf countries. This is not a sustainable employment system, however. At some point, proceeds from oil and gas revenue will no longer be able to support the social welfare system of guaranteed government employment that is in effect in these countries. And because these government jobs do not require workers to learn technological skills or engage in entrepreneurial activities that could help propel the country's economy away from reliance on natural resources, nationals who rely on government employment are not developing the skills needed to compete in the global economy.

The third challenge, which uniformly affects all four study countries, is high rates of unemployment among young first-time workers. No data on unemployment rates by age were available for Oman and the UAE, but this issue was consistently raised in our meetings with officials. Unemployment is even more likely for young females, compared with young males, as they make the transition from school to work. The high unemployment rates signal a problem in matching workers to jobs at these young ages, a problem caused in part by a mismatch between the skills of labor market entrants and the needs of employers, especially those in the private sector.

The skill mismatch is a symptom of the fourth issue, which also affects all four study countries: the perception that the education and training systems do not effectively prepare students for the needs of the 21st century global economy. Our study countries have successfully expanded educational opportunities to all citizens at the primary education level, and literacy rates have risen rapidly through time, but there was general acknowledgment by our interviewees that the quality of the primary and secondary education systems in these countries is not yet up to international standards. Secondary school graduates are considered unprepared to directly enter the labor market with relevant skills or to enter competitive university programs. These concerns were validated in our study (see the individual country chapters, Three through Six) with certain evidence: low performance levels on internationally benchmarked student assessments; the low share of students whose studies at the secondary and post-secondary level concentrate in the critical fields of science, mathematics, engineering, and technology; and low rates of obtaining post-secondary degrees, especially for male nationals in the Gulf states.

Two other issues in Table 7.1 pertain to Lebanon and Oman, the two middle-income countries in our analysis. For Lebanon, the out-migration of university-level graduates in recent decades because of the civil war and ongoing political and economic instability has diminished the benefits to the country of producing graduates from what is considered to be one of the finer higher education systems in the region. In addition, both Lebanon and Oman, with lower per capita income and higher disparities in living standards, must contend with disparities in access to and quality of educational opportunities for their populations.

Active Engagement with Reforms to Education and Training Systems, Labor Markets, and the Economy

The human resource challenges are the motivators of a series of reforms implemented or under way in our four study countries. Our analysis of interviews with officials from the public and private sectors, as well as documentation of policies and other reforms, led us to group reforms into two broad categories: changes in the education and occupational training system designed to raise the skills of the population, and changes to the labor market and economy aimed at facilitating the use of human capital in diverse sectors of the economy. We now summarize the approaches identified for our study countries.

Education and Training Reforms

Table 7.2 summarizes the education and training reforms in place or planned in the four study countries, grouping the various elements of these reforms into three areas: primary and secondary education, higher education, and training systems. These reforms are generally aimed at increasing access to or quality of the education and training provided. It is evident from the pattern of check marks that Lebanon

Table 7.2
Education and Training Reforms in Study Countries

Reform Area and Element	Lebanon	Oman	Qatar	UAE
Primary and secondary education				
Establishment of coordinating bodies			√	√
School organizational change		√	√	√
Standards-based accountability			√	
Restructured curriculum		√	√	
National assessment and evaluation			√	
Participation in international assessments	√		√	
Training for teachers and administrators		√	√	
Integration of information technology		√	√	
Higher education				
Establishment of coordinating bodies				√
Administrative, curricular, and academic standards reforms			√	
International accreditation of higher education programs		√		√
Establishment of private higher education institutions		√	√	√
Scholarship programs		√	√	
University-based job placement program(s)				√
Training systems				
Establishment of coordinating bodies				√
Establishment of technical/vocational colleges		√	√	√
Public-private partnerships to train nationals		√	√	√
Independent certification of post-secondary training institutes			√	

has not been actively engaged in reforms to the education and training system, except for participating in international student assessments (i.e., the 2003 TIMSS). This is not an indication that the country's leadership fails to recognize the importance of an effective education system for future economic success. Instead, it is the recognition that the country's basic infrastructure and pubic-sector institutions need to be rebuilt before fundamental changes can be made to the education and training systems. The three Gulf countries also recognize the importance of advancing their education and training systems. With greater resources to devote to reform at all levels—primary and secondary education, higher education, and training—the three Gulf countries have engaged in more-extensive reforms.

Primary and Secondary Education Reforms. In the primary and secondary education arenas, as summarized in the first panel of Table 7.2, Oman and Qatar are engaged in broad-based reforms to their primary and secondary education systems. Qatar's education reforms are arguably the most comprehensive in the region, with changes initiated in 2002 that address the management and delivery of educational services, the curriculum, and the quality of teachers and other critical resources. Qatar's reform provides for a decentralized, independent system of primary and secondary schools that operates alongside the country's traditional Ministry of Education schools. The schools in the new system, called Independent schools, are overseen by a newly developed Education Institute. Principals in these schools make their own staffing and pedagogical decisions, and the schools use newly developed curriculum standards in mathematics, science, and English (benchmarked to international standards) and in Arabic (the first of their kind). The standards encourage critical thinking and problem solving as part of their learning tools. Training programs for teachers and administrators and investments in information technology further enhance the quality of the educational inputs. Another part of the education reform is a system for evaluating the progress of students in all publicly funded schools; it includes annual standards-based assessments and surveys administered to all students and their parents, teachers, and school administrators. Results from the assessments and surveys are distributed to all schools in the form of a school report card.[1] Qatar is also participating in three international assessments (PISA, PIRLS, and TIMSS) that will allow comparisons among Qatar's students and students around the world. The national and international assessments will enable policymakers to gauge how well the country's education reform efforts are doing through time.

Faced with the prospect of dwindling natural resources and spurred by its Vision 2020 (a map for Oman's economic development that was originated in a conference in 1995) (Oman Ministry of Education, 2004), Oman initiated reforms to its publicly funded education system earlier than the other Gulf countries in this study did. In 1998, Oman's Ministry of Education initiated its Basic education school system, which runs parallel to the Ministry's General education school system, beginning with students in grades 1 and 2 in 17 primary schools; the number of students and schools participating in the Basic education school system grows each year. The Basic system reorganized the structure of schooling into two cycles: Cycle 1 covers students in grades 1 through 5; cycle 2 covers students in grades 6 through 10. After grade 10, students have the option of entering the labor market or continuing their schooling in grades 11 and 12, which prepare them for higher education. Other changes introduced as part of the Basic education reform include lengthening the school year, school day, and class period time; changing the curriculum to emphasize critical thinking, English language, information and communication technology, mathematics, and science; encouraging the use of formative and continuous assessments in the classroom so that teachers can receive feedback on student performance and skills; and raising teacher qualifications and the classroom supports they receive.

In the UAE, policymakers have recently brought primary and secondary education reform to the forefront. The formation of the Abu Dhabi and Dubai Education councils to set new priorities for the government education system was based on recognition that graduates were not prepared to meet the human resource needs of UAE's oil- and gas-associated industries in Abu Dhabi and the rapidly growing

---

[1] Starting in 2007, only Independent schools participate in the student assessments.

and diversifying manufacturing, services, communications, and tourism sectors in Dubai. The Abu Dhabi Education Council authorized a pilot program involving the establishment of government-school clusters administered by a number of carefully selected Education Management Organizations as an alternative governance model, as well as reforms in how the traditional government schools were being run by the Ministry of Education. The Ministry of Education itself, under the leadership of a new minister, began considering whether to grant more autonomy to the individual emirates to manage their own education affairs with the support and guidance of the Ministry. The Ministry of Education also recently scrapped the secondary school exit exam with the goal of developing a more formative and continuous system of assessing student achievement throughout students' school years. Furthermore, the Ministry implemented a new school model in a select number of government schools, termed "Al Ghad schools," with an emphasis on a modern, bilingual curriculum; use of student-centered instructional approaches; greater integration of technology; and the availability of more-continuous professional development and support for school leaders and teachers. These are all signs of the potential for fundamental change to UAE's education system.

Higher Education and Training Reforms. Table 7.2's second panel summarizes the initiatives that address the higher education system. These reform elements consist of a mixture of strategies designed to focus on quality through curricular changes, international accreditation, and other reforms; to expand access by introducing new higher education institutions and providing scholarships; and to strengthen links to the labor market through job placement programs. The three Gulf countries in our study have reexamined the quality of their available post-secondary options and have adopted several approaches to enhance quality within existing institutions and increase the number of quality post-secondary programs available to students. For example, Qatar is implementing reforms to its one national university in an effort to promote faculty research, increase financial transparency, and improve student learning. Higher education institutions in the UAE and Oman have sought international accreditation for all or some of the academic programs in their main institutions. All three Gulf countries have increasingly come to rely on foreign universities and the private sector to meet their growing post-secondary education needs. Qatar and the UAE have instituted education and "knowledge" centers to attract international colleges and universities to establish satellite campuses in their countries. In Qatar's case, the foreign institutions are specifically targeted and subsidized; in the UAE, the centers are open to a wider array of providers that operate on a cost-recovery basis. In addition, scholarships are being used, in Oman to allow students from low-income families to attend higher education, and in Qatar to provide incentives for university students to major in high-priority fields. In the UAE, another focus at the post-secondary level is matching students to jobs. UAE University, HCT, and Zayed University have programs in place to improve the school-to-work transition through the provision of specialized instruction relevant to the private sector and through the use of internships and other job placement programs.

The goal of raising the skills of the current and future workforce has required a focus not just on primary, secondary, and post-secondary education, but on the training system, as well. Table 7.2's third panel lists the various reform elements specific to the training systems in our study countries. While efforts to address training needs are in process in the three Gulf countries, they are not as systematic or sustained as the education reforms. In the UAE, training issues are but one focus of the coordinating education councils, which also concentrate on primary, secondary, and higher education reforms. For all three countries, there is an effort to expand the number of technical and vocational colleges and to forge public-private partnerships to expand opportunities to train nationals, especially in skills required for the private sector. In Qatar, officials have established an independent certification of training programs to ensure their quality.

Reforms to the Labor Market and Economy

The four countries in our study have also engaged in initiatives that target the labor market and the economy more generally; these are summarized in Table 7.3. The labor market reforms are specific to the three Gulf countries and aim to address some of the labor market barriers that have precluded the employment of nationals in the private

Table 7.3
Labor Market and Other Economic Reforms in Study Countries

Reform Element	Lebanon	Oman	Qatar	UAE
Labor market reforms				
Quotas for employment of nationals in private sector		√	√	√
Rewards and sanctions for employment of nationals in targeted sectors		√		√
Elimination of automatic employment of nationals in public sector			√	
Equalization of worker rights or access to benefits in public and private sectors		√	√	√
Training and financial support to start new business		√		
Establishment of job placement/matching and training bureau				√
Other economic reforms				
Incentives to expand peripheral industries		√		√
Divestment of government-owned companies	√	√		
Allowance of foreign ownership of companies in selected sectors		√	√	
Implementation of free trade agreements and free trade zones	√	√		
Establishment of free zones exempt from government requirements		√	√	√
Training and other supports for more efficient public administration	√			

sector. The broader economic reforms seek to diversify and privatize the economy and, in the case of Lebanon, provide for a more efficient public sector. These reforms potentially allow for use of the country's human capital throughout the economy.

The labor market reforms (Table 7.3, top panel) in the Gulf countries consist of approaches geared to give employers incentives to hire nationals through quotas or sanctions. Another approach is to make private-sector employment more attractive to nationals by equalizing employment conditions between the public and private sectors. And yet another approach is to introduce institutions that facilitate the transition of nationals to private sector work through training and financial support or through job matching. For example, in the UAE, Emiratisation has been a goal since the late 1990s. Quotas in the banking sector were subsequently extended to the insurance and trade sectors, and financial penalties may be applied to companies that repeatedly fail to meet Emiratisation targets. Such quotas for targeted industries have been used in Oman and Qatar, as well. To give nationals an incentive to work in the private sector, all three countries have passed laws to equalize workers' rights or access to benefits in the public and private sectors. Qatar also eliminated the entitlement of nationals to jobs in the public sector. Other incentives for workers include training and financial support to start new businesses, as provided in Oman; and Emiratis potentially benefit from publicly sponsored job banks, career counseling, and training programs designed to match workers to private-sector jobs.

Table 7.3 also shows (bottom panel) the variety of measures being pursued by the countries in our study to diversify their economies, promote their private sectors, and raise public-sector efficiency as a way to employ the citizenry and enhance the sustainability of their economies. For example, Oman is diversifying industries by offering tax incentives to foreign companies to open branch offices and plants in the country, and the UAE has targeted expansion of the industrial and manufacturing base related to the oil and gas sectors. A related strategy to diversify the economy, one employed in Oman and Lebanon, is the privatization of public utilities and other government-owned firms, such as petroleum companies. Diversification has also been promoted, in Oman and Qatar, by relaxing restrictions on foreign ownership of companies in targeted sectors. Lebanon and Oman have entered into free trade agreements and used other strategies to promote foreign trade. Related approaches in Oman, Qatar, and the UAE include opening free zones—areas in which companies are subject to reduced taxes, are exempt from government regulations (e.g., labor laws and capital controls), and benefit from well-developed infrastructure and facilities—to expand and create new areas of economic activity, particularly through foreign investment. In Lebanon, in light of its level of public-sector indebtedness, economic reform efforts have focused on creating a more efficient public sector by providing training and developing a more rational human resource strategy for the government sector.

Lack of High-Quality Data and Evaluation Systems

Given the challenges affecting our study countries and the reforms that have been implemented or are under way, it is relevant to ask whether systematic efforts are in place to assess the effects of these reforms and whether there is evidence of their success. Our analysis indicates that there has been no deliberate strategy of evaluating the effects of the reforms covered in our study. For many of these reforms, implementation was recent, so there has been little time to assess their effects. At the same time, for both recent reforms and those that were implemented up to a decade ago, evaluation has generally not been an integral part of planning for or implementing policy changes.

We did find several instances in which formal evaluations accompanied policy changes or there had been limited efforts to assess trends in outcomes before and after reforms were put in place. For example, in Chapter Three, we highlight evidence from Qatar's national student assessments that student performance is higher in the new, Independent schools, which are part of the primary and secondary education reforms under way in the country. In Chapter Five, we cite data on student performance over time to suggest that Oman's education reforms are having their desired effect, although other factors could explain the improved student outcomes. In Chapters Four and Five, respectively, we present figures to suggest that rates of Emiratisation and Omanization are on the rise in key sectors, which may be the result of policies designed to achieve that outcome, although, again, other factors may be responsible for the gains or may be limiting the realized improvements (e.g., conflicting policies, such as the use of free zones, where employers are exempt from quotas for nationals). And in Chapter Four, we cite an evaluation of the UAE University internship program that indicated the program did not lead to the desired types of job placements in the private sector.

Evaluation efforts in the study countries are partly hampered by limited experience with program and policy evaluation and by data gaps. In the Gulf countries, collection of economic and demographic data has been constrained by several historical factors that have left legacies of great mistrust in data collection, as well as a poor infrastructure for implementing data collection activities. The factors include (Mohammed, 2003)

- *Lack of administrative "state" structures.* On the Arabian mainland, small *wadis* were separated by large expanses of uninhabited desert roamed by wandering tribes whose survival depended on trading the produce of their herds and their livestock with coastal towns. Coastal towns, with their settled populations, were led by tribal sheikhs—for example, Doha under the Al Thanis, Abu Dhabi under the Al Nuhayyans—the closest that the region came to having a government structure.[2]
- *Frequent and unmonitored population movements.* Persian traders, African slaves, Bedouins—these are some of the populations making frequent and unmonitored moves, limiting the ability to conduct traditional population-based surveys.
- *Social and cultural norms.* Many of these do not lend themselves to divulging private information.

For countries in the Gulf, collection of statistical information on the population began in the 1940s, when states needed this information to redistribute oil revenues. The first oil shock in 1973 necessitated that censuses be conducted. In the case of Lebanon, our non-Gulf country, collection of census data dates to the early part of the 20th century, although data collection efforts have since been hampered by the civil war and sectarian rivalries, which made accurate data on the distribution of the population politically untenable.

---

[2] Bahrain was the only country in which a rudimentary administrative system existed, managed by a literate minority.

In the last few decades, each country in our study has attempted to establish government entities to oversee the collection of data. These include Lebanon's Central Administration for Statistics; Oman's Ministry of National Economy, which oversees economic data collection and has acquired considerable authority over national policymaking; Qatar's Planning Council; and the UAE's Ministry of Economy and Planning and the National Human Resource and Employment Authority (Tanmia). However, issues of coordination remain. For example, each emirate in the UAE is in charge of its own census—only in 2005 did the seven emirates combine efforts to have the UAE Ministry of Economy and Planning perform the census.

Although the countries in our sample are making strides to develop national sources of data, comprehensive and systematic data collection has only recently been put in place, and gaps in data collection efforts remain. Table 7.4 summarizes the censuses and specialized surveys conducted in our four study countries up to 2006. The specialized surveys we focus on include those covering population and housing (in lieu of a full census or enumeration), labor force participation, and household income and expenditures—topical areas relevant for understanding the human capital accumulation and use of the population. Lebanon has the earliest census of the study countries but has yet

Table 7.4
Censuses and Specialized Surveys in Study Countries

Data Collection Category	Lebanon	Oman	Qatar	UAE
Census	1932	1993 2003	1986 1997 2004	1975 1980 1985 1995 2005
Population and housing survey	1994–1996			
Household labor force survey	1970 1997	1996 2000 2006	2001 2006	
Household income and expenditure survey	2004	1991–1992 1999–2002	1982 1988 2001	

to repeat the enumeration completed in 1932. It has filled in the data gap with other, specialized surveys, but they have been very irregular. Of the Gulf countries, the UAE has the longest and most regular history of conducting censuses, but it has not implemented other surveys to capture labor force activity (beyond what is captured in the census) and household income or expenditures. Oman and Qatar have collected such specialized surveys but only on an irregular schedule.

Other data, beyond those obtained from the sources in Table 7.4, are also relevant for examining human capital development. For example, each of our study countries has administrative data, typically available on an annual basis, on aspects of the primary, secondary, and higher education systems. Qatar is the only country that is also systematically collecting data on student performance in order to evaluate primary and secondary education reforms.

Our study countries generally intend to increase the frequency and quality of their data collection efforts. Future plans call for members of the GCC (which includes the three Gulf countries in our study) to collect census data in a coordinated effort in 2010. Qatar has indicated plans to collect labor force data annually; Oman plans to do the same with income and expenditure data. Each study country, with the exception of the UAE, has also joined the IMF GDDS, which requires the development of systematic data collection efforts following international standards in areas relevant for analyzing human capital development.

While the countries covered in our study should be commended for making efforts to collect data on the population and labor force, significant improvements could be made to many of the data collection processes and goals and to the use of these data. In general, the analysis of data and the use of evaluation results to inform policymaking have not become entrenched activities in the countries we studied. Some government ministries have begun to recognize the value of policy evaluation, but there has not been a strong institutional commitment to using data and evaluation methods in support of policymaking.

The Value of Policy Evaluation

As the Arab countries respond to the human resource challenges they face, tremendous energy and resources are being devoted to initiatives to raise the skills of the population and ensure that the resulting human capital is fully utilized throughout the economy. However, there are some limits to the use of national policy that countries should take into consideration.

Policymaking needs to balance the complex demands of a country's social culture and its economic realities. For example, workforce flows, strife within or directly outside a country's borders, a population's adaptability to major changes in education or labor market structures—these are all part of the context within which policymakers must develop policies. To ensure that resources are used wisely, it is critical to evaluate whether policy changes and other initiatives are having their intended effect and whether reforms are having unintended consequences. For example, the three Gulf countries in our study are in various stages of investing in initiatives to improve the quality of primary, secondary, and higher education. A key issue is whether families and students will respond to the new opportunities so that future students making the transition from school to work do so with the skills required by employers. Related issues include whether education institutions can keep up with demand by young people, and even older workers, for educational opportunities. Furthermore, the extent to which there will continue to be sufficient opportunities in the private sector, with commensurate compensation for higher levels of skill attainment, is unknown. These issues can be investigated by monitoring through time students' academic achievement and educational attainment and the success of new entrants to the labor market. Other investigations can address the factors that are driving choices made by students, workers, and employers and how responsive they are to particular incentives.

Ultimately, for reforms to be their most effective, policy evaluation must become an essential component of the process of change, so that initiatives can be refined and improved based on measured effects. With evaluation also comes the potential to minimize unintended consequences and identify barriers to successful implementation. Moreover, the extensive range of reforms under way throughout the Arab world offers a tremendous opportunity to learn from the cross-county experimentation and build a knowledge base of lessons learned and strategies that can be transferred from one county to another. Countries in the Arab world will then have the information essential for making the best investments in the human capital of their people in the decades to come.

APPENDIX A
Interviews Conducted

We conducted a series of interviews in 2006 in Lebanon, Oman, and the UAE and analyzed interview notes from myriad studies conducted by RAND from 2001 through 2006. This appendix lists the officials and the representatives of the public, private, and quasi-private sectors that we or other RAND researchers interviewed:

- *Manpower and vocational training:* Undersecretary of the Ministry of Manpower (Oman); member of Education Council in Charge of Vocational Education (UAE)
- *Primary, secondary, and post-secondary education:* Minister of Higher Education (Oman); Minister of Education (Oman, Lebanon, Qatar); member of Education Council and Director of Knowledge Village (UAE); Director of Academic City (UAE); University Faculty and Administrators (UAE); President of Qatar University; members of the Supreme Education Council (Qatar)
- *Civil service and labor:* Undersecretary of the Ministry of Civil Service (Oman); Ministry of Civil Service and Housing (Qatar)
- *Economy, finance, and planning:* Minister of Economy (Lebanon); Advisor to the Minister of Finance (Lebanon); Undersecretary of Ministry of National Economy (Oman); Minister and Undersecretary of Ministries of Economy and Planning (Lebanon, UAE); Minister of Planning (Qatar); Ministry of Economy and Planning Statistical Department staff (UAE)
- *Administrative reform and social affairs:* Minister of Reform (Lebanon); Minister of Social Affairs (Lebanon)

- *General government:* Chief Advisor to the Prime Minister (Lebanon)
- *Private or quasi-private sector:* Petroleum-sector representatives (UAE, Qatar); technology, research, and development representative (UAE); director of research center (UAE).

APPENDIX B
Interview Protocol

We conducted a series of semi-structured interviews with officials in Lebanon, Oman, and the UAE. We based the protocol we developed for these interviews on our analysis of notes taken by RAND researchers during interviews conducted from 2001 through 2006 for studies assessing Qatar's education, labor market, and civil service sectors. This appendix provides the generic interview protocol we used for these interviews, both core questions and some supplemental questions. In some cases, the protocol was further tailored to address issues unique to the ministry or organization where we conducted the interview.

Core Questions

Role of the Ministry

1. What are the most important reforms in the area of human capital that have been overseen by this Ministry in the past five years? What are the specific programs that have been implemented in this area?
2. What kinds of studies are conducted or commissioned by this Ministry to understand the human resource needs of the nation?
3. What are the most important current national policy priorities, and what role does this Ministry play in formulating and addressing them?

4. What kinds of mechanisms are in place to provide information and data to you in conducting policymaking?

Trends in Labor Force and Human Capital Initiatives

1. What are the most significant challenges that the country faces in terms of the labor pool? (We are particularly interested in issues related to human skills deficits, and examples of how institutional, social, and political contexts play a role.)
2. What specific economic initiatives and reforms have been embarked upon at the national and local levels to address those human resource needs?
   a. What are the specific goals of these initiatives?
   b. What goals, in your opinion, have been successfully achieved, and what goals remain significant challenges?

Political and Social Context for Reform

1. What are the impetuses for human capital and economic reform and how are the reforms sustained? What is the source of support needed to maintain major reform initiatives?
2. What is the process for formulation and implementation of reform? What institutional structures exist to oversee and carry out these reform initiatives?
3. How are the private sector and community involved in the process of economic reform policy formulation and implementation? (We are particularly interested in learning about politically representative entities, public forums, and non-governmental organizations, if relevant.)

Evaluation of Human Capital and Economic Reform Initiatives

1. Is there a benchmarking or evaluation mechanism in place that measures progress in the achievement of these reform goals?

2. What do you see as the major upcoming challenges to the success of these reforms, and how do factors related to institutional capacity, and resource availability and utilization play a role?
3. What other goals and objectives do you feel should have been or should now be integrated into these ongoing reforms?

Supplemental Questions

Censuses, Other Data Collection Programs, and Their Utilization

1. What kinds of surveys exist that collect data on labor force, training, and education related indicators to identify trends in employment growth and skill needs?
2. What other data collection and research efforts in the areas mentioned above are carried out by either governmental or nongovernmental entities and which ones do you find the most informative and useful to your organization?
3. What electronic or paper publications and reports on reform initiatives are produced, and can you refer us to individuals who can help us to obtain relevant documentation?
4. How are publications that are produced used to inform policymaking?
5. What tangible results have the reforms produced thus far? Which of the following apply:
   a. The gap between educational opportunities and demand for workforce skills is narrowing.
   b. Graduates are prepared to continue successfully into post-secondary study or be productive members of the workforce.
   c. The reforms are showing clear signs of sustainability and continuity.
   d. Nationalization levels are being met without significant compromises made to qualifications or experience.

APPENDIX C
Qatar Higher Education Institute Scholarship Programs

This appendix provides supplementary information for Chapter Three's discussion of scholarship programs administered by the Qatar Higher Education Institute (HEI).

The HEI administers five scholarship programs:

- The *Emiri Scholarship* is awarded to exceptional students, possessing significant academic achievements and the potential to become national leaders, who are accepted into one of the top institutions, as determined by HEI. (Currently, HEI has identified 50 institutions worldwide that meet its criteria as a top institution). There is no pre-determined number of scholarships—they are awarded to everyone who qualifies. Out of 114 current (academic year 2005–2006) recipients of the Emiri Scholarship, six are studying abroad (four males, two females) and the rest are studying at Education City institutions.
- The *National Scholarship* is intended for students with the potential to become future business and professional leaders in targeted fields in Qatar who are accepted into one of the HEI-approved institutions (currently 250 institutions are approved for the National Scholarship). Like the Emiri Scholarship, everyone who qualifies receives a National Scholarship. In academic year 2005–2006, 204 students received this scholarship.
- The *Employee Scholarship Program* is available to high-potential employees who want to pursue additional education and advanced training at HEI-approved universities in areas of critical impor-

tance to Qatar. This program is offered in partnership with public and private employers in Qatar; it currently has 30 slots.

- The *Diploma Scholarship Program* is available to students seeking technical and specialized diplomas in demand in Qatar's labor market, such as diplomas related to nursing, aviation, and other fields. These scholarships are currently available for those attending the College of the North Atlantic (CNA).
- The *Pre-College Grant Program* supports students who need additional academic preparation prior to beginning their post-secondary studies. It is available for students in programs such as the Academic Bridge Program (ABP) and is offered to students with the expectation that they will then be accepted into an HEI-approved college or university.

Table C.1 shows the number of students enrolled in HEI scholarship programs as of academic year 2005–2006. There were 1,445

Table C.1
Number of Students in Qatar HEI Scholarship Programs, 2005–2006

Program	Continuing Students	New Students	Total
Emiri	59	55	114
National	150	54	204
Employee	110	9	119
Pre-college (ABP)	0	127	127
Diploma: CNA-Qatar	66	24	90
Diploma: Qatar Aeronautical College	92	95	187
Pre-HEI: USA/Canada/Australia	87	0	87
Pre-HEI: Europe	256	0	256
Pre-HEI: Middle East/Asia	261	0	261
Total	1,081	364	1,445

SOURCE: Unpublished data made available to authors by officials at the HEI.

students enrolled in all scholarship programs, including 604 students with pre-HEI scholarships.

Table C.2 provides a breakdown of students by field of study for the fields with the highest concentration of HEI scholarship recipients. The HEI scholarship programs cover scholar stipend, tuition and fees, and health insurance, as well as allowances for spouse, children, books, "holiday money," computer, graduation, and more. About 57 percent of scholarship expenses are directed for tuition and fees. Those studying abroad also receive travel expenses and allowances for clothing and relocation.

Table C.2
Highest Concentrations in HEI Scholarships, by Field of Study, 2005–2006

Field of Study	Bachelor's	Master's	Doctorate	Facharzt	Board	Total
Engineering						
Computer engineering	22					22
Industrial engineering	18					18
Electrical engineering	18					18
Petroleum engineering	13					13
Communication/ electronic engineering	36	12				48
Medicine and dentistry						
Medicine	82	2	6	10	13	113
Dentistry	20	1				21
Business, finance, and economics						
Business administration	31	9	3			43
Finance/financial management	16	8	2			26

Table C.2—Continued

Field of Study	Bachelor's	Master's	Doctorate	Facharzt	Board	Total
Investment management/banking	6	2	2			10
Marketing	9					9
Economics	8	1	1			10
Law	45	22	5			72
Graphic design, fine arts, and interior design	56					56
Education	6	19	17			42
Computer science	29	1				30
Political science	14	4	1			19
International relations	9	1				10
Total	438	82	37	10	13	580

SOURCE: Unpublished data made available to authors by officials at the HEI.

APPENDIX D
Private Institutions of Higher Education in Oman

To supplement the discussion in Chapter Five, Table D.1 lists and provides degree field and other information on the private institutions of higher education operating in Oman as of academic year 2006–2007.

Table D.1
Information on Private Institutions of Higher Education Operating in Oman, 2006–2007

Institution	Yr. Est.	Fall 2005 Enrollment	Tourism	Journalism and Communication	Information Technology/ Computing	Engineering[b] and Statistics	English Language/ Linguistics	Business Studies[c]	Social Work	Mathematics and Sciences	Social Sciences and Education	Design	Medicine[d]
								Degree Field[a]					
Majan College	1995–96	1,456			✓		✓	✓					
Caledonian College of Engineering	1996–97	1,197				✓							
Modern College of Business and Science	1996–97	617			✓			✓					
Muscat College	1997–98	497				✓		✓					
Fire Safety Engineering College	1998–99	771				✓							
Al Zahra College for Women (A)	1999–00	882			✓		✓	✓					
Mazoon College	1999–00	794			✓		✓	✓			✓		
Oman College of Tourism	2001–02	181	✓									✓	
Oman Medical College	2001–02	457											✓

Table D.1—Continued

Institution	Yr. Est.	Fall 2005 Enrollment	Tourism	Journalism and Communication	Information Technology/ Computing	Engineering and Statistics[b]	English Language/ Linguistics	Business Studies[c]	Social Work	Mathematics and Sciences	Social Sciences and Education	Design	Medicine[d]
Sohar University	2001–02	1,709		✓	✓	✓	✓	✓			✓		
Sur University College	2001–02	548	✓		✓	✓		✓					
Wajat Colleges of Applied Science	2001–02	927				✓		✓					
Middle East College of Information Technology	2002–03	990			✓	✓		✓				✓	
Al Buraimi College	2003–04	714			✓		✓	✓					
Dhofar University	2004–05	1,824			✓	✓	✓	✓	✓		✓	✓	
Gulf College	2004–05	615	✓		✓			✓				✓	
Oman College of Management and Technology (A)	2004–05	417			✓			✓					
Scientific College of Design	2004–05	230										✓	

Table D.1—Continued

Institution	Yr. Est.	Fall 2005 Enrollment	Tourism	Journalism and Communication	Information Technology/ Computing	Engineering[b] and Statistics	English Language/ Linguistics	Business Studies[c]	Social Work	Mathematics and Sciences	Social Sciences and Education	Design	Medicine[d]
University of Nizwa	2004-05	1,845			✓	✓		✓		✓	✓	✓	✓
International Maritime College Oman	2005-06	171				✓							
Al Bayan College	2006-07	n.a.		✓			✓						
Oman Dental College	2006-07	n.a.											✓

SOURCE: Unpublished data received by authors from Oman Ministry of Higher Education.

NOTES: n.a. = not available. Curriculum taught in English in all colleges and universities unless name listed is followed by "(A)" to designate that Arabic is the medium of instruction.

[a] Degrees are two-year diplomas or four-year bachelor's degrees.
[b] Includes fire safety engineering and marine engineering.
[c] Includes business administration and commerce, finance, and accounting.
[d] Includes dentistry, pharmacy, and nursing.

APPENDIX E
Recent Economic Reform Efforts in Oman

This appendix provides details to supplement Chapter Five's discussion of Oman's recent economic reforms in the areas of economic diversification; promotion of the private sector; development of tax-free zones, ports, and business sectors; and other labor market initiatives.

Economic Diversification

A liquefied natural gas plant opened in 2000 in Sur with production capacity of 6.6 million tons per year, as well as unsubstantial gas liquids, including condensates. Completion of the plant's expansion in December 2005 increased capacity to 10.3 million tons/year. Natural gas production was estimated in 2003 at 16.5 billion cubic meters, and natural gas reserves at 829.1 billion cubic meters (U.S. Department of State, 2007b).

Industrial/manufacturing projects are under way:

- Oman-India Fertilizer Project (commercial production started by 3rd quarter of 2005).
- Sohar International Urea and Chemical Industries.
- Plants for methanol and an oil refinery that will produce propylene, gasoline, aviation fuel, and other oil-based products.
- A polypropylene plant that opened in the last quarter of 2006.
- Aluminum, petrochemical, and ethylene dichloride projects; iron and steel plants (Oman Ministry of National Economy, 2005c).

- Omani Center for Investment Promotion and Export Development (OCIPED): Established in 1996 by Royal Decree, its role is to boost local and international private-sector investment in key economic sectors in Oman and to work in partnership with businesses located in Oman to develop the export of goods and services. It provides information guides for small- and medium-sized exporters in Oman, a directory of exports of Oman companies, and information on investment opportunities and exports from Oman. It also provides assistance to investors to Oman (Oman Ministry of National Economy, 2005c).

Promotion of the Private Sector

- Government divestment:
  - The government has divested 60 percent of its holdings in Al Maha Petroleum Company through a public offering in 2004, and a further 5 percent through private placement. The company is now 100 percent owned by the private sector.
  - The government partially divested its holdings, retaining 51 percent of shareholdings, in such commercial undertakings as Oman Cement Company and Oman Flour Mills, which will be privatized in the future (Oman Ministry of National Economy, 2005c).
- Privatization Act, promulgated by Royal Decree 77/2004 on July 14, 2004 (Oman Ministry of National Economy, 2005c):
  - Allows for 100 percent foreign ownership. Government will form independent regulatory authorities to regulate the market.
  - The company will be deemed as wholly owned Omani Company for tax purposes, attracting a lower tax rate of 12 percent.
- Movement toward privatization of power sector (Fasano and Iqbal, 2003): Royal Decree 78/2004 restructured the electricity and water sectors, allowing for privatization of the power sector. In addition, the decree maps a plan to transfer responsibilities from the Ministry of Housing, Electricity, and Water to ten suc-

cessor companies. On completion of the transfer, regulation will be applied by the newly created Office of Electricity Regulation. Once the power and water sectors are fully commercialized, the government intends to privatize the successor companies by selling the government's shareholdings of the successor companies. Privatization efforts have already taken hold:
- Management of airport services.
- Independent power projects: Manah Power Project (1996), which is presently 100 percent privately owned; Al Kamil Power Project (2003); the Independent Water and Power Project in Barka (2003).
- Salalah power system: Vertically integrated utility—89 percent of project's capital is for foreign investors, 11 percent for Omani founders, and 35 percent to be floated within four years of incorporation.
- Sohar power and water system: Water desalination (2004). Commercial output started in 2007.
- Independent Water Project (2004) in Ash-Sharquiah region: Water desalination. Two committees have been formed to establish companies to operate Al Masarat and Ash-Sharquiah water projects on a commercial basis to be privatized at a later stage.
- Telecommunications: Royal Decree 30/2002 sets the regulatory framework for the telecommunications sector:
  - Thirty percent disinvestments were made in national telecommunications company OMANTEL, offering 30 percent of OMANTEL shares on Muscat Securities Market on June 11, 2005, to Omanis, pension funds, and charitable organizations.
  - A second mobile telephone license was given to Nawras, led by a foreign investor, starting in 2005.
  - Future plans include privatization of a wastewater network to provide recycled water in Salalah and Muscat, hazardous waste disposal, solid waste management in towns, and postal services.

Development of Tax-Free Zones, Ports, and Business Sectors

- Ports:
  - Salalah: 1997 contract to build a container terminal at Raysut near Salalah. The government is now establishing a commercial company (owned by the government) to implement the Salalah Free Zone project.
  - Sohar: Started development of a port in 2002, in tandem with Sohar Industrial Zone.
  - Duqum: Opened in 2006.
- Manufacturing and industrial zones dot the country—in Rusayl, Sohar, Raysut, Sur, Nizwa, Buraimi, and Al Muzanah Free Trade Zone.
- The Public Establishment for Industrial Estates (PEIE): Established by Royal Decree 4/93 on January 3, 1993. It is responsible for developing industrial land. It acts as a liaison for manufacturing businesses and the Omani government to help companies assemble sites, develop buildings, facilitate issuing permits, assess infrastructure needs, and review incentives available for projects, and to help firms market and promote their products. It works closely with Ministry of Commerce and Industry; Oman Chamber of Commerce; Oman Center for Investment, Promotion, and Export Development; permit issuing and regulatory organizations; and utility providers.
- Al Mazunah Free Zone: Operating since November 1999, it is located in Oman's southern region of Dhofar, close to the border with Yemen. It lies outside Oman's tax boundaries; business personnel can enter Al Mazunah without a visa.
- Foreign Capital Investment Law: Royal Decree 102/94, amended by Royal Decrees 90/96 and 56/2003, stipulates that
  - Non-Omanis can conduct a business with a license from the Ministry of Commerce and Industry.
  - The foreign share cannot exceed 49 percent of the total capital. Exceptions, up to 65 percent, are granted by a "Foreign Capital Investment Committee" of the Minster of Commerce and

Industry. The share can be further increased to 100 percent for "projects which contribute to the development of the national economy upon the approval of the Development Council" (Oman Ministry of National Economy, 2005c, p. 47).
- Companies in the following activities are exempt from taxes for five years, and exemption may be renewed for another five years: industry and mining; export of locally manufactured or processed projects; tourism promotion (operation of hotels and tourist villages); production and processing of farm products (animal husbandry, processing of animal products, and agro-industries); fishing and fish processing, culturing, and breeding; exploitation and provision of services (public utility projects, excluding management and project execution contracts).

Other Labor Market Initiatives

- A uniform minimum wage for Omanis was established to replace the previous two-tiered (skilled versus unskilled) minimum wage (Fasano and Iqbal, 2003).
- A labor law adopted in May 2003 gives employees more rights.

References

Abdelkarim, Abbas, and Hans Haan, *Skills and Training in the UAE: The Need for and the Dimensions of Institutional Intervention*, Policy Research Paper No. 5, CLMRI, National Human Resource Development and Employment Authority, Dubai, UAE: CLMRI, 2002.

Abdul Aziz, Ahmed, "30 New Schools in Abu Dhabi Soon," *Khaleej Times*, July 28, 2006. As of August 1, 2008:
http://www.khaleejtimes.com/DisplayArticleNew.asp?xfile=data/theuae/2006/July/theuae_July945.xml&section=theuae&col=

Abu Dhabi Education Council, "The Abu Dhabi Education Council," homepage, Abu Dhabi, UAE: Government of Abu Dhabi, Abu Dhabi Education Council, 2007. As of August 1, 2008:
http://www.adec.ac.ae/en

Abu Dhabi Retirement Pensions and Benefits Fund, "The Insured Obligations Towards the Fund," website, Abu Dhabi, UAE: Government of Abu Dhabi, Abu Dhabi Retirement Pensions and Benefits Fund, 2008. As of August 1, 2008:
http://www.pension.gov.ae/dynamicpages/index.aspx?id=262&main_id=317&sub_id=323

Ahmad, Abdul Hamid, "Stage Set for Country's First FNC Elections," gulfnews.com, September 14, 2006. As of August 1, 2008:
http://archive.gulfnews.com/articles/06/09/14/10067399.html

Ahmed, Osama S., *Assessing Relevance of Work Placement Schemes of Higher Education Institutes in the UAE*, CLMRI, National Human Resource Development and Employment Authority, Careers, Skills, and Training Survey Series No. 3, Dubai, UAE: CLMRI, 2003.

Al Baik, Duraid, and Shireena Al Nowais, "Ministers Welcome Smooth Transfer of Power," gulfnews.com, January 6, 2006. As of July 27, 2008:
http://archive.gulfnews.com/articles/06/01/06/10009667.html

Al-Fakhri, Jamal Jassem, "The Demographic Structure of the GCC States," *The Gulf in a Year—2003*, Dubai, UAE: Gulf Research Center, 2004, pp. 68–80.

Al-Hafidh, Nuri, *Qatar Education Profile*, Paris, France: UNESCO, 1973.

Al Mazroo'i, Muhammad Salem, "Legislative Institutions in the GCC States: Analysis and Assessment," *Gulf Year Book 2004*, Dubai, UAE: Gulf Research Center, 2005, pp. 39–53.

Al Roken, Mohammed Abdullah, "Constitutional and Legal Developments," *Gulf Yearbook 2004*, Dubai, UAE: Gulf Research Center, 2005, pp. 29–37.

Al Shaiba, Abdullah, "Change Is Around the Corner," gulfnews.com, September 9, 2006. As of August 2, 2008:
http://www.gulfnews.com/notes/Education/10066206.html

Al-Shamsi, Fatima, "Economic Performance and the Challenges of Non-Oil Economic Growth," *Gulf Year Book 2004*, Dubai, UAE: Gulf Research Center, 2005, pp. 57–71.

Autor, David H., Lawrence F. Katz, and Melissa S. Kearney, "The Polarization of the U.S. Labor Market," *American Economic Review Papers and Proceedings*, Vol. 96, No. 2, May 2006, pp. 189–194.

Bahry, Louay, and Phebe Marr, "Qatari Women: A New Generation of Leaders?" *Middle East Policy*, Vol. 12, No. 2, Summer 2005, pp. 104–119.

Beblawi, Hazem, and Giacomo Luciani (eds.), *Nation, State and Integration in the Arab World; Vol. 2: The Rentier State*, London, United Kingdom: Croom Helm Ltd., 1987.

Becker, Gary S., *Human Capital: A Theoretical and Empirical Analysis with Special Reference to Education*, Chicago, Ill.: The University of Chicago Press, 1964.

Bhandari, Rajika, and Patricia Chow, *Open Doors 2007: Report on International Educational Exchange*, New York: Institute of International Education, 2007.

Bolle, Mary Jane, "U.S.-Oman Free Trade Agreement," *Congressional Research Service Report to Congress RL33328*, Washington DC: Congressional Research Service, Library of Congress, October 10, 2006. As of August 1, 2008:
http://fpc/state/gov/documents/organization/75249.pdf

Brewer, Dominic J., Catherine H. Augustine, Gail L. Zellman, Gery Ryan, Charles A. Goldman, Cathleen Stasz, and Louay Constant, *Education for a New Era: Design and Implementation of K–12 Education Reform in Qatar*, MG-548-QATAR, Santa Monica, Calif.: RAND Corporation, 2007. As of July 20, 2008:
http://www.rand.org/pubs/monographs/MG548/

Budd, Bruce, "An Overview of the Demographic and Labour Trends of the Member Nations of the Cooperation Council for the Arab States of the Gulf," Working Paper Series No. 10, CLMRI, National Human Resource Development and Employment Authority, Dubai, UAE: CLMRI, 2002.

Cecil, Charles O., "Oman's Progress Toward Participatory Government," *Middle East Policy*, Vol. 13, No. 1, 2006, pp. 60–68.

Centre for Labour Market Research and Information, *UAE Human Resources Report, 2005*, Dubai, UAE: National Human Resource Development and Employment Authority (Tanmia), 2005.

Centre of Excellence for Applied Research and Training, "About CERT," Abu Dhabi, UAE: CERT Technology Park, 2008a. As of August 1, 2008:
http://www.certonline.com/CorporateInfo_AboutUs.aspx

———, "Our Partners," Abu Dhabi, UAE: CERT Technology Park, 2008b. As of August 1, 2008:
http://www.certonline.com/CorporateInfo_Partners.aspx#CTI

CERT—*See* Centre of Excellence for Applied Research and Training

CLMRI—*See* Centre for Labour Market Research and Information

Cohn, E., and J. Addison, "The Economic Returns to Lifelong Learning in OECD Countries," *Education Economics*, Vol. 6, 1998, pp. 253–307.

Collelo, Thomas (ed.), *Lebanon: A Country Study*, 3rd edition, Washington DC: U.S. Government Printing Office, 1989. As of July 21, 2008:
http://lcweb2.loc.gov/frd/cs/lbtoc.html#lb0068

Cooper, Peter J., "Abu Dhabi, New Education Council," *AME Info*, September 12, 2005. As of August 1, 2008:
http://www.ameinfo.com/67291.html

Dubai Education Council, "The Council," Dubai, UAE: Government of Dubai, Dubai Education Council, 2007. As of May 1, 2007:
http://www.dec.gov.ae/english/About%20DEC/default

Dubai Knowledge Village, "Dubai Knowledge Village," Dubai, UAE: Dubai Knowledge Village, 2004a. As of August 2, 2008:
http://www.kv.ae/en/default.asp

———, "Dubai Knowledge Village Services," Dubai, UAE: Dubai Knowledge Village, 2004b. As of August 2, 2008:
http://www.kv.ae/en/cms/showcontent.asp?menu=side&menuid=75&DocumentID=49

Eken, Sena, Paul Cashin, S. Nuri Erbas, Jose Martelino, and Adnan Mazarei, "Economic Dislocation and Recovery in Lebanon," IMF Occasional Paper No. 120, Washington DC: IMF, December 1995.

El Khazen, Farid, "Lebanon—Independent No More: Disappearing Christians of the Middle East," *Middle East Quarterly*, Winter 2001. As of August 5, 2008:
http://www.meforum.org/article/16

El-Quqa, Omar M., Shailesh Dash, Chandresh Bhatt, Dinker Mattam, and Raghu Sarma, *Qatar Economic and Strategic Outlook—III*, Kuwait City, Kuwait: Global Investment House, December 2005. As of July 24, 2008:
http://www.globalinv.net/research/Qatar-Economic-III.pdf

Emirates Institute for Banking and Financial Studies, "Emiratization Chart," Abu Dhabi, UAE: Emirates Institute for Banking and Financial Studies, 2006. As of August 2, 2008:
http://www.eibfs.com/EIBFS/HRDEmiratizationChart

European Training Foundation, *Lebanon: Country Analysis 2005*, Torino, Italy: European Training Foundation, 2006. As of August 2, 2008:
http://www.etf.europa.eu/pubmgmt.nsf/(getAttachment)/2F2485B6DE9B72F4C1 2570FF003B361F/$File/NOTE6LBEN5.pdf

Fasano, Ugo, "Sluggish Growth, Declining Oil Reserves Prompt Qatar to Diversify Economy Away from Oil," *International Monetary Fund Survey*, Vol. 30, No. 20, 2001, pp. 382–384.

Fasano, Ugo, and Zubair Iqbal, "GCC Countries: From Oil Dependence to Diversification," Washington DC: IMF, 2003. As of August 5, 2008:
http://www/imf.org/external/pubs/ft/med/2003/eng/fasano/index.htm

Frank, Lone, "Qatar Taps Wells of Knowledge," *Science*, Vol. 312, April 2006, pp. 46–47.

Golden, Lara Lynn, "Trading Companies Offered Three-Month Grace Period to Comply with Emiratisation Target for 2005," *AME Info*, February 12, 2006. As of August 2, 2008:
http://www.ameinfo.com/77661.html

Gonzales, Patrick, Juan Carlos Guzman, Lisett Partelow, Erin Pahke, Leslie Jocelyn, David Kastberg, and Trevor Williams, *Highlights from the Trends in International Mathematics and Science Study (TIMSS) 2003*, NCES 2005-005, Washington DC: National Center for Education Statistics, 2004. As of August 2, 2008:
http://nces.ed.gov/pubsearch/pubsinfo.asp?pubid=2005005

Haddad, Rola, "Education in Lebanon," Beirut, Lebanon: Center for Sponsored Research and Development, Lebanese American University, 2004. As of November 2, 2006:
http://csrd.lau.edu.lb /Publications/StudentReports/Education%20in%20 Lebanon.htm

Hanafi, Atef, "More Women Should Serve Private Sector," *Al Khaleej Times*, May 17, 2006. As of August 1, 2008:
http://www.khaleejtimes.com/DisplayArticle.asp?xfile=data/theuae/2006/May/ theuae_May655.xml&section=theuae

Hanka, Wadih Ali, "503 Expat Teachers Will Be Replaced by Nationals," Abu Dhabi: Ministry of Education, UAE, February 6, 2006. As of August 2, 2008:
http://www.moeya.ae/ministry/article_view.asp?language=English&id=2376&school_id=

His Highness Mohammed Bin Rashid Al Maktoum, "Education," official website of the Ruler of Dubai, UAE, 2008. As of August 1, 2008:
http://www.sheikhmohammed.co.ae/vgn-ext-templating/v/index.jsp?vgnextoid=1e8c4c8631cb4110VgnVCM100000b0140a0aRCRD

Hutton, Sue, "Nationalization of the Omani Workforce," *Oman Economic Review*, September 2003. As of August 2, 2008:
http://www.oeronline.com/

IMF—*See* International Monetary Fund

International Monetary Fund, "General Data Dissemination System: A Factsheet," Washington DC: IMF, undated. As of August 5, 2008:
http://dsbb.imf.org/vgn/images/pdfs/GDDS_factsheet_web.pdf

———, "General Data Dissemination System: Oman Metadata," Washington DC: IMF, 2005. As of August 5, 2008:
http://dsbb.imf.org/Applications/web/gdds/gddscountrycategorylist/?strcode=OMN

———, "Qatar Formally Begins Participation in the IMF's General Data Dissemination System," Press Release No. 06/04, Washington DC: IMF, January 5, 2006. As of August 5, 2008:
http://www.imf.org/external/np/sec/pr/2006/pr0604.htm

Jebel Ali Free Zone, "Jafza at a Glance," Dubai, UAE: Jafza, Jebel Ali Free Zone, 2008. As of August 2, 2008:
http://jafza.ae/en/about-us/jafza-at-a-glance.html

Jolo, Hend, *Human Capital Formation in the State of Qatar with Special Reference to Oil and Gas Based Industries*, Doctoral dissertation, Exeter, United Kingdom: University of Exeter, 2004.

Kasparian, Choghig, *L'Entrée des Jeunes Libanais dans la Vie Active et l'Émigration: Les Libanais Émigrés Depuis 1975* [*The Transition of Young Lebanese to the Labor Force and Emigration: Lebanese Emigrants Since 1975*], Vol. 3, Beirut, Lebanon: Presses de l'Université Saint-Joseph, 2003 (in French).

Kerr, Simeon, "Strike Risk to Dubai's Building Bonanza," Financial Times.com, November 10, 2007. As of August 2, 2008:
http://www.ft.com/cms/s/0/b4454018-8f31-11dc-87ee-0000779fd2ac.html?nclick_check=1

Khaleej Times Online, "Bid to Lift Standard of Public Education," *Al Khaleej Times*, January 30, 2006a. As of August 2, 2008:
http://www.khaleejtimes.com/DisplayArticle.asp?xfile=data/theuae/2006/January/theuae_January709.xml&section=theuae

———, "President Okays New Cabinet," *Al Khaleej Times*, February 10, 2006b. As of August 2, 2008:
http://www.khaleejtimes.com/DisplayArticle.asp?xfile=data/theuae/2006/February/theuae_February276.xml&section=theuae

Khouairy, Antoine, *The War in Lebanon, 1975—Part I*, Beirut, Lebanon: Dar Al-Abjadieh, 1976 (in Arabic).

Knowledge and Human Development Authority, "About KHDA," Dubai, UAE: Government of Dubai, 2008. As of August 2, 2008:
http://www.khda.gov.ae/en/AboutUs/AboutKHDA.aspx

Knowledge Oasis Muscat, official website, 2008. As of August 2, 2008:
http://www.kom.om/

KOM—*See* Knowledge Oasis Muscat

Korpi, Tomas, and Michael Tahlin, *Skill Mismatch, Wages, and Wage Growth: Overeducation in Sweden, 1974–2000*, SE-106 91, Sweden: Swedish Institute for Social Research (SOFI), Stockholm University, 2006.

Krayem, Hassan, "The Lebanese Civil War and the Taif Agreement," in Paul Salem (ed.), *Conflict Resolution in the Arab World: Selected Essays*, Beirut, Lebanon: American University of Beirut, 1997, pp. 411–435. As of August 2, 2008:
http://almashriq.hiof.no/ddc/projects/pspa/conflict-resolution.html

Lebanese American University, "Lebanese American University: Questions and Answers," official university website, Beirut, Lebanon: Lebanese American University, 2008. As of August 2, 2008:
http://www.lau.edu.lb/about/qanda.php

Lebanon Central Administration for Statistics, *2004 Living Conditions National Survey: First Statistical Results*, Beirut, Lebanon: Central Administration for Statistics, 2005. As of July 23, 2008:
http://www.cas.gov.lb/Download/Tables%20Living%20conditions.xls

———, *Living Conditions of Households: The National Survey of Household Living Conditions, 2004*, Beirut, Lebanon: Central Administration for Statistics, 2006. As of July 22, 2008:
http://www.cas.gov.lb/Newsrep_en.asp

Lebanon Ministry of Economy and Trade, *Lebanon's Economic Accounts 1997–2002*, Beirut, Lebanon: Ministry of Economy and Trade, July 2005. As of August 2, 2008:
http://www.economy.gov.lb/NR/rdonlyres/7D1FCF7D-C0BD-4BDD-B84B-695E417E48E4/0/English9702NA.pdf

———, *Select Macro Economic Indictors*, Beruit, Lebanon: Ministry of Economy and Trade, 2007. As of August 2, 2008:
http://www.economy.gov.lb/MOET/English/Panel/EconomicResearchAndPrices/EconomicResearch/Misc/MacroEconomicIndicators.htm

Lebanon Ministry of Education and Higher Education, *Annual Statistics Bulletin: 2001/2002*, Beirut, Lebanon: Ministry of Education and Higher Education, Center for Education, Research, and Development, 2003 (in Arabic). As of August 2, 2008:
http://www.crdp.org/CRDP/Arabic/a_default.htm

———, *Annual Statistics Bulletin: 2004/2005*, Beirut, Lebanon: Ministry of Education and Higher Education, Center for Education, Research, and Development, 2006 (in Arabic). As of August 2, 2008:
http://www.crdp.org/CRDP/Arabic/a_default.htm

Lebanon Ministry of Environment, *State of the Environment Report 2001*, Beirut, Lebanon: Republic of Lebanon Ministry of Environment, 2001. As of August 2, 2008:
http://www.moe.gov.lb/Reports/SOER2001.htm

Lebanon Ministry of Social Affairs, *Mapping of Living Conditions in Lebanon: Analysis of the Housing and Population Database*, 2nd edition, Beirut, Lebanon: Ministry of Social Affairs, 2001. As of August 2, 2008:
http://www.undp.org.lb/programme/pro-poor/poverty/povertyinlebanon/molc/main.html

———, *The Socio-Economic Situation in Lebanon: Reality and Possibilities*, Beirut, Lebanon: Ministry of Social Affairs, 2004 (in Arabic).

Lebanon Office of the Minister of State for Administrative Reform, *Strategy for the Reform and Development of the Public Administration in Lebanon*, Beirut, Lebanon: OMSAR, 2001. As of August 2, 2008:
http://msib.omsar.gov.lb/Cultures/en-US/Strategies/Reform+and+Development/

———, *Annual Report, 2004-2005*, Beirut, Lebanon: OMSAR, April 2006 (in Arabic). As of August 2, 2008:
http://msib.omsar.gov.lb/Cultures/en-US/Publications/Annual+Reports/Annual+Report+2004-2005.htm

Lussier, Jocelyn, *Oman Economics*, Ottowa, Canada: Export Development Canada, November 2007. As of August 2, 2008:
http://www.edc.ca/English/docs/goman_e.pdf

Maktabi, Rania, "The Lebanese Census of 1932 Revisited: Who Are the Lebanese?" *British Journal of Middle Eastern Studies*, Vol. 26, No. 2, November 1999, pp. 219–241. As of August 2, 2008:
http://www.jstor.org/stable/195924

Manacorda, Marco, and Barbara Petrongolo, *Skill Mismatch and Unemployment in OECD Countries*, Economica, Vol. 66, 1999, pp. 181–207.

McInerney, James, "Oman's Blue City: Tourism and Jobs," *AME Info*, June 13, 2005, updated May 2007. As of August 2, 2008:
http://www.ameinfo.com/62292.html

Metz, Helen C. (ed.), *Persian Gulf States: Country Studies*, 3rd edition, Washington DC: U.S. Government Printing Office, 1994. As of August 1, 2008:
http://www.country-studies.com/persian-gulf-states/

Mohammed, Nadeya Sayed Ali, *Population and Development of the Arab Gulf States: The Case of Bahrain, Oman and Kuwait*, Hampshire, United Kingdom: Ashgate Publishing, 2003.

Mullis, Ina V. S., Michael O. Martin, Eugenio J. Gonzalez, and Steven J. Christowski, *TIMSS 2003 International Mathematics Report: Findings from IEA's Trends in International Mathematics and Science Study at the Fourth and Eight Grades*, Chestnut Hill, Mass.: International Association for the Evaluation of Educational Achievement and TIMSS and PIRLS International Study Center, Boston College, 2004. As of August 1, 2008:
http://isc.bc.edu/timss2003i/mathD.html

Najjar, Ghanim, "Internal Political Developments: A General Overview," *Gulf Year Book 2004*, Dubai, UAE: Gulf Research Center, 2005, pp. 17–28.

National Science Foundation, *Science and Engineering Indicators: 2004*, NSB 04-01C, Arlington, Va.: NSF, 2004. As of August 1, 2008:
http://www.nsf.gov/statistics/seind04/

———, *Science and Engineering Indicators: 2006*, NSB 06-01C, Arlington, Va.: NSF, 2006. As of August 1, 2008:
http://www.nsf.gov/statistics/seind06/

Novakovic, Janeta, "Dubai Education Council Announces 'Dubai Schools,'" *AME Info*, October 10, 2005, updated October 23, 2006. As of August 2, 2008:
http://www.ameinfo.com/69673.html

NSF— *See* National Science Foundation

OECD—*See* Organisation for Economic Co-operation and Development

Oman Chamber of Commerce and Industry, "Sanad," Muscat: Oman Chamber of Commerce and Industry, 2008. As of August 2, 2008:
http://www.chamberoman.com/sanad_occi_sanad.asp

Oman Cultural Office, "Education in Oman," Washington DC: Oman Cultural Office, 2008. As of August 2, 2008:
http://www.omani.info/education.htm

Oman Ministry of Education, *Basic Education in the Sultanate of Oman: The Theoretical Framework*, Muscat: Sultanate of Oman Ministry of Education, 1998.

———, *National Report on Quality Education in Oman*, Muscat: Sultanate of Oman, Ministry of Education, 2004. As of August 2, 2008:
http://www.ibe.unesco.org/International/ICE47/English/Natreps/reports/oman_part_1.pdf

———, *Educational Statistics Yearbook (2005/2006)*, Muscat: Educational Statistics Department, Sultanate of Oman Ministry of Education, 2006. As of August 2, 2008:
http://82.178.29.32/statistical/english/aqwal.html

Oman Ministry of Higher Education, *General Statistical Book for Higher Education Institutions in the Sultanate of Oman, Academic Year 2004/2005*, 3rd edition, Muscat: Sultanate of Oman, Ministry of Higher Education, 2005a.

———, *Guide to Higher Education Institutions*, Muscat: Sultanate of Oman, Ministry of Higher Education, 2005b.

Oman Ministry of Information, "Omanisation Policy," Muscat: Ministry of Information, Sultanate of Oman, 2008a. As of August 2, 2008:
http://www.omanet.om/english/misc/omanise.asp

———, *The Complete Information of Oman*, Muscat: Ministry of Information, Sultanate of Oman, 2008b. As of August 2, 2008:
http://www.omanet.om/english/home.asp

Oman Ministry of Manpower, Comment letter—personal correspondence with authors, Muscat: Sultanate of Oman, Ministry of Manpower, December 2006.

Oman Ministry of National Economy, *Oman Human Development Report, 2003*, Muscat: Sultanate of Oman, Ministry of National Economy, January 2004. As of July 22, 2008:
http://www.moneoman.gov.om/book/hdr03/Final_en/ind_1.htm

———, *The Address of His Excellency The Minister of National Economy to the Honorable Majlis A'Shura on the Outcomes of the Assessment of the Sixth Five-Year Development Plan Performance During the Period (2001–2004) and the Directions of the Seventh Five-Year Development Plan*, Muscat: Sultanate of Oman, Ministry of National Economy, 2005a.

———, *First Volume—Census Results at the Sultanate Level*, Muscat: Sultanate of Oman, Ministry of National Economy, 2005b. As of July 22, 2008:
http://www.omancensus.net/english/first_publication.asp

———, *Oman: The Development Experience and Investment Climate, 2005*, 5th edition, Muscat: Sultanate of Oman, Ministry of National Economy, 2005c.

———, *Census 2003 Data*, Muscat: Sultanate of Oman, Ministry of National Economy, 2005d. As of July 22, 2008:
http://www.omancensus.net/english/index.asp

———, official website, Muscat: Sultanate of Oman, Ministry of National Economy, 2008a. As of July 23, 2008:
http://www.moneoman.gov.om

———, *Ministry of National Economy, Statistics*, Muscat: Sultanate of Oman, Ministry of National Economy, 2008b. As of July 23, 2008:
http://www.moneoman.gov.om/mainStat.asp.

———, *Statistical Yearbook 2007*, Muscat: Sultanate of Oman, Ministry of National Economy, 2008c. As of July 22, 2008:
http://www.moneoman.gov.om/book/syb2007/index_Index.htm

Oman Society for Petroleum Services, "Official Portal of Oman Society for Petroleum Services," Muscat: Oman Society for Petroleum Services, 2008. As of August 2, 2008:
http://www.opaloman.org/

OMSAR—*See* Lebanon Office of the Minister of State for Administrative Reform

OPEC—*See* Organization of the Petroleum Exporting Countries

Organisation for Economic Co-operation and Development, *OECD in Figures: 2005 Edition*, Paris, France: OECD Publications, 2005.

Organization of the Petroleum Exporting Countries, *Annual Statistical Bulletin 2004*, 2005. As of July 21, 2008:
http://www.opec.org/library/Annual%20Statistical%20Bulletin/interactive/2004/FileZ/Main.htm

———, *Annual Statistical Bulletin 2005*, 2006. As of July 21, 2008:
http://www.opec.org/library/Annual%20Statistical%20Bulletin/interactive/2005/FileZ/Main.htm

Ozden, Caglar, "Brain Drain in Middle East and North Africa: The Patterns Under the Surface," Paper presented at United Nations expert group meeting on international migration and development in the Arab region, Population Division, Department of Economic and Social Affairs, United Nations Secretariat, Beirut, Lebanon, May 15–17, 2006. As of August 2, 2008:
http://www.un.org/esa/population/migration/turin/index.html

Panizza, Ugo G., and Marianne El-Khoury, "Social Mobility and Religion: Evidence from Lebanon," Inter-American Development Bank and World Bank working paper, October 2001. As of August 5, 2008:
http://papers.ssrn.com/sol3/papers.cfm?abstract_id=293012

Peninsula, "Qatar Could Become a Model in Labour Policies: Experts," April 11, 2006.

Population Reference Bureau, "Country Statistics and Reports: Lebanon," Washington DC: Population Reference Bureau, 2005. As of August 2, 2008:
http://www.prb.org/Datafinder/Geography/Data.aspx?category=11&region=126&region_type=2

———, *DataFinder*, Washington DC: Population Reference Bureau, 2006. As of July 22, 2008:
http://www.prb.org/datafind/datafinder7.htm)

Powell, Walter, and Kaisa Snellman, "The Knowledge Economy," *Annual Review of Sociology*, Vol. 30, 2004, pp. 199–220.

Psacharopoulos, George, "Returns to Education: A Further International Update and Implications," *Journal of Human Resources*, Vol. 20, 1985, pp. 583–604.

———, "Return to Investment in Education: A Global Update," *World Development*, Vol. 22, 1994, pp. 1325–1343.

Qatar Ministry of Education, *National Report on the Development of Education in the State of Qatar*, Doha: Qatar Ministry of Education, 1996.

———, *Ministry of Education Annual Statistics Report 2004/2005*, Doha: Qatar Ministry of Education, 2005.

Qatar Petroleum, "Qatarization," Doha: Qatar Petroleum, 2008. As of August 5, 2008:
http://www.qatarization.com.qa

Qatar Planning Council, *Sample Labour Force Survey, 2001*, Doha: State of Qatar Planning Council, April 2002.

———, *Annual Abstracts 2005: Labor Force*, Doha: State of Qatar Planning Council, 2005a. As of July 21, 2008:
http://www.planning.gov.qa/AnnAbs/annabst_2005/annabst/2005/First-Section/LabourFource/Labour_Index.htm

———, *Qatar Census 2004*, Doha: State of Qatar Planning Council, 2005b. As of July 21, 2008:
http://www.planning.gov.qa/Qatar-Census-2004/Flash/introduction.html

———, *Qatar in Figures: 2005*, Doha: State of Qatar Planning Council, October 2005c. As of July 21, 2008:
http://www.planning.gov.qa/QIF/2005/QIF2005_PDF.pdf

———, "Chapter II: Labour Fource," *Annual Abstract: 2006, Labor Force*, Doha: State of Qatar Planning Council, 2006a. As of July 23, 2008:
http://www.planning.gov.qa/AnnAbs/2006/First-Section/LabourFource/Labour_Index.htm

———, *Gross Domestic Product, 2005*, Doha: State of Qatar Planning Council, 2006b. As of July 23, 2008:
http://www.planning.gov.qa/GDP/2005/GDP_2005_E.pdf

———, *Qatar in Figures*, 25th issue, Doha: State of Qatar Planning Council, October 2006c. As of July 23, 2008:
http://www.planning.gov.qa/QIF/2006/QIF2006_PDF.pdf

———, *Sample Labour Force Survey, 2006*, Doha: State of Qatar Planning Council, 2007. As if August 5, 2008:
http://www.planning.gov.qa/labour_force_2006/Bulletin_Labour_Force_2006.pdf

———, "Qatar Planning Council," Doha: State of Qatar Planning Council, 2008. As of July 23, 2008:
http://www.planning.gov.qa/

Qatar Supreme Council for Family Affairs, *Women and Men in Qatar: Statistical View 2004*, Doha: State of Qatar Supreme Council for Family Affairs, 2004.

Qatar Supreme Education Council, *Evaluation System, An Overview of Results, Progress, and Plans: QCEA and QCSS 2004*, Doha: State of Qatar Supreme Education Council, 2005a. As of August 5, 2008:
http://www.english.education.gov.qa/files/1544_file_Adel_English.pdf

———, *Fact Sheet on Higher Education Institute*, Doha: State of Qatar Supreme Education Council, 2005b. As of August 5, 2008:
http://www.english.education.gov.qa/content/resources/detail/1543

———, *All Government Schools to Be Independent Soon*, Doha: State of Qatar Supreme Education Council, 2006a. As of August 5, 2008:
http://www.english.education.gov.qa/content/resources/detail/2959

———, *Scholarship Guide 2006–2007*, Doha: State of Qatar Supreme Education Council, 2006b. As of August 5, 2008:
http://www.english.education.gov.qa/newsletter/scholarg.pdf

———, *Parents Move Quickly to Register Children for Admission to Independent Schools*, Doha: State of Qatar Supreme Education Council, 2007a. As of August 5, 2008:
http://www.english.education.gov.qa/content/resources/detail/5146

———, *QCEA 2007: Arabic, English, Mathematics, and Science in Grades 4 to 11*, Doha: State of Qatar Supreme Education Council, 2007b. As of August 5, 2008:
http://www.english.education.gov.qa/section/sec/evaluation_institute/assessment/_qcea_2007

———, *International Tests Results Underscore Urgency of Present Education Reform*, Doha: State of Qatar Supreme Education Council, 2008. As of August 5, 2008:
http://www.english.education.gov.qa/content/resources/detail/5807

Rabi, Uzi, "Majlis al-Shura and Majlis al-Dawla: Weaving Old Practices and New Realities in the Process of State Formation in Oman," *Middle Eastern Studies*, Vol. 38, No. 4, 2002, pp. 41–50.

Rassekh, Shapour, *Education as a Motor for Development: Recent Education Reforms in Oman with Particular Reference to the Status of Women and Girls*, Innodata Monographs 15, Geneva, Switzerland: UNESCO, International Bureau of Education, 2004. As of August 2, 2008:
http://unesdoc.unesco.org/images/0014/001411/141188eo.pdf

Salama, Samir, Ahmed A. Elewa, and Bassam Za'za', "President Endorses New UAE Cabinet Presented by Mohammad," gulfnews.com, February 17, 2008. As of July 27, 2008:
http://archive.gulfnews.com/articles/08/02/17/10190481.html

Sfakianakis, John, "An Overview of the Gulf Economies: Challenges and Prospects in a Global Marketplace," *Gulf Yearbook 2004*, Dubai, UAE: Gulf Research Center, 2005, pp. 79–92.

Sharma, Manu, "Jafza Sees 10pc Growth in Companies in 2006," *Al Khaleej Times*, January 28, 2007. As of August 2, 2008:
http://www.khaleejtimes.com/DisplayArticleNew.asp?section=business&xfile=data/business/2007/january/business_january653.xml

Stasz, Cathleen, Eric R. Eide, and Francisco Martorell, *Postsecondary Education in Qatar: Employer Demand, Student Choice, and Options for Policy*, MG-644-QATAR, Santa Monica, Calif.: RAND Corporation, 2007. As of July 20, 2008:
http://www.rand.org/pubs/monographs/MG644/

UAE—*See* United Arab Emirates

UAE HCT—*See* United Arab Emirates Higher Colleges of Technology

UNDP—*See* United Nations Development Programme

UNESCO—*See* United Nations Education, Scientific, and Cultural Organization

United Arab Emirates Council of Ministers, "Council of Ministers Order No. (259/1) Year 2004," Abu Dhabi: Council of Ministers Resolutions on Training and Employment of UAE Citizens in the Private Sector, UAE, 2004. As of August 2, 2008:
http://www.mol.gov.ae/PAges-EN/documents-en/
TrainingAndEmploymentOfUAECitzenInThePrvateSector.htm#a

United Arab Emirates federal e-government portal, "About Industry," Abu Dhabi: Government of the UAE, 2006a. As of August 2, 2008:
http://www.government.ae/gov/en/biz/industry/about.jsp

———, "e-Government Strategy," Abu Dhabi: Government of the UAE, 2006b. As of August 2, 2008:
http://www.government.ae/gov/en/gov/projects/strategy.jsp

———, "Employment and Social Security," Abu Dhabi: Government of the UAE, 2006c. As of August 2, 2008:
http://www.government.ae/gov/en/biz/employment/employment.jsp

———, "Oil and Gas," Abu Dhabi: Government of the UAE, 2006d. As of August 2, 2008:
http://www.government.ae/gov/en/biz/industry/oil.jsp

United Arab Emirates Higher Colleges of Technology, "HCT at a Glance," Abu Dhabi, UAE: HCT, 2008a. As of August 1, 2008:
http://www.hct.ac.ae/misc/aspx/hct_at_a_glance.aspx

———, "About HCT," Abu Dhabi: HCT, 2008b. As of August 1, 2008:
http://www.hct.ac.ae/misc/aspx/about_us.aspx?abthct

———, "General Education," Abu Dhabi: HCT, 2008c. As of August 1, 2008:
http://www.hct.ac.ae/programs/aspx/general_education.aspx

United Arab Emirates Ministry of Economy, *Census 2005 UAE*, Abu Dhabi: Ministry of Economy, UAE, undated. As of August 3, 2008:
http://tedad.ae/english/index.html

———, *Statistics Abstract,* Dubai: Ministry of Economy, UAE, 2000, 2003, 2004, 2005, 2006 (in Arabic). As of July 23, 2008:
http://www.economy.ae/Arabic/EconomicAndStatisticReports/StatisticReports/StatisticAbstract/Pages/default.aspx

———, *Preliminary Results of Population, Housing and Establishments Census 2005*, UAE, 2006. As of August 1, 2008:
http://www.tedad.ae/english/results.pdf

———, *UAE Figures 1997, 2001, 2002, 2007*, Dubai: Ministry of Economy, UAE, 2007. As of August 2, 2008:
http://www.economy.ae/English/EconomicAndStatisticReports/StatisticReports/Pages/UAEinNumbers.aspx

United Arab Emirates Ministry of Education, "History of Education in the United Arab Emirates," Abu Dhabi: Ministry of Education, UAE, 2006a (in Arabic). As of March 14, 2008:
http://www.moe.gov.ae/Arabic/Pages/%D8%AA%D8%A7%D8%B1%D9%8A%D8%AE%D8%A7%D9%84%D8%AA%D8%B9%D9%84%D9%8A%D9%85.aspx

———, "Kindergarten Department," Abu Dhabi: Ministry of Education, UAE, 2006b. As of September 3, 2006:
http://www.moe.gov.ae/r_atfal/index.htm

———, "Minister of Education and a Comprehensive Discussion with the Gulf Newspaper," Abu Dhabi: Ministry of Education, UAE, 2006c (in Arabic). As of September 10, 2006:
http://www.moe.gov.ae/news/news2006/3_9_06_2.htm

———, "Suggested System for the General Secondary Examination," Abu Dhabi: Ministry of Education, UAE, 2006d (in Arabic). As of August 25, 2006:
http://www.moe.gov.ae/ministry/new_high%20school%20academic%20system.htm

———, MoE Minister Reviews Education Reform Strategy," Abu Dhabi: Ministry of Education, UAE, 2008a. As of June 21, 2008:
http://www.moe.gov.ae/English/Pages/h040508_2.aspx

———, "MoE Strategic Objectives," Abu Dhabi: Ministry of Education, UAE, 2008b. As of June 21, 2008:
http://www.moe.gov.ae/English/Pages/StrategicObjectives.aspx

———, "Principal Advisor Program Develops Leadership Skills," Abu Dhabi: Ministry of Education, UAE, 2008c. As of June 21, 2008:
http://www.moe.gov.ae/English/Lists/Reports/Display.aspx?ID=27

United Arab Emirates Ministry of Information and Culture, *UAE Yearbook 2006*, Abu Dhabi: Ministry of Information and Culture, 2006. As of July 21, 2008:
http://www.uaeinteract.com/uaeint_misc/pdf_2006/index.asp#year

United Arab Emirates Tanmia, "Tanmia Board of Trustees Approves Budget and Work Plan for 2006," Dubai, UAE: Tanmia, December 21, 2005. As of August 4, 2008:
http://www.tanmia.ae/tanmia/general/News.aspx

———, "Tanmia Records 100pc Increase in Jobs for Emiratis," Dubai, UAE: Tanmia, July 31, 2006. As of August 4, 2008:
http://www.tanmia.ae/tanmia/general/News.aspx

———, "The National Human Resource and Development and Employment Authority," Dubai, UAE: Tanmia, 2008. As of August 4, 2008:
http://www.tanmia.ae/tanmia/general/aboutus.aspx

United Arab Emirates University, "Institutional Accreditation for UAE University," Abu Dhabi: UAE University, 2007a. As of August 1, 2008:
http://www.uaeu.ac.ae/irpsu/irpsu_uaeu_accreditation.shtml

———, *United Arab Emirates University Statistical Year Book*, Vols. 2002/2003, 2003/2004, and 2004/2005, Al 'Ayn, UAE: Institutional Research and Planning Support Unit, UAE University, 2007b. As of August 1, 2008:
http://www.uaeu.ac.ae/irpsu/irpsu_publications.asp

———, "What Is Institutional Research?" Al 'Ayn, UAE: Institutional Research and Planning Support Unit, UAE University, 2007c. As of August 1, 2008:
http://www.uaeu.ac.ae/irpsu/irpsu_what_ir.shtml

United Nations Development Programme, "Living Conditions of Households in Lebanon in 1997," undated. As of August 2, 2008:
http://www.undp.org.lb/programme/pro-poor/poverty/povertyinlebanon/conditions97.cfm

———, *A Profile of Sustainable Human Development in Lebanon*, New York, N.Y.: UNDP, 1997. As of August 2, 2008:
http://www.undp.org.lb/programme/governance/advocacy/nhdr/nhdr97/

———, *Arab Human Development Report: Creating Opportunities for Future Generations*, New York, N.Y.: UNDP, Regional Bureau for Arab States, 2002.

———, *Arab Human Development Report: Building a Knowledge Society*, New York, N.Y.: UNDP, Regional Bureau for Arab States, 2003.

———, *Human Development Report 2005: International Cooperation at a Crossroads, Aid, Trade and Security in an Unequal World*, New York, N.Y.: Oxford University Press, 2005.

———, *Human Development Report 2006: Beyond Scarcity—Power, Poverty, and the Global Water Crisis*, New York, N.Y.: Oxford University Press, 2006.

United Nations Education, Scientific, and Cultural Organization, *The Dakar Framework for Action, Education for All: Meeting Our Collective Commitments*, Text adopted by the World Education Forum, Dakar, Senegal, April 26–28, 2000, ED-2000/WS/27, Paris, France: UNESCO, 2000a. As of July 17, 2008:
http://www.unesco.org/education/efa/ed_for_all/dakfram_eng.shtml

———, *Education for All in the Arab States: Renewing the Commitment, The Arab Framework for Action to Ensure Basic Learning Needs in the Arab States in the Years 2000–2010*, Adopted by the Regional Conference on Education for All for the Arab States, Cairo, Egypt, January 24–27, 2000, Paris, France: UNESCO, 2000b. As of July 17, 2008:
http://www.unesco.org/education/efa/wef_2000/regional_frameworks/frame_arab_states.shtml

———, "Country Profiles," Paris, France: UNESCO Institute for Statistics, 2006. As of July 22, 2008:
http://www.uis.unesco.org/profiles/selectCountry_en.aspx

U.S. Department of Labor, Bureau of Labor Statistics, *Labor Force Statistics from the Current Population Survey (1998–2008)*, Washington DC: U.S. Department of Labor, February 2008. As of August 2, 2008:
http://data.bls.gov/PDQ/servlet/SurveyOutputServlet?data_tool=latest_numbers&series_id=LNS11300000

U.S. Department of State, *Background Note: Lebanon*, Washington DC: U.S. Department of State, November 2007a. As of August 1, 2008:
http://www.state.gov/r/pa/ei/bgn/35833.htm

———, *Background Note: Oman*, Washington DC: U.S. Department of State, June 2007b. As of August 1, 2008:
http://www.state.gov/r/pa/ei/bgn/35834.htm

———, *Background Note: United Arab Emirates*, Washington DC: U.S. Department of State, June 2007c. As of August 1, 2008:
http://www.state.gov/r/pa/ei/bgn/5444.htm

———, *Background Note: Qatar*, Washington DC: U.S. Department of State, June 2008. As of August 1, 2008:
http://www.state.gov/r/pa/ei/bgn/5437.htm

Vijayan, K., "Nationals Prefer Private Schooling for Children," Ministry of Education News website, March 3, 2006. As of August 5, 2008:
http://www.moeya.ae/ministry/article_view.asp?language=English&id=2385

Winckler, Onn, "Population Growth, Migration, and Socio-Demographic Policies in Qatar," *Data and Analysis*, Israel: Tel Aviv University, Moshe Dayan Center for Middle Eastern and African Studies, July 2000.

World Bank, *Unlocking the Employment Potential in the Middle East and North Africa*, Washington DC: World Bank, 2004.

———, *Country Assistance Strategy for the Republic of Lebanon*, Report No. 34463-LB, Washington DC: World Bank, International Bank for Reconstruction and Development, November 22, 2005. As of August 2, 2008:
http://www-wds.worldbank.org/external/default/WDSContentServer/WDSP/IB/2006/05/19/000160016_20060519103442/Rendered/PDF/34463.pdf

———, "United Arab Emirates," *Engendering ICT [Information and Communication Technology] Toolkit*, 2006. As of July 23, 2008:
http://web.worldbank.org/WBSITE/EXTERNAL/TOPICS/EXTGENDER/EXTICTTOOLKIT/0,,contentMDK:20272159~pagePK:64168445~piPK:64168309~theSitePK:542820,00.html

———, *World Development Indicators Online*, Washington DC: World Bank, 2007 (subscription only). As of August 5, 2008:
http://go.worldbank.org/B53SONGPA0

———, *The Road Not Traveled: Education Reform in the Middle East and Africa*, MENA Development Report, Washington DC: World Bank, 2008.

Zahlan, Rosemarie Said, *Making of the Modern Gulf States: Kuwait, Bahrain, Qatar, the United Arab Emirates and Oman*. Reading, United Kingdom: Ithaca Press, 1998.

Zayed University, "About Zayed University," Abu Dhabi and Dubai, UAE: Zayed University, 2007a. As of August 2, 2008:
http://www.zu.ac.ae/html/aboutzu.html

———, Student Recruitment website, Abu Dhabi and Dubai, UAE: Zayed University, 2007b. As of August 1, 2008:
http://www.zu.ac.ae/studentrecruitment/admissions.htm

Za'za', Bassam, "Dubai Academic City Promises to Be Global Destination," gulfnews.com, May 1, 2006. As of August 2, 2008:
http://archive.gulfnews.com/articles/06/05/01/10036837.html